Technology of Modern Rice Milling and Basmati Rice

Technology of Modern Rice Milling and Basmati Rice

Written By

EIRI BOARD OF CONSULTANTS & ENGINEERS

ENGINEERS INDIA RESEARCH INSTITUTE

4449, Nai Sarak, Main Road, Delhi - 110 006 (India)

Ph:. 91-11- 23918117, 23916431, 23840361, 31082370

Fax: 91-11- 2391 6431, 2391 8117

* E-Mail : eirisidi@bol.net.in

* Website: www.eiriindia.org

Sole Distributor :

INDIAN INSTITUTE OF CONSULTANTS, 4/27 ROOP NAGAR, DELHI - 07

PRINTED & PUBLISHED BY

ENGINEERS INDIA RESEARCH INSTITUTE

4449, Nai Sarak, Main Road, Delhi - 110 006 (India)
Ph:. 91-11- 23918117, 23916431, 23840361, 31082370
* Fax: 91-11- 23916431, 23918117
* E-Mail : eirisidi@bol.net.in
* Website: www.eiriindia.org

DISTRIBUTED BY

SMALL INDUSTRY RESEARCH INSTITUTE (SIRI)
INDIAN INSTITUTE OF CONSULTANTS

ISBN : 81-86732-69-1
Printed in New Delhi (INDIA)

Rs. 600

Printed & Published by Sudhir Gupta for "Engineers India Research Institute" 4449 Nai Sarak, Main Road, New Delhi - 110 006

Preface

*The book **Technology of Modern Rice Milling and Basmati Rice** covers almost all the basic and advanced details to setup own Rice Milling Industry. The new edition of the book is covering latest methods including Botany of the Rice Plant, Processing of Rice, Rice Milling, Modern Conventional Milling, Properties of Parboiled Rice, Huller Use for Milling Parboiled Rice is the Chief Obstacle, Technology of Basmati Rice Processing, Marketing of Basmati Rice, Speciality Rice, TRIPS and WTO, Details of Technology and Technology Providers, Directory of Basmati Rice Exporters/Importers, Important Details, Plant Economics of Rice Puff, Plant Economics of Rice Bran Oil, Plant Economics Rice Polishing and Packing, Plant Economics of Modern Rice Mill, Plant Economics of Modern Rice Mill, Plant Economics of Modern Rice Mill, Plant Economics of Basmati Rice Trading, Plant Economics of Rice Sorting / Grading Plant, Suppliers of Plant and Machineries, Suppliers of Packaging Materials*

The book has been written for the benefit and to prove an asset and a handy reference guide in the hands of new entrepreneurs & well established industrialists.

Director
ENGINEERS INDIA RESEARCH INSTITUTE
Nai Sarak, New Delhi (INDIA)
E-Mail : eirisidi@bol.net.in

CONTENTS

4

5

1

Botany of the Rice Plant

Cultivated rice *(Oryza sativa)* belongs to the Gramineae or grass family and the tribe Oryzeae. Unlike the other cereal crops, rice is a semiaquatic plant which thrives under flooded soil conditions. There are 24 chromosomes (2N) in *Oryza sativa*. Among the wild species, both 24 and 48 chromosome types have been reported. Wild rice belongs to a different genus.

Over 60 species of *Oryza* have been reported, but only 23 valid species are generally recognized. Most of the wild species are found in Southeast Asia and Africa, but several of them have been discovered in the Western Hemisphere. Cultivated rice does not cross freely with most wild species except that *O. sativa* and *O. glaberrima* intercross freely. Further cytogenetic studies of interspecific hybrids are needed before the relationship between cultivated rice and the various wild species can be established.

It has been said that over 8,000 botanically different varieties of rice are in existence in the world and that more than 4,000 varieties have been identified in India. It was also reported that over 8,000 varieties and selections were introduced into the U.S. for testing purposes during the 50-yr period 1903 to 1852. At the present time, over 18,000 varieties are maintained in the World Rice Collection of the International Rice Research Institute.

Varieties of *Oryza sativa* are usually divided into two subspecies, japonica and indica. Ghose *et al.* based their classification on morphological differences and responses to temperature and length of day. All of the japonica varieties have essentially the same grain and panicle type. Crosses between japonica and indica varieties show different degrees of sterility. Some investigators have concluded that the two types probably had a common origin many centuries ago, and that gene mutations and chromosomal rearrangement are responsible for these incompatibilities. In the U.S., the japonica and indica subspecies have been intercrossed and several important commercial varieties developed. In Asia, subspecies crosses have frequently produced plants with a high degree of sterility. The difference in results is explained by the theory that fertility is largely determined by the genetic structure of the indica parent. All (or most) crosses made with certain indica varieties will yield fertile offspring, while other varieties will cause sterility regardless of the japonica variety used as the other parent.

The rice plant has a branched panicle type of inflorescence. The spikelets are borne on the panicle branches, and each spikelet contains a single ovule and six anthers. The ovule, when fertilized, forms the rice grain, the latter being covered by loose outer hulls, the lemma and palea. Hulls remain adherent when the grain is threshed and are removed as a first step in the milling operation. At the base of the lemma and palea are two outer sterile glumes which are usually greatly reduced in size and remain attached to the grain when threshed.

The rice florets usually bloom after the panicles emerge from the leaf sheath. Blooming usually occurs at about the same time of day in each region where grown, but the exact time depends upon the daily fluctuations in temperature and humidity. In the U.S., this occurs between the hours of 8:00 AM and 4:00 PM, with most of the blooming occurring between 10:00 AM and 12:00 noon. Blooming is characterized by opening of the lemma and palea. Simultaneously with the opening of the glumes, there is a rapid elongation of the styles bearing the anthers. Pollination takes place as the anthers dehisce, liberating the pollen grains which fall on the feathery stigma attached to the ovule. The glumes usually remain open about one hour. Rice is a self-fertilized plant, but some natural crossing occurs. Natural crossing has been reported to vary from a fraction of 1% to over 3%.

According to Juliano (1985B), "Traditional rice varieties of tropical Asia are tall and slender, with droopy leaves, photoperiod sensitivity, and strong grain dormancy. The introduction of modem semidwarf varieties in the mid 1950s resulted in widespread adoption of these shorter plants by farmers in Asia. Because of its reduced height (from about 160 to 100 cm), its erect leaves, and its heavy tillering, the modem variety is able to absorb nutrients without lodging but is comparable in yield to traditional varieties at low levels of input. Some of the new varieties are of short duration, requiring less than 100 days from seeding to harvest; these had to be nonsensitive to changes in the photoperiod. . .Adoption of semidwarf varieties has been concentrated in the 25% of the area that is lowland (irrigated)."

The Culture of Rice

Optimal conditions for rice culture include high temperatures during the growing season, a dependable fresh water supply for the irrigation period, soil that is comparatively level and underlaid with impervious subsoil, and good drainage. Areas in the U.S. which meet these requirements are found in the Coastal Prairie region of southwestern Louisiana and southeastern Texas, eastern Arkansas and northwest Mississippi, and the central valleys of California (particularly the Sacramento Valley). It is in these three regions that the major production of rice occurs.

Climate

Rice can be grown successfully under a wide range of climatic conditions. It generally requires a minimum growing season of 4 to 5 months, during which the mean temperature must average at least 70ºT. Although rice culture extends from 45°N to 40°S latitude, most of the world's rice crop is grown between the Equator and 40°N latitude. The crop is commonly associated with tropical regions, but it is also widely grown in temperate areas. The many types of rice which have evolved through the centuries of extensive rice culture vary widely in their range of adaptability. Rice is grown at altitudes from sea level to over 5,000 ft.

In tropical humid regions, tall rank-growing long-season varieties are usually cultivated. In tropical Asian countries, varieties requiring a growing season of over 180 days are common. These tropical varieties grow tall, tiller profusely, and produce rank vegetative growth on soils that are are annually cropped to rice. In low-lying flood plains, deep-water rices (commonly called floating rices) are grown. These varieties elongate as much as 12 inches per day as the waters rise and may reach a length of 12 to 20 ft.

In temperate regions, short-season varieties maturing in 85 to 145 days are grown. They are usually hardy, somewhat short stature types that can withstand wide variations in daily temperatures and produce satisfactory yields even when grown in cold irrigation water.

It has been reported that yield of grain is correlated with the amount of sunlight (measured in calories per square centimeter per day) received over the last 4 to 6 weeks before harvest. Different varieties vary in the efficiency of their use of radiant energy.

Soil Types

Rice is grown on a wide range of soil types. The lack of adequate irrigation water is more apt to be a limiting factor than is soil type. Soil pH can vary from 4.0 to 8.0 without serious damage to the plant's growth. The rice plant has a high tolerance for alkaline soils and is sometimes grown for reclaiming such lands.

Soils with impervious subsoils capable of holding flood water or level prairies that can be readily flooded make ideal rice lands. Deep soils tend to give higher yields than soils that have an impenetrable layer at a shallow depth. This effect must be balanced against the advantage of an impervious subsoil for retaining the irrigation water. Experiments at International Rice Research (IRRI) in the Philippines showed that, as the depth of the soil was increased to about 40 cm, grain yield increased proportionately. Beyond 40 cm depth there was some yield improvement, but it was relatively slight. The soil in question was a fertile clay soil. Fertilizer nitrogen was much more effective on shallow than on deep soils. The disadvantages of shallow soils could be largely eliminated by suitable fertilizer application.

The lands used for commercial rice production in the U.S. are usually comparatively level and have reasonably good surface drainage. Medium or heavy clays, clay loams, silt loams, or fine sandy loams with slowly permeable subsoils are preferred. Such soils can be flood-irrigated more efficiently and will support heavy mechanized equipment under a wide range of soil moisture conditions. Soils of this type occur in the coastal prairie region of southwest Louisiana and southeastern Texas. They also occur in the Grand Prairie and other areas in eastern Arkansas, elsewhere in the south central states and in the interior valleys of California.

Water Requirements

The commercial rice crop of the U.S. is grown with irrigation, and fields are kept flooded throughout the greater part of the growing season. The rice plant requires abundant soil moisture and usually thrives under continually flooded soil conditions. This necessitates an abundant supply of irrigation water for a rather long period. Flooding of fields provides a means of controlling many serious weed pests and assures adequate moisture at all times for optimum growth and development of the rice plant.

The total water requirements of a rice crop can vary greatly depending on the type of soil, climatic conditions, and the efficiency of the irrigation equipment. Typically, from 4 to 10 acre-ft of water are required to produce a rice crop in California, 40 to 45 inches of water are required in Texas and Louisiana, and about 33 inches are required in Arkansas. Water supplied by rainfall during the growing season amounts to about 15 inches in Texas and Louisiana, about 11 inches in Arkansas, and only a negligible amount in California. In the southern states the land may be drained one or more times during the growing season, but in California the land is rarely drained from the time the seed is sown until harvest.

The rice plant also grows well under nonflooded or "upland" conditions. In parts of South America, much rice is grown under nonflooded or upland conditions, and, while this practice is also known throughout Asia, it constitutes only a small proportion of the total acreage. Short-season varieties, those usually maturing in 100 to 125 days, are commonly planted in these fields. The land is cleared and the rice grown during seasons of frequent rainfall. After several crops, yields normally decrease due to reduced fertility and the intrusion of weeds. The field is then abandoned and another area cleared. Yields are low, but little effort is required to produce a crop.

Prior to World War II, small acreages of upland rice were grown in Alabama, Florida, Georgia, Mississippi, and South Carolina, but production was less than 1% of the total U.S. rice crop. Upland rice was grown as a cultivated crop sown in rows 1.5 to 3 ft apart. Today, this type of rice cultivation is practically nonexistent in the U.S.

Rotation Practices

In tropical Asian countries, lands are cropped continuously to rice. Two crops per year are grown when sufficient water is available. This has been the practice for centuries, and yields are low. However, it has been demonstrated that yields of 3,560 to 5,340 lb per acre can be produced on these same lands during the monsoon season by growing short stiff-strawed nitrogen-responsive varieties in combination with nitrogen fertilizer and good cultural and management practices. Similar results have been obtained in many tropical Asian countries.

In Japan, lands produce a rice crop every year, but rotation with soil-building crops and other forms of fertilization are used, and adequate irrigation water is provided. Under these conditions, yields hold up very well. In Spain, Italy, and Portugal, rice is grown in rotation with pasture and green manure crops combined with heavy applications of fertilizer to both the rice and pasture crops.

In The U.S., frequency of rice cropping in the rotation system varies with the soil type and with the economic conditions affecting the price or demand for rice. Rotation systems include a wide variety of other crops. As a general rule, heavy clay soils are cropped more frequently than are lighter soils. Since acreage controls were enacted in 1955, fewer rice crops are grown in the rotation systems throughout the country. More emphasis is being placed upon those practices which result in higher acre yields of rice and more efficient production.

Since the beginning of rice production in Texas and Louisiana, it has been a common practice to grow one or, possibly, two rice crops, followed by one or more years of grazing beef cattle on the vegetation that volunteers between the rice crops. With this system, little effort was made to drain the fields between crops. As better drainage facilities became available, more acres were put into improved pasture in the off-years. While unimproved pasture rotation systems can still be found, improved pastures are now much more common. In Texas and Louisiana, rice following improved pastures yielded 648 to 810 lb more rice than crops planted following unimproved pastures, when fertilizer applications were kept at the same level in each.

Improved pastures are usually followed by two or more rice crops. Due to the high cost of developing improved pastures, fields are cropped to improved pastures at least three years before planting rice. Costs of converting rice lands, to improved pastures can be reduced by seeding pasture crops immediately following rice without seedbed preparation. The rice irrigation and drainage systems are maintained when the land is in improved pasture. The leading plants for improved pastures include Bermudagrass, Dallisgrass, and White, Persian, and Hop clovers. Hay crops such as lespedeza, Alyce clover, and rye grass are sometimes planted in rotation with rice, particularly on the better-drained soils. Soybeans have been grown in rotation with rice in Texas and Louisiana. Rice in rotation with fish production is practiced on areas used as reservoirs in Arkansas. The land is kept flooded for two seasons and stocked with fish. Two rice crops then follow.

It is difficult to grow cultivated crops following rice in California because the soils are heavy clays that are difficult to work following the long flooding period. Wheat and barley, the crops which were grown on rice lands prior to the upsurge in rice culture in California, are sometimes grown in a 3-yr rotation with rice, with one year of summer fallow following the rice crop. Rice and summer fallow in alternate years are also used. In such cases, the land is spring-plowed following rice and then summer-fallowed until prepared for rice the following spring. In some cases, the land is not summer-fallowed and the volunteer vegetation is grazed by cattle or sheep.

As a result of a survey of rotation practices in the U.S. (Anon. 1990A), the USDA concluded these patterns varied widely. In Arkansas and Louisiana, common rotations are rice-soybeans-rice and rice-soybeans-soybeans. In these states, 20% of the 1988 rice acreage had been planted to soybeans during the previous two years, and another 20% was planted to soybeans in 1987 and rice in 1986. In the Delta states, disease, insect, and weed problems prohibit rice production every year. In California, about 72% of the 1988 rice land had been continuously planted to rice, while 8% followed a rice-fallow-rice rotation and 6% a rice-fallow-fallow. The reasons for this situation are that most California rice is grown on heavy soils that offer few economic alternatives to the primary crop and on land specifically leveled for rice production.

Field Irrigation and Drainage Systems

In the U.S., most irrigation water is obtained from bayous and streams, but about 40% originates from deep wells. In Texas and Louisiana, surface water obtained from bayous and streams is pumped into canals and from them usually flows by gravity into laterals leading into the rice fields. Size of the irrigation systems varies from a few thousand acres to over 60,000 acres, and the water may be lifted as much as 50 ft into the canals. In some sections of Arkansas, Louisiana, and Texas, small pumping systems are installed to elevate surface water from streams and ditches into reservoirs during periods of abundant surface water supply. As it is needed, water from the reservoir is either pumped or allowed to flow by gravity to the rice fields. In California, most of the water used for rice irrigation is obtained from large streams. Since the water may be rather cool, warming basins are frequently employed to raise the water's temperature before it is moved into the rice fields. Hardy japonica types are grown in California to help overcome the cool water problem.

One of the first steps in preparing land for rice production in the U.S. is the laying out of field lateral channels and drainage ditches. It is essential that irrigation laterals and drainage ditches be situated properly if they are to provide uniform submergence and timely drainage of fields. Contour levees which divide the fields into subfields or paddies are located by survey and are usually placed at grade differences of 0.2 or 0.3 ft. Contour levees are located after the land has been plowed and leveled.

The contour levees can be constructed in several ways, the choice depending on the soil type and irrigation practices to be used. On the lighter soils in Arkansas, Louisiana, Mississippi, and Texas, disk levee builders are used. They require two or more passes to form a suitable levee. On the heavier soils in Louisiana and Texas, hydraulically controlled steel blade pushers are used. The levee area is plowed to the center using a moldboard or disk plow before pushing. A second plowing and pushing is required in most cases. When possible, levees should be formed in the fall or early winter to prevent washouts when the fields are flooded.

Extremely large pushers or dikers are commonly used in California. These form a levee in one or two operations. They require much motive power or the equivalent of two large track-type tractors. In California, the levees are usually 14 to 16 ft wide, including bar-ditches, and are 3 to 4 ft high. In the Southern States, levees are seldom over 10 to 12 ft wide and 2 ft high.

Tillage

In tropical Asia, essentially all rice is produced by intense hand methods of production. The land is usually plowed and puddled under flooded conditions, using oxen for motive power. In many areas, rainfall is depended upon for irrigating the crop. Harvesting, threshing, and milling are hand operations. As a result, there is an average labor requirement of over 200 man-days to fully service an acre of rice.

In the U.S., highly mechanized production methods are used to cut the labor requirement to less than two man-days for each acre of rice. Much the same general type of equipment is used as for other small grain crops, except that the special requirements resulting from flood irrigation must be met. Flood irrigation is accomplished by smoothing the land and then building contour levees or dikes which are located by survey and usually placed at elevation differences of 0.2 ft in the southern states and 0.3 ft in California.

Rice lands may be plowed in the summer, fall, winter, or even in the spring just prior to seeding. Summer and fall plowing are practiced when the land cannot be used profitably for growing another crop. In the southern states, some of the heavier soils are plowed when wet, particularly during seasons of above normal rainfall.

Much rice land is leveled using land planers up to 60 ft in length. If there is considerable slope to the land, shorter planes are used. Land leveling has proved to be extremely profitable, since level land is easier to drain and irrigate. Rice fields should be drained at the time the young rice seedlings are emerging from the soil, and again when the fields are ready for harvest. Poor stand establishment results from improperly drained fields. It is important to have a uniform depth of irrigation water on the fields to control grass and weeds.

Plowed lands are made ready for seeding by disking and harrowing. Heavy offset disks perform best on the heavier type of soil. Custom built spiketooth harrows made from pipe are frequently used along with springtooth harrows as a final operation prior to seeding. Heavy clay soils are usually left rough or slightly cloddy, since finely prepared seedbeds are more likely to crust following flooding or rains. Crusting tends to stimulate the germination of small seeded grasses and other weeds.

Seeding Procedures

Most of the U.S. rice crop is sown in April and May. In Texas and Louisiana, where a longer growing season prevails, some rice is sown in early March and some after mid-June. There is a choice of seeding methods. In California, airplanes are used for seeding practically all of the crop. This has been the practice for many years. In the southern states, both conventional grain drills and airplanes are used.

Rice is sown in both flooded and dry seedbeds. When sown in flooded fields, the airplane is used exclusively, but for sowing on dry land grain drills and the airplane are both used. Dryland seedbed preparation and seeding operations follow closely those used with other cereal crops. When the airplane is used for dryland seeding, the seeds are usually covered by means of a light spiketooth harrow.

Water-seeding methods vary greatly in the different states. The procedure was first used in California as a means of controlling water grasses (*Echinochloa* and *Leptochloa* species). The California method consists of holding flood water from 6 to 8 inches deep on the fields until the rice seedlings have emerged through the water. The water depth chosen depends upon the kind and abundance of water grasses. It is important to maintain adequate and uniform water depths for the first 21 to 28 days following seeding, as the weeds can emerge through shallower depths. Under California conditions, the deep water also serves as a temperature regulator and thus compensates for the wide variation between prevailing day and night temperatures. After the rice seedlings emerge, an average water depth of 5 to 7 inches is usually maintained throughout the growing period. In cases of excessive vegetative growth by the rice, which may occur on highly fertile land, fields may be drained when the rice is 60 to 75 days old. Herbicides are widely used to control water grasses.

Seeding procedures followed in the southern states depend upon the type of soil, the weed and grass problem, and seasonal conditions. Where weeds and grass are not serious, and weather conditions permit, rice is often sown with a grain drill in rows 7 to 8 inches apart. In clay soils, shallow seeding depths are used and the fields are irrigated following seeding. In sandy loam, the rice is sown two or more inches deep in moist soil and the seedlings emerge without irrigation.

Broadcast seeding on dry soil by airplane or various types of broadcase seeders is frequently practiced on the heavier soils. When sown in this way, seedbeds are left rough and harrowed with a lightweight spiketooth following seeding but prior to irrigation. Irrigation water is then applied and drained off as soon as possible. Thorough drainage of fields is essential, as rice seeds covered with soil cannot emerge through water.

Controlled experiments by the IRRI have failed to demonstrate any advantage in terms of grain yield of transplanting as compared to drilled or broadcast planting. Weed control is, however, more difficult with direct-seeded crops because early flooding to smother the weeds is not possible and the young seedlings do not compete as effectively with the weeds as do the larger transplanted seedlings. Transplanting also has the advantage that, under continuous cropping conditions, the fields are available for maturing crops while new seedlings are being raised in the seed bed.

Water-seeding is used in the southern states for controlling certain water grasses and red rice, a variety which volunteers from one rice crop to the next by remaining viable in the soil. In the southern states, rice has more difficulty emerging through water than it does in California due to the warmer water, cloudy weather, seedling diseases, varieties used, and possibly other factors. In Louisiana and Texas, the flood water is drained off immediately following seeding, or it is dropped to shallow depths, until seedlings have emerged and the rice root systems are firmly established in the soil.

A method of water-seeding commonly employed in Texas consists of dropping dry or sprouted seeds by airplane into flooded fields that have been harrowed or slightly puddled prior to seeding. Light weight spiketooth or springtooth harrows, pulled by wheeled tractors operating in shallow flooded fields are used for this operation. Seeds are dropped 12 to 36 hr after puddling and fields are drained 12 to 36 hr after seeding. The young seedlings develop rapidly under such conditions, ahead of the weeds and grass. Fields are flushed again a week to 10 days later, depending on the weather conditions and the growth of the rice. The fields are flooded as soon as weed and grass seedlings emerge, which may be before the rice seedlings reach a height of 3 to 4 in. If weeds are not a serious problem, it is better to wait until the rice seedlings are 5 to 6 inches tall before flooding the field, regardless of the method of seeding used.

In some sections of Arkansas, Louisiana, and Texas, water-seeding is used and the land is not worked following irrigation. The water is held for several days after dropping sprouted or dry seed. In most cases, the fields are then drained or the water is lowered to shallow depths to allow the root systems of the young seedlings that are on the surface of the soil to become established.

In the southern states, wet seedbed preparation or water cultivation is sometimes necessary during seasons of heavy rainfall. Disks and harrows are used to work the land under flooded conditions, and seeds are then dropped by airplane into the flooded fields.

Sprouted seeds, when used in water-seeding, should be at the stage where the sprout is just breaking the husk. If the sprouts are longer, they are likely to be damaged in handling or seeding. Seeds are sprouted in small water-tight bins or in sacks placed in canals or ditches for 12 to 48 hours, followed by a draining period of 12 to 24 hours. Optimum length of the soaking and draining period is dependent upon prevailing temperatures. It may be necessary to sprinkle or pour water on the rice to lower its temperature during warm weather. In California, soaking vats are generally used for sprouting the seeds.

Much of the seed rice used in the southern states is treated with fungicides. Insecticides are sometimes used as seed treatments in the southern states to control insects which attack rice in the seedling stage. The increasing stringency of Federal and state control of chemical treatments has created many problems for farmers and manufacturers alike.

Seeding rates vary from 80 to 140 lb per acre in the southern states. Seeding rates as low as 60 lb per acre have been used in the western part of the Texas rice area. Seedling rates vary from 125 to 150 lb per acre in California.

Fertilizers

Commercial fertilizers are widely used throughout the rice regions of the U.S. The use of commercial fertilizers dates back to the early 1900s, when basic slag and superphosphate were used to a limited extent on relatively new lands in the southern states. The importance of nitrogen fertilizers became generally recognized prior to World War II, and today large quantities of nitrogen and phosphate fertilizers, as well as a limited amount of potash, are being used.

In Texas and Arkansas, up to 80 lb of nitrogen per acre are being applied, along with approximately 40 lb of phosphate. In Louisiana and Mississippi, slightly lower nitrogen rates are employed. When very early maturing varieties (about 100 days from seeding to maturity) are being grown, as much as 120 lb of nitrogen per acre may be used. In California, 60 lb of nitrogen per acre are generally used on soils of average fertility. Lower amounts of fertilizer are required on more fertile soils. Rice responds best to ammonia forms of nitrogen, a fact that is recognized throughout the world.

In the southern states, most fertilizers are broadcast by airplane after the rice has been sown, since experience has shown better weed and grass control is obtained by fertilizing after the rice has emerged from the soil and just ahead of the first flood water. It has been recommended that all fertilizer be applied as a top-dressing 35 to 40 days after seeding if grass and weeds are troublesome. In California, most of the fertilizer is broadcast just prior to seeding.

Pests of Rice

Weeds.—Weeds are a constant threat to rice growers. Control practices such as rotation systems, grazing, summer tilling, water-seeding, and timely irrigation and drainage have long been used in the rice-growing regions. Almost any kind of weed can be adequately controlled by chemical herbicides, usually with minor effects on the rice plant, provided the chemical is applied at the proper time, in the proper concentration, and under proper conditions. Unfortunately, the proliferation of Federal and state restrictions on the application of herbicides to food crops continually decreases the options available to the farmer. Many other countries have more liberal views on this problem and allow a greater variety of effective herbicides. The following discussion will deal with insecticides in general, without consideration of the current legal status of individual chemicals.

Until the development of phenoxy based herbicides in the late 1940s, broad-leaved weeds were difficult to control on heavily cropped lands, particularly in the southern states. Many farms were so badly infested that it was no longer profitable to grow rice. Today, many of the water-loving broad-leaved weeds so common in rice fields are no longer a threat to the farmer.

Chemical means to prevent crop destruction by weeds and other pests are well known, but suggestions for treatment are often made obsolete as different herbicides, insecticides, etc. become legally unacceptable depending on which one is the demon of the moment in the eyes of environmental activists. According to Mikkelsen and DeDatta (1980), pre-emergence weed control with herbicides such as 2,4-D and 2-methyl-4-chlorophenoxyacetic acid (MCPA) usually provide good control of annual broadleaf weeds but do not eliminate grasses. Selective' herbicides such as butachlor, butralin, and thiobencarb are effective against a wide spectrum of weeds. Propanil and molinate are useful in direct-seeded rice production. A mixture of piperophos and dimethametryne has been used with great effectiveness for weed control in Asian rice fields.

Diseases.—There are several diseases affecting the rice plant in the southern states, but they seldom cause heavy losses. The only serious disease in California is seedling blight.

One of the most serious diseases in the southern states is straighthead, a physiological disorder which is most prevalent on lighter soils or where large quantities of organic matter have accumulated in the soil. Straighthead is characterized by panicles that remain erect because the grains have failed to develop properly. Panicles may be distorted and the glumes deformed. In extreme cases, the plants may fail to head. This disease can be controlled or greatly reduced by draining the field at about the jointing stage of growth or by growing resistant varieties.

Several leaf spot diseases caused by fungi such as *Helminthosporium oryzae*, *Cercospora oryzae*, and *Entyloma oryzae* are common in the southern states, but they seldom cause significant economic losses. Stem rot (*Sclerotium oryzae*) occasionally causes rather severe losses from lodging and from failure of grains to fill properly.

Blast, one of the most destructive diseases of rice, is caused by the fungus *Pyricularia oryzae*. It can attack plants either at the seedling stage (leaf blast) or at time of flowering (neck rot). Different races predominate in different regions, and they are identified on the basis of varietal susceptibility or resistance. The varieties of rice now grown in the U.S. are moderately resistant to blast but on new lands, or when extremely high levels of nitrogen are present, the disease can cause heavy losses. This is particularly true during periods of cloudy, humid weather.

White tip, a disease caused by a seedbome nematode, can lead to rather severe losses of susceptible varieties. Most of the varieties now grown are at least moderately resistant to white tip. The most satisfactory control measures are hot water treatment of seed, and the use of resistant varieties.

Some of the virus diseases of tropical Asia are grassy stunt, orange leaf, yellow dwarf, tungro, and transitory yellowing. Most of these are known by different names in different countries, and the identification of distinct diseases may be difficult, especially since the symptoms may also vary from country to country. These viruses are transmitted by insect vectors, most of them quite specific, such as the rice green leafhopper. Control measures include use of resistant varieties and control of the vectors. Hoja blanca, a virus disease occurring in Central and South America, has also been observed in Florida and Louisiana, but has not caused damage to the crop in important rice producing states. It has caused heavy losses in Cuba, Venezuela, and Colombia. Varieties resistant to hoja blanca are available, but the leading long grain varieties in the U.S. are susceptible to the disease. The virus of hoja blanca is carried by a leafhopper.

Bacterial leaf diseases which occur in most tropical Asian countries are bacterial leaf blight (*Xanthomonas oryzae*) and bacterial leaf streak (*X. translucens f. sp. oryzae*). Neither of these diseases has been positively identified as occurring in the Western hemisphere. Sheath and stem blights found in the U.S. have been attributed to two *Rhizoconia* species and a species of *Ophiobolus*. Figure 1.1 illustrates the leaf lesions typically observed when the rice plant has been damaged by seven rice diseases (Source IRRI).

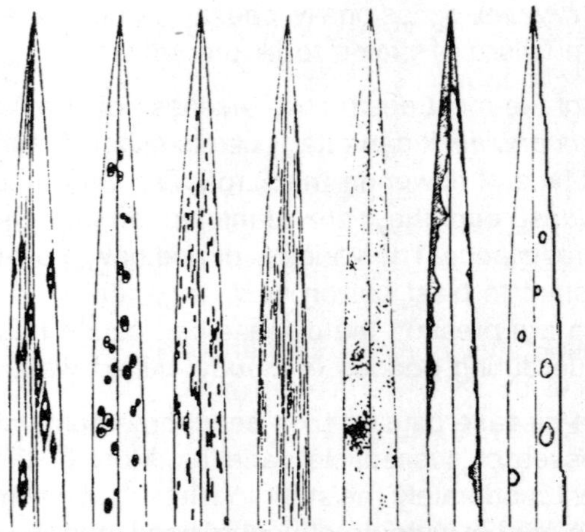

Fig. 1.1. Typical leaf lesions of seven rice diseases.

Insects.—Several species of field insects attack the rice plant, particularly in the southern states. The most common rice insect pests are rice water weevils, army worms, rice stalk borers, rice stinkbugs, leaf miners, sugarcane beetles, and grasshoppers. The rice water weevil, or root maggot (*Lissorhoptrus oryzophilus*), attacks young seedlings by feeding on their leaves in the adult stage and by feeding on the roots in the larval stage. The adults deposit their eggs in the roots of the rice plant immediately after the first flood water has been applied. The field must remain flooded for the larval stage (maggots) to develop. The maggots feed on the young roots and cause serious damage to the root system. Control measures include timely draining of fields, use of insecticides such as aldrin or dieldrin for treating the seed, and spraying the fields with insecticide. The water weevil has developed resistance to dieldrin.

Army worms cause serious damage to rice by devouring the leaves and stems. They can be controlled by aerial application of various insecticides. The two stalk borers affecting rice in the U.S. are the sugarcane borer (*Diatrae saccharalis*) and the rice stalk borer (*Chilo plejadellus*). Heavy losses seldom occur, but borers can be found in most rice fields. They feed within the rice stems during the jointing and heading stages of development and cause the panicles to dry up and turn white. This usually occurs before the grains are fully developed. In tropical countries with year around growing seasons, stem borers cause heavy losses. Control is by means of systemic insecticides.

The rice stinkbug (*Solubea pugnax*) and several other related species cause serious losses to the developing rice grain by puncturing the kernel in the milk or the dough stage. Losses result from grain failing to develop and from the discoloration caused by the puncture and the accompanying fungal infection on kernels which do develop. Many of these damaged grains are poorly filled and break up in the milling operation, thus reducing yields of head (whole grain) rice. Such kernels are commonly referred to as "pecky" rice. Stinkbugs and similar insects can be controlled by airplane spraying of recommended insecticides such as aldrin, dieldrin, and toxaphene.

Grasshoppers cause damage to rice by feeding upon the glumes and other floral parts of the developing rice grain. They are also controlled by airplane spraying with insecticides. Leaf miners affect rice plants in the seedling stage and, in cases of heavy infestation they cause serious reduction in stands. The sugarcane beetle (*Euetheola rugiceps*) is most severe in southwest Louisiana but also occurs in other southern rice-growing states. Adult beetles attack rice plants in both the seedling and the mature plant stages by feeding on the lower stems when the fields are not flooded.

The difficulty in reaching larvae concealed within the plant, and of maintaining adequate concentrations of insecticide on the plant throughout the growth cycle, has directed attention away from the foliar sprays into the direction of systemic insecticides such as lindane (the gamma isomer of benzene hexachloride). It has been shown by IRRI reseach workers that stem borers can be controlled by two applications of 2 to 3 kg per hectare of lindane to the paddy water 50 and 80 days after transplanting. This treatment is, however, comparatively ineffective against the pink borer, and does not control the green leafhopper. Use of carbaryl at 1 to 2 kg per hectare in conjunction with lindane gave protection against leafhoppers. Diazinon seemed to be almost as effective as the lindane and carbaryl combination in preliminary tests.

The use of insecticides in U.S. fields depends upon the regulations in effect at the time, a situation which cannot be predicted by the author since logic seems to play a small or no role in the establishment and execution of these laws and rules. The increasing stringency and prevailing influence of fanaticism in formulating Federal and state regulations on pesticide use is placing the rice growing industries, as other agricultural industries, in a position very vulnerable to serious damage when a concatenation of conditions leads to a season when heavy infestation with insects having high tolerance to insecticides combines with weather conditions favoring rapid growth.

Harvesting

Rice is harvested from iate July to late October in Texas and Louisiana. In Arkansas and California the harvest season is shorter due to the shorter growing season. The time must be chosen so that the grain is mature, high in quality, and has the proper moisture content. The soil should be sufficiently dry and firm to support the harvesting equipment and field transport vehicles.

According to Steffe *et al.* (1980), the production of early-maturing varieties is often desirable because they allow longer optimum harvesting periods, permitting the grain to be gathered under the most favorable weather and field conditions. In California, the rice head yields of early maturing varieties may be reduced by high daytime temperatures and dry north winds which can dry the field rapidly and make it difficult to harvest the crop at an optimum moisture content. Later maturing varieties are not exposed to the extreme variations in day-night temperatures and humidities which cause rapid field drying.

Although, it is said, most of the rice grown in the world is harvested manually, virtually all U.S. production is combined. Self-propelled combines are commonly used for harvesting rice in all of the rice-growing regions. Most harvesters are self-propelled units on rubber tires; others either use half-tracks or have full tracks with independent hydrostatic drives to improve flotation and maneuverability under wet soil conditions.

Conventional combines are used throughout the southern states and parts of California, with minor changes being made to adapt them to muddy harvesting conditions. These combines consist essentially of a pickup reel, a single or double sickle bar for cutting the stems, and auger conveyors or draper belts for carrying the harvested grain into the threshing cylinder. The cylinder rotates so that its rows of spike-toothed pins can carry the straw and grain panicles between stationary rows of spiked teeth. In this way, the grain is torn from the stems.

Most of the grain, and some small debris, falls through a grate beneath the cylinder and is conveyed to an oscillating cleaning device provided with a fan. The leaves, chaff, and other light scrap are blown away from the grain, Other devices in the combine reprocess whole or partial panicles which have avoided earlier breaking and then eject the straw from the rear of the machine. Adjustments which can be made by the operator include forward velocity, speed of the pickup reel, cylinder speed, cylinder clearance, and fan speed.

In California, large custom built full-track combines are sometimes used. These machines are built in farm shops in the rice areas. Pickup reels to catch low-lying stalks are now standard equipment on most rice combines because lodging is frequent, especially where high rates of nitrogen fertilizers are used.

Rice is usually harvested when the moisture content of the grain is between 18 and 25%. Therefore, it is necessary to dry the grain artificially before placing it in permanent storage. Steffe *et al.* (1980) state that most early maturing rice grown in California should be harvested at an average moisture content of 24 to 26% when the highest daytime temperatures are over 75° F if maximum yields of head rice are to be obtained. Drier rice tends to crack when combined, or even in the field.

Figure 1.2. shows an experimental plot of mature rice plants, illustrating the growth habit of this cereal (Source IRRI).

Fig. 1.2. Rice plants.

Rice grown in tropical and semitropical climates does not encounter wide variations in daily temperatures and humidity, and may be allowed to reach considerably lower moisture contents before harvesting and still yield a high percentage of whole rice kernels. Steffe and his coworkers advise that cylinder speeds of the combines should be set at the minimum when moisture contents drop below 22% and daytime temperatures exceed 75°F; this precaution is not as important when the moisture content is betwen 24 and 26%. Of course, in many parts of the world, rice is still manually harvested. This allows great flexibility in setting the harvesting date and probably reduces the amount of grain lost from shattered panicles.

Drying and Storage

Since combined rice is harvested at a relatively high moisture content, it must be dried before it can be placed in storage. Usually, a moisture content of 12 to 13.5% is aimed for, since this will give good protection against mold growth during storage. Head rice, i.e., whole kernel rice, sells for more than broken rice since it is considered more desirable by the consumer. Therefore, it is important that a minimum amount of the grains be fractured or otherwise damaged during the drying process. Driers of the fixed-bed type can be used for complete on-farm drying or for finish-drying after most of the moisture has been removed in a continuous flow drier. Fixed-bed driers are provided with fans to circulate heated, or sometimes unheated, air through the grain mass. These units can be either circular (cylindrical) or rectangular in design.

Continuous flow driers using heated air and of large column-configuration are being widely used. These are generally high-capacity units handling up to about 120,000 cwt of rough rice annually. Maximum temperature of the air stream seldom exceeds 140°F. The two main types are the mixing driers and the non-mixing driers. In the latter design, the grain flows by gravity in a straight path between two screens. The flow rate is controlled by a variable speed discharge roll, and the grain is taken away by a screw conveyor. The mixing type of columnar drier uses baffles over which the grain flows in its descent from the top. Grain is usually passed through these driers several times, its moisture content being reduced 2 to 4% each time. Between passes, the grain is allowed to rest so that its moisture can, to some extent, equilibrate. If the drying rate is excessive, the rice will check or break. Nearly all these designs use cross-current air, but newer types are appearing with counter-flow air circulation systems.

Rice cracking during drying, transport, or storage is a problem because it reduces the yield of head rice when the grain is milled and therefore reduces the value of the finished products. Cracking can, of course, occur simply due to excessive force exerted on the individual kernel at some time in the process. On the other hand, cracking sometimes appears to occur spontaneously in kernels that have been handled relatively gently. This cracking, or checking, is evidently due to stresses that are set up in the kernel due to moisture gradients or temperature gradients. If the endosperm is in a relatively plastic condition because of a fairly high moisture content, these stresses are relieved by distortion of the endosperm, resulting in microscopic changes in shape which cause no further harm. If, however, the endosperm is hard, brittle, and unyielding, the stresses may be relieved by the formation of fractures. Preventing of checking, then, requires gradual and uniform drying, especially as the kernel reaches low moisture contents.

At one time, some rice was dried in sacks in tunnel driers, using heated air. Due to high handling costs, sack drying has been largely abandoned except perhaps for seed rice where it provides a means for preventing mixing of lots.

Practically all of the U.S. rice crop is stored in bulk. Prior to World War II, most of the Texas and Louisiana crop was sacked as it was threshed by stationary threshing machines. The grain was stored in sack warehouses. When combine harvesting and artificial drying replaced the binder-thresher method of harvest, there was a rapid shift to bulk storage. Several different types of storage structures are used, including bins made of wood, concrete, and steel. They are described as "flat" or "vertical" depending on the relationship of height to width. Vertical bins have hopper bottoms and are unloaded by gravity flow. Flat bins are unloaded by power shovels, sweep augers, or similar means.

Suitable storage buildings must provide proper air flow to prevent spontaneous heating of the grain. They must prevent the absorption of water so the rice will not rise above about 13.5% moisture and become susceptible to fungal attack. Of course, they must also protect the grain from rodents, insects, birds, and whatever other animal pests are around. They must prevent contamination by chemicals, toxic fumes, etc. Aeration to prevent accumulation of moisture from natural respiration of the grain and to reduce temperature increases due to the same reactions is accomplished by a system of fans and ducts. Ambient—unheated and uncooled—air is used.

Varieties

Considerations Affecting the Grower

The first concern of the farmer in selecting seed must always be the reliability of the cultivar; will the variety sprout, survive to maturity, and yield well under the conditions it will encounter in his fields? If the seeds germinate poorly, succumb to unavoidable contacts with disease vectors and insects, can be damaged or killed by normal fluctuations in climatic conditions, or fail to survive other vicissitudes of a normal crop year, all other characteristics are irrelevant. The actual yield under the conditions of fertilizer application and cultural practices which will be applied is the next consideration; obviously the farmer is interested in obtaining the largest amount of grain possible with the treatments he intends to apply—fertilizers, cultivation, insecticides, herbicides, etc. If the grower intends to sell all, or most, of his yield rather than using all of it to feed his family, he must also factor into his decision the demands of the marketplace—is the buyer willing to pay a premium for long grain, short grain, or medium grain rice? Is some other quality factor important to consumers or processors? What are the relationships of these quality characteristics to yield? And, of course, cost of the seed must always be considered.

For thousands of years, rice growers had little choice. They grew the same varieties their fathers had grown, not genetically pure strains by any means, but each lot of seeds held over from the preceding harvest containing a collection of varieties more or less suited to the conditions of the locality in which the farmer lived. If any improvement occurred over the centuries, it was due to selection of seeds from the most vigorous or best yielding plants. Most farmers probably attempted a kind of crude seed improvement of this type.

Eventually, two species of cultivated rice achieved predominance—*Oryza sativa* and *O. glaberrima*. The former, Asian rice, probably originated somewhere in the area between north India and the Pacific coast of Asia adjoining Vietnam and China. *O. glaberrima*, or African rice, may have originated in the swampy area of the upper Niger River or to the southwestnear the Guinean coast.

Our principal concern is *O. sativa*, which can be separated into the important races Indica, Japonica, and Javanica, the last being grown primarily in Indonesia and not entering much into international commerce, if at all. The terms long, medium, and short (used in referring to kernel conformation) must be considered in relation to variety. The FAO of the UN has classified milled rices by length into sizes of extra long (more than 7 mm long), long (6.0 to 7.0 mm), medium (5.0 to 5.9 mm), and short (less than 5.0 mm). Most japonicas have short and relatively round kernels, while grains of indica rice are generally long, slender, and rather flat. There are places in the world where japonicas are grown in the same areas (sometimes in the same fields) as indicas.

The subsequent sections will deal with the development of improved varieties of *O. sativa* in modern times.

Structure and Composition

The composition of typical samples of rice and rice products is shown in Table1.1. The changes that occur as the grain is milled reflect the uneven distribution of its components relative to the distance from the surface of the kernel. As layers are successively removed, the proportion of protein, fats, and vitamins in the remaining kernel decreases, while the proportion of carbohydrates decreases. Both brown rice and milled rice are common articles of human food, rice polish and rice bran are predominantly used as animal feeds.

Table 1.1. Representative Composition of Rice Products[1]

Component and unit	Brown rice	Milled rice	Rice polish	Rice bran
Carbohydrates, %	87.2	91.5	66.8	46.6
Protein, %	8.3	7.6	13.2	14.6
Ash, %	1.7	0.5	7.1	10.6
Fat, %	2.0	0.3	10.7	13.4
Crude fiber, %	1.1	0.4	3.3	12.7
N-free extract	82.4	88.8	62.5	45.0

[1]Compiled from a number of sources, see especially Matz and Beachell (1969). Data reported on moisture-free basis.

Structure of the Rice Kernel

As harvested, rough rice consists of the outer covering tissues comprising the hull, or husk, and the inner kernel, i.e., the caryopsis, or brown rice. The caryopsis is enveloped by the caryopsis coat consisting of the pericarp, seed coat, and nucellar layers. The fibrous pericarp consists of compressed cells and is about ten microns thick. Just inside it is the seed coat, a layer of cells having a thick cuticle and representing what

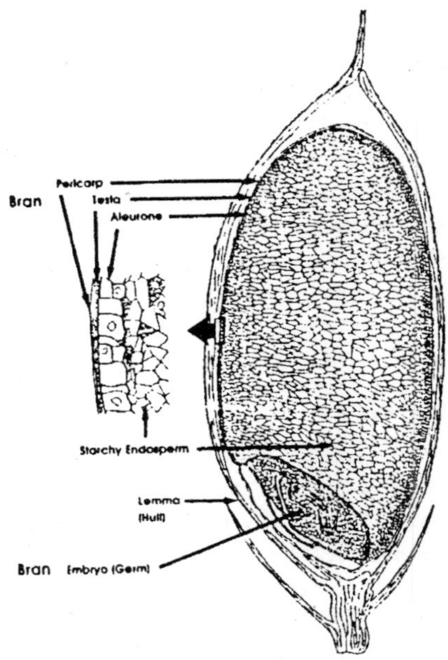

Fig. 1.3. Cross-section of a grain of rough rice.

remains of the inner integument. Proceeding inwardly, the next layer, only about 2.5 microns thick, consists of the remains of the nucellus; it has a thick cuticle adjacent to the seed coat cuticle. Inside the nucellus layer is the aleurone, which completely encloses the endosperm and the embryo. It is composed of 1 to 7 layers of rectangular parenchyma cells and varies in thickness in different parts of the caryopsis. The structure of a typical rice kernel is shown in the drawing reproduced here as Figure 1.3 (obtained from the Rice Bran Institute).

The aleurone cells that surround the endosperm are filled with protein-rich aleurone grains with a single membrane containing globoids or phytate bodies in a protein-carbohydrate matrix, and lipid droplets or spherosomes around a nucleus that is centrally located (Juliano 1980). Aleurone cells that surround the embryo are modified, lacking aleurone grains, and having fewer spherosomes than other aleurone cells. They also contain filament bundles.

The embryo or germ is relatively small and is located on the ventral side of the caryopsis. Within the germ are embryonic leaves and an embryonic primary root joined together by a very short stem. The embryo is bound to the endosperm by the scutellum (cotyledon). Immature cells of scutellum and mesocotyl are found between differentiated parenchyma cells.

The endosperm, which in the mature caryopsis is much larger than all the other tissues combined, consists of thin-walled, radially-elongated parenchyma cells, which are packed with compound starch granules and protein bodies. Protein bodies, which are covered by single membranes, are more abundant in the outer cell layers where the compound starch granules are small. The compound starch granules are in double-membraned amyloplasts. The husk constitutes perhaps 18 to 28% of rough rice, while the remaining 72 to 82% is brown rice. The weight distribution of the brown rice grain components is pericarp 1 to 2%, nucellus and seed coat 4 to 6%, embryo 2 to 3%, and endosperm 89 to 94%. About 6 to 10% of brown rice is removed in abrasive milling, the by-products being bran and polish.

Important Components

Proteins.—The nutritional quality of rice protein is high relative to that of most other cereal proteins. This is due to rice's relatively high content of lysine, which is the first limiting amino acid. Most of the so-called storage proteins in rice kernels are found in discrete protein-rich bodies (aleurins) in the endosperm, similar to the situation in many other seeds. This protein is largely insoluble in water. Most of it—80% or more in milled rice— is the type called glutelin, soluble only in dilute acids or alkalies. The second most abundant type of protein is the salt-soluble globulin. Both globulins and glutelins are composed of an unknown number of molecular species which are generally isoelectric around pH 7.

Table 1.2. Amino Acids in Rice Products[1]

	Ranges*			
Amino acid	Brown rice	Milled rice	Rice bran	Rice polish
	grams of amino acid per 16 grams of N			
Alanine	5.5	5.3-5.5	5.9-6.4	5.9-6.0
Arginine	8.1-8.6	8.2-8.3	7.8-8.3	8.1-8.2
Aspartic acid	8.6-9.0	8.7-9.1	9.0-10.0	8.8-9.7
Cystine	2.2-2.3	1.7-2.5	2.3-2.6	2.5-2.6
Glutamic acid	16.1-16-8	17.4-17.6	13.2-13.6	14.6-16.0
Glycine	4.5-4.6	4.3-4.6	5.2-5.6	5.0-5.1
Histidine	2.3-2.5	2.2-2.6	2.7-3.0	2.6-2.7
Isoleucine	3.4-4.4	3.5-4.6	2.7-4.1	2.7-3.8
Leucine	7.9	8.0-8.2	6.9-7.6	6.6-7.6
Lysine	3.7-4.1	3.2-4.0	4.8-5.0	4.2-4.7
Methionine	2.2-2.4	2.2-2.9	1.7-2.3	2.2-2.8
Phenylalanine	4.8-5.0	5.0-5.2	4.5-4.8	4.2-4.6
Proline	4.6-4.9	4.4-4.9	4.2-5.5	3.8-5.1
Serine	5.1-5.5	5.0-5.6	4.7-5.4	4.5-5.3
Threonine	3.7	3.5-3.7	3.8-4.2	3.5-4.0
Tryptophan	1.2	1.2-1.7	1.2	1.2
Tyrosine	3.8-4.4	4.2-5.2	3.1-3.4	3.4-4.9
Valine	5.1-6.3	5.0-6.5	4.9-6.0	4.4-5.6
Ammonia	2.7-6.5	2.9-6.7	1.9-6.9	2.0-5.9

The amount of protein and the amino add composition of the protein of rice will vary with growing conditions and variety. It has been found that the same variety of rice grown at different locations will vary considerably in amino acid composition. As the percentage of nitrogen increases in the grain, due to growing conditions for example, there is a tendency for the percentage of lysine in the protein to decrease. Different rice varieties grown at the same location will also contain proteins varying in amino acids composition. Furthermore, the distribution of the different amino acids is not uniform within the grain. Milling not only causes a decrease in the total protein of the kernel, but also a change in the amino acid pattern of the remaining protein. Generally, the decrease of lysine on milling is disproportionately large, while there is a relative increase of isoleucine, leucine, and valine.

Table 1.2. gives values for ranges in the amino add composition of brown rice, milled rice, rice bran, and rice polish, as found by one investigator (adapted from Juliano 1980).

Starch.—Milled rice will contain from about 84 to over 90% starch (dry basis). This component is present in the form of angular granules measuring about 2 to 7 microns in their largest dimension. Many of these particles are roughly pentagonal in outline. In size and shape, they are somewhat like the granules of oat starch, but differ in that few if any rounded particles occur. The hilum is centric and indistinct, and birefringence is weak.

In the seed, starch exists in compound granules containing up to about 150 of the smaller particles. These clusters are firmly bound together by a water-insoluble protein matrix which can be dispersed, and the granules released, by various alkaline steeping methods.

Samples of commercial rice starch obtained from U.S. sources lose their birefringence between 144° and 169ºF and gelatinize in the range of 154 to 172ºF when cooked on a Kofler hot stage. The viscosity behavior is similar to that of corn starch. Nonwaxy starch from indica rice contains 21 to 33% amylose, while that from japonica rice will contain a lower amount (17 to 19%) of the linear fraction.

There is a wide variation in iodine affinity and viscometric molecular weight depending on the variety from which the amylose is taken. For example, Century Patna amylose has an iodine affinity of 18.1% as compared to Caloro's 15.0%; Rexoro linear fraction starch has an apparent molecular weight of 325,000 while the equivalent figure for Century Patna is 100,000.

Rice starch preparations contain small amounts of lipid. Fats determined by acid hydrolysis amount to about 0.7 to 0.8%. A large part of this material consists of fatty adds which cannot be removed by petroleum ether but dissolve readily in methanol or 80% dioxane.

Waxy (glutinous) rice has been grown in Asia for many centuries. In some countries, the major portion of the crop consists of these varieties. The principal differences between waxy rice and normal rice depend upon the starch, that from waxy rice consisting of almost 100% amylopectin and thus staining red with iodine solution, while non-waxy starch contains a substantial amount of amylose, and stains blue with iodine. Typically, waxy rice will contain 2% or less of amylose. Both the flour and the purified starch from waxy rice has been found to have advantages for certain food and industrial uses. Gravies, sauces, and puddings based on this starch are very resistant to syneresis during freezing and thawing.

Lipids.—There is very little lipid material in milled rice, perhaps 0.3 to 0.4% by acid hydrolysis could be considered average. Rice bran contains a much higher percentage of lipids, perhaps 21%. Nearly all the studies of rice lipids have concentrated on rice bran oil, and there is a substantial trade in the fatty materials extracted from rice bran and refined.

The glycerides of rice bran oil contain mostly fatty acids having even numbers of carbon atoms from 14 to 20 as well as the odd-numbered fatty acids of chain length 11, 13, and 15. The odd-numbered chains were present in the small amounts of 0.2, 0.6, and 0.9%, respectively, in one sample. Gas-liquid chromatography indicates that bran lipids have significantly higher mean contents of linoleic and linolenic acids, but lower contents of myristic, palmitic, palmitoleic, and stearic acids, than the lipids of milled rice. The iodine values of bran lipids were reported to be significantly higher than for milled rice lipids, and the lipids of indica varieties had lower iodine values than did this component in japonica rice.

Table 1.3 describes some of the characteristics of rice bran oil.

Table 1.3. Some Characteristics of Rice Bran Oil[1]

Characteristic and unit	Crude oil	Characteristics after refining & bleaching	
Rice wax, %	1-4	Smoke point, °F	415
Free fatty acid, %	5-120	Flash point, °F	615
Specific gravity, 25°C	0.916-0.921	Fire point, ‘F	665
Refractive index, 40°C	1.465-1.467	Cloud point, °F	34
Iodine value	92-115	Solid point, °F	28
Saponification value	175-192		
Unsaponifiables, %	3.0-8.0	After refining, bleaching & winterizing	
Volatile matter, %	1.5		
Hechner number	92.1-96.5		
Reichert-Meissel value	0.59-1.75	Cold test, hours	9
Energy value, kcal/kg	9438	Cloud point, °F	20
		Pour point, °F	18

[1] Chang et al. (1980) and Mickus (1959).

Vitamins.—So far as vitamins are concerned, rice is an important source of only thiamin and niacin. The following data are mg per 100 g, first figure for raw, second for parboiled rice. Thiamin was present at levels of 0.13 and 0.15, niacin at levels of 1.54 and 3.2, pyridoxine at a level of 0.14 for raw, and riboflavin at levels of 0.04 and 0.044 (Kennedy 1980). According to Kennedy, "When compared on an energy basis with the RDA for adult women and when rice is a large part of the diet (2000 Kcal), brown rice would give more than sufficient niacin, thiamin, and phosphorus. . .Protein needs would be nearly enough— 91%. . .but calcium and riboflavin needs would be low, both about 23% [zinc about 60%]. Milled rice, however, would be deficient in all nutrients with only protein, niacin, and phosphorus supplying more than 50% of the RDA." A more complete survey of reported values of vitamins in rice and rice components is given in Table 1.4. This table is based on a compilation by Juliano and Bechtel (1985), but with only the medians of the ranges being taken being taken from the original data.

Table 1.4. Vitamin Content of Rice and Rice Products[1]

Vitamin	Brown rice	Milled rice	Rice polish	Rice bran
Retinol (A)	0.06	tr	0.40	1.80
Thiamin	4.50	0.60	11.00	18.00
Riboflavin	0.90	0.40	2.00	3.00
Niacin	44.00	18.00	306.00	383.00
Pyridoxine	7.00	8.00	18.00	18.00
Pantothenic acid	12.00	5.00	40.00	41.00
Biotin	0.07	0.04	0.40	0.40
Inositol, total	1000.00	100.00	3800.00	6000.00
Choline, total	950.00	630.00	1060.00	1190.00
p-aminobenzoic acid	0.30	0.13	0.60	0.65
Folic acid	0.30	0.08	1.40	0.90
Cyanocobalamin*	4.00	1.40	3.00	0.40
Alpha-tocopherol	17.00	tr	70.00	78.00

[1]Values calculated as mg per kg, 14% moisture basis, except * micrograms per kg.

Minerals.—Milled rice is not an important source of minerals by any reasonable standard. The content of ash in a large series of samples ranged from 0.26 to 1.95%, dry basis, with a mean of about 0.65%. There is a considerably higher concentration of minerals in the bran, but the availability of at least some of these is adversely affected by the high concentration of phytin in the bran. Table 1.5 summarizes the mineral and phytate content of rice kernels.

Calcium, iron, potassium, sodium, silicon, magnesium, sulfur, phosphorus, and minor amounts of other elements have been found in rice ash. Potassium and phosphorus are the most abundant mineral elements in rice. Representative figures would be 88 mg and 140 per 100 g dry weight, respectively. Appreciable amounts of silicon are found in the mature rice plant, and slight amounts in milled rice; the function of this element in the plant and its value, if any, in human nutrition is unknown.

Table 1.5. Mineral and Phytate Content of Rice Kernels[1]

Element or compound and unit	Content in kernel or part			
	Whole kernel	Germ	Endosperm	Pericarp
Total P,%	0.31	1.30	0.110	1.04
Phytate P, %	0.25	0.98	0.004	0.95
Zn ppm	19.50	147.00	10.600	56.70
Fe ppm	24.30	321.00	13.000	51.20
Mn ppm	42.40	110.00	6.800	139.00
Cu ppm	4.80	18.00	5.330	10.30
Ca ppm	154.00	1144.00	41.000	721.00
Mg %	0.12	0.56	0.020	0.51
K, %	0.20	0.61	0.080	0.45

[1]O'Dell *et al.* 1972. The kernel was composed of 2% germ, 77% endosperm, and 21% pericarp. All analyses reported on an air dry weight.

Sodium, magnesium, and calcium were found at mean concentrations of 8.1, 28, and 25 mg, respectively, in the whole kernels of six varieties of milled rice.

Of the trace minerals, iron is present in brown rice and white rice at 1,8 and 0.9 mg per 100 g, dry weight basis, respectively, and zinc is present at 1.6 and 1.4 mg per 100 g, as is basis, respectively.

Other Constituents.—Sugars, hemicellulose, nucleic acids, pigments, phytin, and numerous other substances have been found in small amounts in rice. Phytin, the principle phosphorus compound in rice is said to constitute more than 8% of the bran in some samples.

There is a small, but important, amount of sugar in rice. Brown rice will contain about 0.8 to 1.4% total sugars. Reducing sugars are typically near 0.1%. Parboiled rice can be expected to contain around 0.7 to 1.1%

total sugars, and about 0.16% reducing sugars. Milled rice will typically contain much lower amounts of total sugars, about 0.4%, and perhaps 0.06% reducing sugars.

The amount of fiber found in rice varies greatly, depending on the method of analysis, the variety of rice and its growth conditions, the processing which has been applied to the rice, and other factors. Among the reported values for fiber in brown, milled, and parboiled rices are 0.9, 0.3, and 0.2%, respectively.

A concise summary of nutrients and other components to be found in a typical sample of long grain brown rice is included in Table 1.6.

Quality Factors

U.S. Standards

No discussion of rice quality can be complete without consideration of the U.S. Standards for Rice. These specifications control commercial definitions of rice and thus serve as the foundation for any purchasing specifications for rice and rice products. There are actually three different sets of standards: U.S. Standards for Rough Rice, U.S. Standards for Brown Rice for Processing, and U.S. Standards for Milled Rice.

Rough rice is defined as "Rice (*Oryza sativa L.*) which consists of 50 percent or more of paddy kernels of rice." Paddy kernels are further defined as "Whole or broken unhulled kernels of rice." There are four classes: Long-grain, Medium-grain, Short-grain, and Mixed. And, there are six numbered grades (i.e., Grades 1 through 6) and a U.S. Sample grade. The grade is established by determining the total amount of seeds and heat-damaged kernels, the separate amount of heat damaged kernels and objectionable seeds, red rice and damaged kernels, chalky kernels, and color.

Brown rice for processing is defined as "Rice (*Oryza sativa L.*) which consists of more than than 50.0 percent of kernels of brown rice, and which is intended for processing to milled rice." There are four classes: Long-grain, Medium-grain, Short-grain, and Mixed, for each of which there are five numbered grades and a U.S. Sample grade. The grade is largely determined by the percentage content of paddy kernels, seeds and heat-damaged kernels, red rice and damaged kernels, objectionable seeds, chalky kernels, broken kernels, other types, and well-milled kernels.

Milled rice is defined as "Whole or broken kernels of rice (*Oryza sativa L.*) from which the hulls and at least the outer bran layers have been removed and which contain not more than 10.0 percent of seeds, paddy kernels, or foreign material, either singly or combined."

Table 1.6. Nutrients and Other Components in Long Brown Rice[1]

	Unit	Amount		Unit	Amount
Proximate:			**Amino acids:**		
Water	g	10.37	Tryptophan	g	0.101
Food energy	kcal	370.	Threonine	g	0.291
	kJ	1,548.	Isoleucine	g	0.336
Protein (N x 5.95	g	7.94	Leucine	g	0.657
Total lipid (fat)	g	2.92	Lysine	g	0.303
Carbohydrate, total	g	77.24	Methionine	g	0.179
Crude fiber	g	1.32	Cystine	g	0.096
Ash	g	1.53	Phenvlalanine	g	0.410
Lipids:			Tyrosine	g	0.298
Fatty acids:			Valine	g	0.466
Saturated, total	g	0.584	Arginine	g	0.602
12-0	g	0.003	Histidine	g	0.202
14-0	g	0.011	Alanine	g	0.463
16:0	g	0.498	Aspartic acid	g	0.743
18:0	g	0.052	Glutamic acid	g	1.618
Monounsaturated, total	g	1.056	Givcine	g	0.391
16:1	g	0.010	Proline	g	0.372
18:1	g	1.046	Serine	g	0.411
Polyunsaturated, total	g	1.044	**Minerals**:		
18:2	g	1.000	Calcium	mg	23.
18:3	g	0.044	Iron	mg	1.47
Vitamins:			Magnesium	mg	143.
Ascorbic acid	mg	0.	Phosphorus	mg	333.
Thiamin	mg	0.401	Potassium	mg	223.
Riboflavin	mg	0.093	Sodium	mg	7.
Niacin	mg	5.091	Zinc	mg	2.02
Pantothenic acid	mg	1.493	Copper	mg	0.277
Vitamin B-6	mg	0.509	Manganese	mg	3.743
Folacin	mcg	20.			

[1]Where no values are stated for a component, or component has been omitted from the listing, there are inadequate data available. All values are from USDA Handbook 8-20 (1989).

There are seven classes of milled rice, four of which are based on the type of rice and three of which are based on the percentages of whole kernels and broken kernels of different sizes. Names of the former are Long-grain, Medium-grain, Short-grain, and Mixed (all followed by the term "Milled Rice"), and of the latter are Second-head Milled Rice, Screenings Milled Rice, and Brewers Milled Rice. The former each have six possible number grades and a sample grade while the latter each have five numbered grades and a sample grade.

The types of rice—long grain, medium grain, and short grain—are based on the length:width ratio of kernels of rice that are unbroken, with limits as defined in the Rice Inspection Handbook.

There are also special grades, "Coated milled rice," "Granulated brewers milled rice," "Parboiled milled rice," and "Undermilled milled rice." Table 1.7 includes details of the grades and grade requirements for Brewers Milled Rice.

Additional Quality Factors

It is rather obvious that the U.S. Standards for rice are too general to serve the needs of the average commercial processor, although they may be suitable for packagers of raw rice. Further evaluation of the quality of a sample of rice must depend to a considerable extent upon the use for which it is intended. Of course, there are some general quality factors, such as freedom from insect infestation and absence of toxic chemicals which will apply to virtually all food uses. Since most consumers buying rice for home preparation expect to find nearly 100% whole kernels in their package and regard this as a quality factor, the number of broken grains must be taken into consideration. If the rice is intended to be milled into a flour, used in brewing, or otherwise comminuted, the percentage of whole grains is obviously much less of a factor and processors for such uses will buy broken grains at a considerable discount from the head rice price.

Long grain rice is characterized by a comparatively high amylose content and a moderately high gelatinizing temperature. Milled kernels of high quality long-grain varieties usually cook dry and flaky with a minimum of splitting, and the cooked grains tend to remain separate. Short and medium grain varieties are more moist and firm when cooked, and the grains tend to stick together. They are characterized by lower amylose content than long grain rices and they have lower gelatinization temperatures. The data in Table 1.8 illustrate the differences between long-, medium-, and short-grain rice so far as their chemical and physical characteristics related to food quality are concerned. Data are based on measurements of fully mature rice of typical varieties within each grain type.

Table 1.7. Grades and Grade Requirements for Brewers Milled Rice

Grade	Maximum limits of— Paddy kernels and seeds: Total (singly or combined) (Percent)	Objectionable seeds (Percent)	Color requirements[1]	Minimum milling requirements[2]
U.S. No. 1 [3, 4]	0.5	0.05	Shall be white or creamy	Well milled.
U.S. No. 2 [3, 4]	1.0	0.01	May be slightly gray	Well milled.
U.S. No. 3 [3, 4]	1.5	0.2	May be light gray or slightly rosy	Reasonably well milled.
U.S. No. 4 [3, 4]	3.0	0.4	May be gray or rosy	Reasonably well milled.
U.S. No. 5	5.0	1.5	May be dark gray or very rosy	Lightly milled.

U.S. Sample Grade shall be milled rice of this class which: (a) Does not meet the requirements for any of the grades from U.S. No. 1 to U.S. No. 5 inclusive; (b) contains more than 15.0 percent of moisture; (c) is musty, or sour. or heating; (d) has any commercially objectionable foreign odor; (e) has a badly damaged or extremely red appearance; (f) contains more than 0.1 percent of foreign material; (g) contains more than 15.0 percent of broken kernels that will pass through a 2½ sieve; (h) contains live or dead weevils or other insects, insect webbing or insent refuse; or (i) is otherwise of distinctly low quality.

[1]For the special grade Parboiled milled rice, see 68.315(c).

[2]For the special grade Undermilled milled rice, see 68.315(d).

[3]GradesU.S. No. 1 to U.S. No. 4, inclusive, shall contain not more than 3.0 percent of heat-damaged kernels, kernels damaged by heat and/or parboiled kernels in nonparboiled rice.

[4]Grades U.S. No. 1 to U.S. No. 4, inclusive, shall contain not more than 1.0 percent of material passing through a 30 sieve. This limit does not apply to the special grade Granulated brewers milled rice.

Table 1.8. Some Characteristics of Rice Grain Types[1]

Endosperm characteristics, and units	Grain Type: Long	Medium	Short
Amylose content, %	23-26	15-20	18-20
Alkali spreading value, av.	3-5	6-7	6-7
Gelatinization temp., °C	71-74	65-68	65-67
Gelat. temp. class	Medium	Low	Low
Water uptake at 77ºC, ml/100g	121-136	300-340	310-360
Protein (N X 5.95), %	6-7.5	6-7	6-6.5
Parboiling-canning stability, solids loss %	18-21	31-36	30-33
Amylographic paste viscosity, BU			
Peak	765-940	890-980	820-870
Cooked 10 min at 95ºC	400-500	370-420	370-400
Cooked to 50ºC	770-880	680-760	680-690
Brewing cookability with malt diastase, Zahn sec	120+	5-15	5-10

[1]Webb (1985). See that reference for original sources.

The suitability of rice for culinary use is related to the variety and to the expectations of the consumer. For example, some ethnic groups demand glutinous rice while most U.S. consumers find this type of rice gives far too sticky and lumpy a finished product to be satisfactory. This characteristic is inherent in the variety and cannot be changed by any set of growing conditions or any practical processing method. Fortunately, a simple evaluation, or even visual .examination, of the lot is sufficient to allow a judgment to be made as to the glutinous quality, but an actual use test or more sophisticated chemical and physical tests are required to determine other important quality factors. Some of these tests will be described in the chapter "Rice Processing."

"Chalkiness" is a kernel characteristic that is undesirable in nearly all forms of rice because it detracts from overall appearance and indicates a mechanical weakness which will lead to greater breakage during the milling process. Parboiling, which strengthens the kernel, may overcome some of the defects. The extent of chalkiness is determined largely by visual examination and it may affect different parts of the grain. The opposite of chalkiness is described as clear, vitreous, translucent endosperms. Specialty waxy varieties will, however, be characterized by opaque endosperms.

The following list of quality factors has been adapted from a table to be found in an article by Webb:

1. Hull and bran color
2. Grain characteristics
    a. Size, shape, weight, and uniformity
    b. Translucency vs. Chalkiness
3. Milling quality
    a. Yield of head rice
    b. Total yield of milled rice
    c. Milling uniformity
4. Cooking and processing quality factors
    a. Amylose content
    b. Alkali spreading value
    c. Protein content
    d. Gelatinization temperature
    e. Water-uptake capacity
    f. Parboil-canning stability
    g. Brewing cookability of rice with diastase
5. Other grading factors
    a. Moisture content
    b. Test weight
    c. Degree of milling
    d. Color
    e. Dockage
    f. Damaged grains
    g. Odors
    h. Red rice

Milling yield is a very important criterion of rice quality. To determine the milling yield of rough rice, foreign material is first removed, then the rice is shelled to remove the hulls, milled to remove most of the bran layers and hulls, and, finally, sized to determine the yield of whole and broken grains. Data are generally expressed as yield of whole rice and total yield, the latter figure representing the quantity of whole plus broken grains.

Standard milling methods are too detailed to reproduce here; they can be found in the USDA Rice Inspection Handbook.

Food, Feed, and Beverage Applications of Rice

The main use of rice the world over is as a boiled or steamed product which serves as a bulk carbohydrate food, in much the same way as bread, pasta, or potatoes have been used in western cuisines. Cooking results in starch gelatinization and water absorption. Some soluble materials are removed. It can be observed that the gross visual effects are an increase in volume and a change in shape of the grain; usually, there are also slight changes in color and visual texture. Most varieties show the greatest expansion in width, but a few types exhibit a pronounced lengthwise expansion during cooking (e.g., Basmati varieties from India).

There are very many other applications of rice, as an ingredient in more complex foods and in beverages, which will be discussed briefly in the following paragraphs. For more complete explanations of processing methods and ingredient specifications, the reader should consult references given in the bibliographies of this chapter and of the chapter on Rice Processing. Breakfast foods made with rice, nutritional foods having rice as one of the important ingredients, and some types of snack foods containing rice will be described in other chapters.

Animal Feed

Rough rice has almost no use as an animal feed. The cost is too high and the nutrient value too low compared to such feeds as corn, sorghum, and the like, especially when such high carbohydrate components are supplemented with soybean meal. Rice hulls are sometimes used as roughage or filler in animal feeds even though their low nutritive value, abrasive nature, low bulk density (about 0.1 g per ml), and high ash content do not make them particularly suitable for this application.

Rice bran is a significant source of nutrients: it contains proteins, oils, some vitamins, and carbohydrates. Protein contents of many samples showed a range of 11.5 to 17.2% protein, 12.8 to 22.6% fat, 6.2 to 14.4% fiber, 8.0 to 17.7% ash, and 33.5 to 53.5% nitrogen-free extract. These figures indicate potential value as an animal feed. Rice bran tends to become rancid fairly quickly, but it can be stabilized by dry or moist heat treatment. According to Barber and Barber, its principal disadvantages as a feed ingredient are high fiber content, high content of fat rich in unsaturated fatty acids, proportion of calcium and phosphorus is not ideal, great fluctuation of composition from lot to lot, and instability. Also, some samples of bran may include mycotoxins, although this type of contamination can also be found in many other feedstuffs.

Rice bran has been used as part of the diet for fattening pigs, but was not recommended for immature pigs. Up to 40% rice bran can be used in growing and finishing rations for swine; larger percentages led to reduced weight gain and lower feed efficiency. The quality of fat in the meat was also poor at the higher levels. It has also been reported that up to 40% bran can be used in the total diet of poultry, but the presence of oxidized fats can cause serious problems to develop; therefore, the bran should be stabilized to prevent the development of rancidity during storage. Growth suppressing factors may be present, but these have not been identified with any certainty.

Use of rice bran in the ration of dairy cows appears to be satisfactory up to a level of 15 to 20%; other workers say up to 60% is acceptable. This ingredient seems to lead to increases in milk and butterfat production, but large percentages can adversely affect properties of the milk. Rice bran has been used as an adsorbent for the liquid and semi-solid waste obtained from processing fish, to give a feed material.

Canned Rice

Rice puddings, Spanish rice, and other canned products consisting mainly of this grain have been offered on the U.S. market from time to time. They do not appear to have ever been a major factor in consumer menu planning. One problem which plagued this type of product was the texture change in the rice kernels, which often led to a quite unpleasant mouthfeel in the food after it had been stored for a few days or weeks. The necessity for high heat treatment, i.e., retorting, of the cans after filling, either caused complete breakdown of the kernels with the formation of a granular mush in the can or the adhering of the rice kernels into large clumps. Use of parboiled rice helps prevent the disintegration of kernels. Gerdes and Burns (1985) suggested use of instant parboiled rice and a cold water quench following blanching to eliminate sticking and clumping.

Large amounts of canned rice soups, such as chicken and rice soup, are sold, either as ready to eat or condensed types. They seem to be perfectly satisfactory to a large number of consumers. The difference between these items and those previously discussed is that in soups the rice forms a minor ingredient with widely separated grains which do not have much opportunity to adhere together.

Fermented Rice Foods

There are probably hundreds of different rice foods made in the Orient by fermenting (in the broad sense of subjecting to the action of microorganisms) rice. Many of these involve slight variations on a few basic themes. Only a few examples can be discussed here.

Fermented sweet rice (tieng-chiou-niang) is made with an inoculum containing yeasts, molds, and bacteria. The most important microorganism appears to be a mold species of the *Rhizopus genus*. Many changes occur as a result of the action of the inoculum on rice grains, but the final result is a mixture of rice grains and a sweet liquid containing some alcohol and acid. One method of serving is to add fresh or canned fruits to the fermented sweet rice to make a dessert.

Yellow rice is made by allowing the naturally contaminating microorganisms to react with unhusked, undried rice. During fermentation, the grain acquires a yellowish or brownish color which is retained by the milled rice. Also, enzymes break down part of the starch and probably other components of the kernel, and partially "cook" the rice as a result of the heat developed during the microbial reactions. *Bacillus subtilis* and *Aspergillus spp.* are important factors.

Miso is a fermented paste of rice, soybeans, salt, and an inoculum. It is used by the Japanese primarily to make soup, but is also used as an ingredient in some other foods. The principal active agent in the inoculum is apparently *Aspergillus oryzae*, but several other important microorganisms such as lactic bacteria, osmophilic and halophilic bacteria, and a yeast, *Saccharomyces rouxii*, are present in most of these preparations. A similar seasoning paste, chiang, is used in China.

Idli and dosci are Indian foods made by fermentation of rice and a pulse called black legume. Tape, and variations of this name, refer to Indonesian foods resulting from microbial reactions on mixtures of glutinous rice and a culture or of cassava and a culture.

Fermented and Distilled Beverages from Rice

Very large quantities of broken rice are used as a carbohydrate source by the U.S. brewing industry. There is a federal standard for "Brewers milled rice" which states this material shall consist of milled rice, which, when determined in accordance with applicable sections of the regulations contains not more than 25.0% of whole kernels and which does not meet the kernel-size requirements for the class Second Head Milled Rice or Screenings Milled Rice. Other requirements are also established by this regulation. Medium- and short-grain rice are preferred; long grain rice can be used by some brewers, but it tends to cause gelatinization and viscosity problems in the cooker. Long storage or certain other conditions may cause the rice to gelatinize slowly to give a highly viscous cooker mash. Brewers rice will contain an average of about 1.5% lipids, which is an acceptable level provided they have not become rancid; higher lipid contents are a negative factor because they can lead to increased yeast growth, reduced foam in the finished beer, and off-flavors.

Shao-hsing wine is made in Taiwan from glutinous rice, wheat, and water. Two kinds of "starters" are used, one made from wheat and the other from rice. Mold is grown on the grain to produce an enzyme preparation that can convert the starch of the raw materials to sugars that can be fermented by yeasts. Mash is prepared from the starters, water, steamed rice, and wheat. The method is described in detail by Wang (1980). Sake, the rice wine of Japan, is a clear, pale yellow liquid with a specific gravity of 1.0 and a typical alcohol content of 15 to 16%. Brewing of sake involves using koji to enzymatically convert the starch of rice to fermentable sugars (and perform other changes), while simultaneously fermenting the mixture with sake yeast. Hong (red) wine of China is made from a rice mash which has been digested and fermented in a manner somewhat similar to the beverages previously discussed, but late in the fermentation the liquid is changed to a red color by the addition of a *Monascus* culture.

A number of distilled beverages are made from mashes consisting principally of rice. The mashes are generally treated with fungal preparations to hydrolyze the starch into fermentable sugars, although malt may also be used. For Taiwanese rice liquor, the most active molds are thought to be Rhizopus spp. and the yeast *Saccharomyces spp.*, as *S. peka*.

Rice Cake

This is a wet product made from either glutinous or nonglutinous rice. The rice is milled, refined, washed, and soaked. It is then drained of excess moisture, kneaded, made into various forms, packed in a plastic film, heat pasteurized, and cooled. The cake is further manipulated and cooked by the consumer. Seasonings include various combinations of salt, pepper, radish, MSG, and sugar. There is a fermented version made in Taiwan from rice, sugar, and a biological leavener.

According to Bums and Gerdes (1985), Japanese rice cakes are roughly classifed into "namagashi" (pastry or unbaked cake) and "higashi" (dried cake). Dango, a dumpling of steamed rice, mochi (rice paste), mochigashi, a processed rice paste, and uiro, a kind of rice pudding. are representative forms of namagashi.

Completely different from the above are the cakes formed of puffed rice kernels which have been commercially available for many years in the U.S., but which have attained added popularity in recent years. Practical methods of forming expanded rice kernels are discussed in considerable detail in the chapter on Breakfast Cereal Manufacture, which will be found later in this volume.

Bread

Flat breads of the unleavened "chapati" type can be made from rice instead of the traditional wheat flour, but, of course, the texture and flavor of the product are entirely different. Red rice has been used in some places in Pakistan for making rice bread, because the product remains softer for a longer period of time than when ordinary rice is used.

Rice flour is far from ideal as the structural component of leavened bread rolls or loaves. The grain contains none of the gluten which gives wheat flour its unique ability to form highly expanded, tender, white, and flavorful yeast-leavened or chemically-leavened baked products. Nonetheless, much research has been done into ways of preparing bread substitutes from rice flour. Part of this interest has been the result of the demand from persons who are allergic to wheat flour. Some of the experiments reported in the literature of this field have been summarized by Bean and Nishita. Many gums have been tested as gluten replacements; only certain hydroxypropyl methylcelluloses gave promising results in bread formulas. Only flour from short- and medium-grain rice had the necessary physicochemical properties to give soft-textured bread crumb.

Noodles

Rice noodles have been consumed in Japan, China, and other Asian countries since ancient times. Instant rice noodles are a more recent development. Nonglutinous rice is the main ingredient in both types. After soaking in water, the rice is mashed into a paste, excess water is squeezed out, the resultant cake is steamed for, e.g., 80 minutes then extruded. The strands are dried on racks with hot air for the required period of time. To prepare for consumption the noodles may either be fried, mixed with meat and cooked, or used in soups.

Oriental-style Snack Foods

There seems to be a large number of varieties of oriental snack crackers. In Japan, rice crackers made from glutinous rice are called "Arare" or "Okaki," while those made from nonglutinous rice are called "Senbei." The doughs are not yeast-leavened and, apparently, no chemical leavener is added either. There is a considerable expansion due to steam leavening, however. As described by Li and Luh, the glutinous rice dough is "quick frozen" during one stage of the processing. Crackers can be seasoned with seaweed, sesame, red peppers, sugar, and spices, and colored with natural or artificial pigments.

Chien tsong is said to be a very popular food in China and Japan. Glutinous rice is treated with an alkali (soda ash), then a portion is wrapped in bamboo leaves and boiled. After the wrapping is removed, the boiled rice is served with honey or sugar.

Vinegar

Rice vinegar is an ancient and common product in the Far East, but it is a minor item of commerce in the U.S. because other forms of vinegar (cider, malt, and distilled), are better known here and are usually cheaper.

Recently, there has been a mild upsurge of interest in this condiment because it somehow fits into the pattern of a healthier universe as envisaged by natural food enthusiasts. The flavor is pleasant and mellow, but is easily masked by other ingredients when the vinegar is used as an ingredient in blended foods.

Rice vinegar is made by a series of steps which include saccharification of the starch to give fermentable sugars, fermentation of the sugars to yield alcohol, and conversion of the alcohol to acetic acid by other microbial reactions. The rice which is used as the main ingredient can be low quality rice, broken rice, etc. In Japan, the aqueous extract from rice wine fermentation is sometimes mixed with alcohol from other sources to form the substrate for the acetic acid fermentation.

In traditional methods, the rice is first steamed to gelatinize the starch and denature the protein. An inoculum of *Aspergillus* is then used to hydrolyze the starch, yielding primarily glucose. The inoculum is generally the preparation known as "koji," which consists of the fungus as grown on steamed rice. This material will contain very many different kinds of enzymes, but it is a particularly potent source of amylases. The yeast used for the alcoholic fermentation is *Saccharomyces sake*, which is evidently prepared in the factory from a culture medium consisting of steamed rice, koji, water, lactic acid, and phosphates which has been inoculated with an impure source of the yeast and then fermented for 15 to 20 days. The "wine" mash is pressed and filtered, then inoculated with seed vinegar from a previous batch to provide the necessary microorganisms for the acetic acid fermentation. Completion of this step can take 1 to 3 months. The raw vinegar is stored in a separate tank for 2 to 3 months for ripening, then filtered through diatomaceous earth (or the like) before being pasteurized at 140°F for 30 min. The rice vinegar is then ready for bottling. A lengthy and complete discussion of this topic was published by Lai *et al.*

2

Processing of Rice

Introduction

Nearly all rice consumed as food has undergone some type of milling operation during its preparation. Rice milling differs considerably from the milling of wheat, rye, or corn, because the preferred form of rice for culinary purposes is the whole grain rather than a flour or meal. It is true that pulverized forms of rice are sometimes used in the kitchen, but only as minor ingredients in sauces and the like. Fairly large amounts of broken kernels and small pieces are sold for manufacturing purposes, as for brewing and for manufacturing puffed breakfast cereals or snacks, but these are obtained as by-products from the production of whole kernel rice. In the aggregate, the demand for whole kernel rice far exceeds that for smaller piece sizes, and the market value of the former is correspondingly greater.

The earliest type of rice milling relied on a mortar-and-pestle type of operation, although the "mortar" may have been merely a hole in the ground. Pounded grain was poured from one vessel to another, allowing the interaction of gravity and the wind to separate fragments of hulls, chaff, bran, and germ from the kernels. In the natural progression of improvement, mortars and pestles became larger, and arrangements were made for moving the pestles by animal power, windmills, or water power. Such simple methods of milling persisted for millenia, and are still used in many parts of the world, but a mechanical semiautomatic system based on different principles started to be used in Europe in the eighteenth century.

The belief is widespread that rice is of major importance as a crop only in countries where its per capita consumption is high and where it is the basic energy food for the inhabitants. It is, however, one of the principal grain crops in the U.S. and the U.S. is one of the largest exporters of rice although this country does not have a very high per capita consumption of this cereal.

Vitreous long-grain rices are preferred in the domestic market for cooking and for processing into canned products such as soups. The softer short-grain or pearl types are sold to some extent for home use, but are raised mainly to supply trade requirements in foreign markets, particularly in the far east, and they are probably the only type used for making puffed rice. Both long- and short-grain rice may be manufactured into dry breakfast cereals and both are used in parboiling operations. The principal difficulty with culinary applications of soft-grain rice is that it tends to become sticky when cooked and usually does not have as firm a texture as long-grain rice. These disadvantages are overcome for the most part when precooked rice is canned or made into dry quick-cooking products. In some instances, the soft characteristic of short-grain rice is an advantage—the brewing industry uses broken grains of rice as a source of carbohydrates and prefers short-grain types because they disperse more readily in the kettles.

Some parts of this chapter are based on the Kester and Matz article cited in the bibliography.

Quality of Rice

Rice trading in the U.S. is based on Standards promulgated by the USDA. Under these Standards, each lot of rough, brown, or milled rice can be provided with a designation which helps to fix its commercial value. In general, the designation will consist of the letters "US" followed by either a number from 1 to 6 or the words "Sample Grade," the name of the class, and the name of the special type (if any). An example is, "US No. 3 Medium Grain Brown Rice Parboiled." Each grade is separately defined for rough, brown, and milled rice. The grade for any lot of rice is determined by limitations on the presence of damaged kernels, chalky kernels, red rice, and certain other undesirable forms or conditions.

The classes for rough and brown rice are long grain, medium grain, short grain, and mixed. Milled rice adds to these four types the additional ones: head, screenings, and brewers.

The special grade designation which forms the final term in the description are: (1) for rough rice, (a) parboiled, (b) weevily; (2) for brown rice, parboiled; (3) for milled rice, (a) undermilled, (b) parboiled, (c) coated, (d) granulated brewers.

The U.S. Standards are very general specifications which are useful as basic requirements for purchase and sale of lots of rice, but they do not fully characterize the rice in terms of its acceptability to the consumer. If the rice will be used to prepare food for the table, a number of special considerations come into play. The processor or retailer must consider the needs or expectations of different ethnic groups, markets of different economic levels, packaging alternatives, and storage life. Some of these factors have been discussed in the chapter on rice grain. Others will be treated in moderate detail in the following paragraphs.

In general, it can be said that consumer satisfaction depends not only on the appearance, flavor, and texture of the finished food, but on appearance of the raw product, cost, convenience of the container, and ease and reliability (tolerance to variations in cooking conditions) of preparation. Perception of nutritive value may also be a factor, though this is often taken for granted, and does not necessarily reflect the true contribution of the raw product to the health and happiness of the ultimate consumer.

A general treatment of this subject will be found in the USDA Technical Bulletin No. 1331, "Quality evaluation studies of foreign and domestic rices," published in 1965. A later discussion was written by Webb, who listed the following major components of rice quality:

Hull and bran (pericarp) color
Grain dimensions, weight, and uniformity
Test weight (weight per unit volume)
General appearance-
  -chalkiness
  -translucency Milling yields
Cooking and processing behavior
Moisture content

The basic requirements for rice, like those for nearly all staple foods—potatoes, pasta, bread, porridge, tortillas—are that the finished food be bland in flavor, light in color, and soft and smooth in texture so that it can act as an extender to the condiments, sauces, additives, and toppings with which it is served and can be consumed in quantity without causing physiological or psychological discomfort. Stickiness, strong or unexpected flavors, uneven or dark colors, and hard textures are seldom appreciated in bulk nutrients of this sort. Allowances must be made for the special requirements of different ethnic groups which may desire, for example, a certain degree of stickiness in the cooked rice, more pronounced flavors, special visual features, etc.

Results of a preference test conducted with a panel of California women give an insight into the factors that consumers believe are most important in determining rice desirability.

According to Reyes and Jindal, texture largely determines the consumer acceptance of rice, although this statement must be based to a large extent on the assumption that aberrant lots of the grain, those with obviously out-of-the-ordinary organoleptic characteristics, are removed from the distribution system before they can reach the ultimate consumer. Hardness of cooked rice, a negative quality factor, is significantly correlated with amylose content. Stickiness correlates negatively with amylose content.

Several instrumental techniques have been used to evaluate the texture of cooked rice. Most are best suited for lots of rice at least several grams in weight, but others can be applied to single kernels.

3

Rice Milling

The paddy seed contains a rough outer covering, called husk. The husk accounts for about one-fifth to one-fourth the weight of paddy. The inner kernel, called brown rice or dehusked rice, contains some soft outer layers, jointly called bran. It accounts for some 8 to 10% of the brown rice weight, including the small germ (1-2% by weight) located at one end of the grain (figure 3.1).

Paddy cannot be directly eaten. The hard, woody husk is not edible and must be removed first. A part of the bran (including the germ) also should preferably be removed to make the rice easy to cook and digest. Rice milling is the process of removing the husk and part of the bran from paddy in order to produce edible rice.

Rice milling is a gigantic industry in India. India currently produces about 108 million tonnes of paddy. A small amount out of this is used for making various rice products (puffed and flaked rice) and another small amount for seed. The rest is all milled for consumption, either as raw or after parboiling. The milling is accomplished by a large number of systems from very small to very large scale. Some of these use complex machines based on intricate scientific principles.

But the rice milling industry does not only mill rice. It also carries out many other essential functions, such as procurement, drying, storage, quality control, utilisation of by-products, etc.

Intake Paddy: its Handling

Cleaning

Paddy after harvesting and threshing contains some 'foreign matter'depending upon harvesting, threshing and handling methods. The foreign matter may be other crop seeds, straw, chaff, sand, stones, dust, pieces of mud and iron particles. Paddy received in the mill must be first cleaned to remove these foreign matters before it can be properly stored. Otherwise they may cause deterioration of the paddy during storage or may damage or obstruct the conveying and milling machinery. Cleaning also helps to reduce storage space.

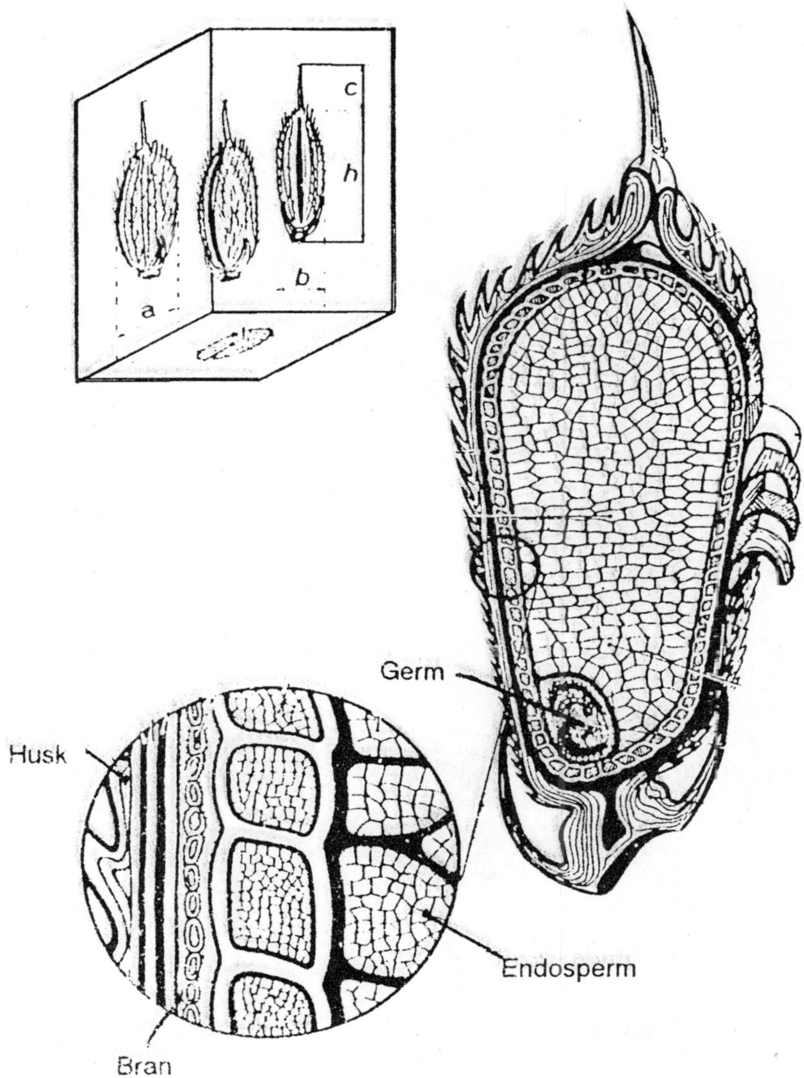

Figure 3.1 : Structure of Paddy Grain

The first cleaning operation of paddy after threshing is called 'Scalping'. It removes the bulk of the foreign matter. But the paddy is not completely cleaned (figure 3.2). The small amount of impurities that still remain are later removed during the next cleaning operation during the rice milling process. Scalper cleaners use both sieves and aspirators.

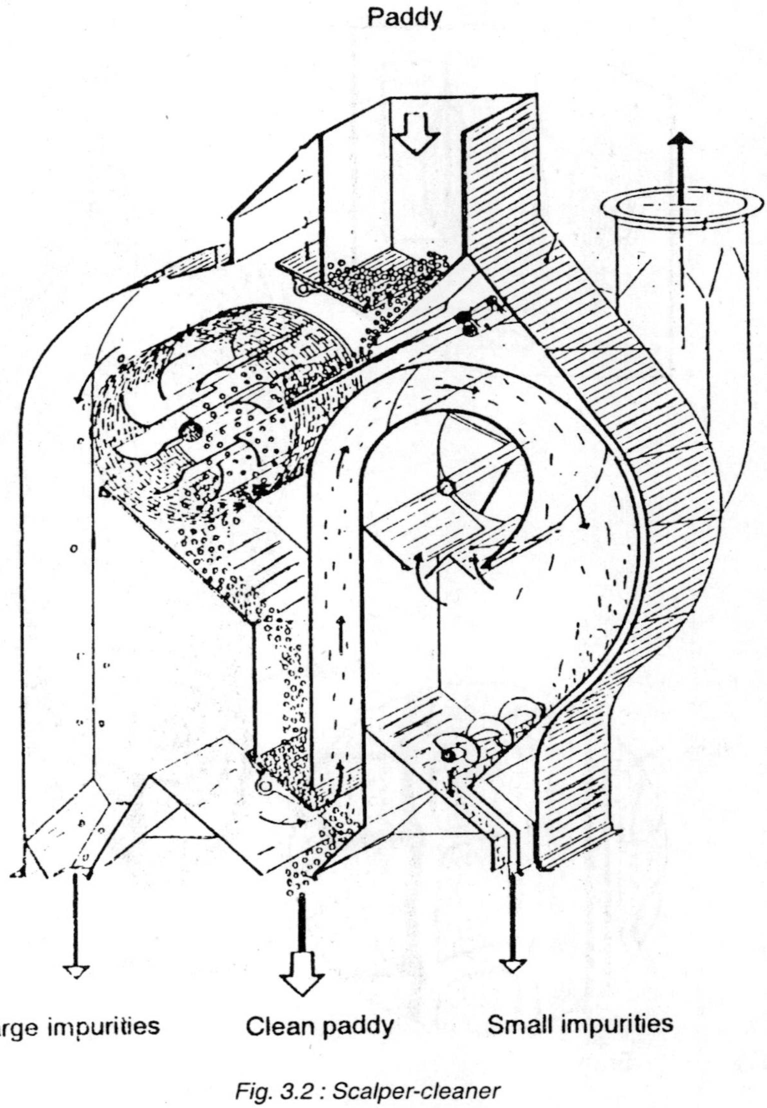

Fig. 3.2 : Scalper-cleaner

Drying

Intake paddy also generally contains more moisture than is safe for storage and has to be dried. Freshly harvested paddy normally has a moisture content of 18-25%. This moisture must be brought down by drying to ensure a good storage quality. A moisture content of 14% is considered safe for short periods of storage. For longstorage, the grain should be dried to 13% moisture or less.

In the drying process, heat supplied by hot air or by the sun evaporates the moisture from the grain, while the moving air carries away the evaporated moisture.

Cracking of Paddy during drying and how to prevent it

In drying of paddy, another point, in addition to removal of moisture, is most important. Drying may cause cracks in paddy. Cracks in paddy are dangerous, for they may later lead to breakage of rice during milling. Therefore, the drying process must be so adjusted that cracks do not develop in the grains.

Why does paddy grains crack during drying? When paddy is dried, moisture evaporates from grain surface only. Moisture in the interior of the grain moves by diffusion to the surface, and only then it can be evaporated. Diffusion is a slower process compared to evaporation. Therefore, during fast drying with hot air or in sun, the rate of moisture loss from the grain surface is greater than the rate of diffusion of moisture from the interior to the surface. The surface, therefore, gets overdried in relation to the centre which remains moist. In other words, whenever paddy is rapidly dried, a moisture difference (or moisture gradient) develops between the grain centre and the surface. This gradient of moisture causes stress to the paddy grain. If the stress becomes too much due to a steep moisture gradient, the grain cracks. This is the principle of grain cracking during drying.

How are we then to prevent the cracks? Clearly, we have to avoid moisture gradient in grain. One way would be to dry slowly. Then evaporation will be slowed to balance diffusion of moisture and there will be no gradient. But paddy is handled in tonnes, not in kilograms. Therefore, paddy must be dried fast, not slowly in shade. The only alternative is to stop drying before the moisture gradient becomes excessive. That means, the drying should not be continuous but should be in stages, with rest periods between the drying stages. These rest periods are called "tempering". During tempering, evaporation of moisture from the paddy surface stops, but diffusion of moisture from inside continues. So moisture gets equalised throughout the grain after some time and the moisture gradient is thus removed (figure 3.4).

Hence, the grain can now be again dried without the danger of cracking. This is the principle of fast drying of paddy without its cracking.

It is generally considered that not more than 2-4% moisture should be removed in one drying stage in the case of mechanical drying with hot air. Paddy may be dried for, say, half-an-hour, then tempered for 6 hours, then dried again, and so on in cycles until it is fully dried. As sun drying is not as fast as mechanical drying, less number of stages may be sufficient for drying in sun.

Methods of Drying

Sun drying : The most common method of drying is sun drying. The paddy is spread over paved yards in 3-5 cm thick layers. It is occasionally turned to prevent the top layers from over drying and to permit the bottom layers to receive heat and air movement. Sun drying is best done in dry weather with low humidity. Tempering of paddy by heaping between stages of drying and frequent turning over during drying can make sun drying quite effective. Two stages of drying with one tempering are generally satisfactory, for sun drying is not as fast as mechanical drying.

Mechanical drying : The alternative to sun drying is mechanical drying. Here paddy is held in a container and hot air is blown through the paddy mass. The dryer may be either batch type or continuous-flow type.

Batch dryers : A batch dryer can be used when the amount of paddy to be dried is small. It consists of a bin which holds 1-2 tonnes of paddy. The floor of the bin is perforated. Paddy is spread 0.6-1.2 meters deep over the perforated floor and heated air is blown through the paddy from below. Air that has passed through the paddy is discharged as cooler, more humid air. After the drying is complete, paddy is removed and the dryer is ready for another batch (figure 3.4).

Continuous-flow dryers : When large volumes of paddy are to be dried quickly, this is the type used. The continuous flow dryers are of two kinds: nonmixing and mixing types (figure 3.5 & 3.6).

In the nonmixing type, paddy flows down between two parallel screens 15-25 cm apart. Hot air is blown through the screen as the paddy moves from the top of the dryer to the bottom. The dryer is usually operated such that the paddy stays for 15-30 minutes in the dryer, i.e., the paddy takes 15-30 minutes to move from the top to the bottom of the dryer. Because the grain flows straight down the column, the grains do not get intermixed during drying. Hence there is chance of overdrying on the side in which hot air enters and under-drying on the side in which the air goes out. However mixing occurs when the paddy is discharged and conveyed from the dryer.

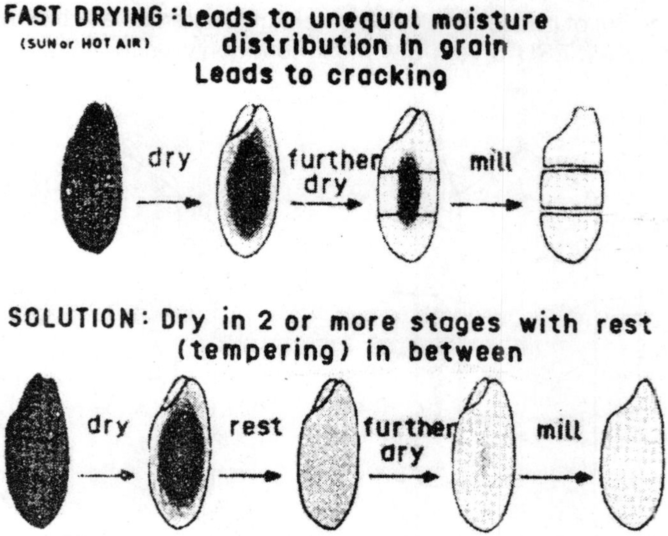

Fig. 3.3. Cracking during Drying and how to avoid it

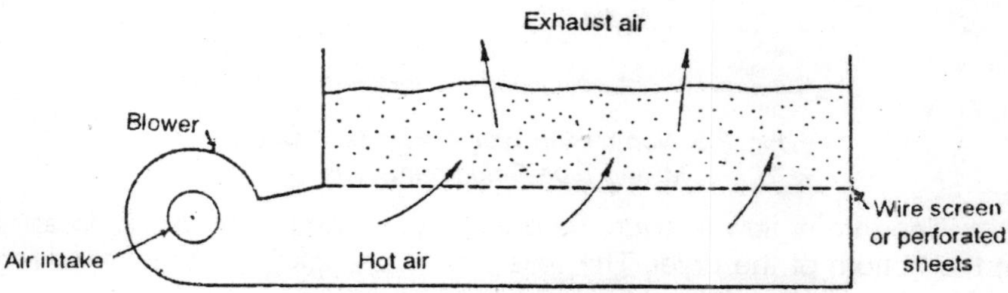

Fig 3.4. Flat Bed Dryer

Mixing type columnar dryers are again of two designs. Baffle type mixing dryer is similar in design to the nonmixing dryer above except that there is arrangement of alternate baffles. The baffles cause the paddy to mix as it flows down.

Louisiana State University (LSU) type dryer is another mixing type dryer. It consists of a vertical, rectangular box with rows of air channels shaped like inverted 'V's. One end of the 'V's is closed, the other open.

The rows alternately open on one side for hot air to enter and then on the next for the air to go out. The rows of'V's are also staggered so that there is good mixing of paddy. Chaff and other light materials are blown out with the exhaust air. LSU dryers are most commonly used in India.

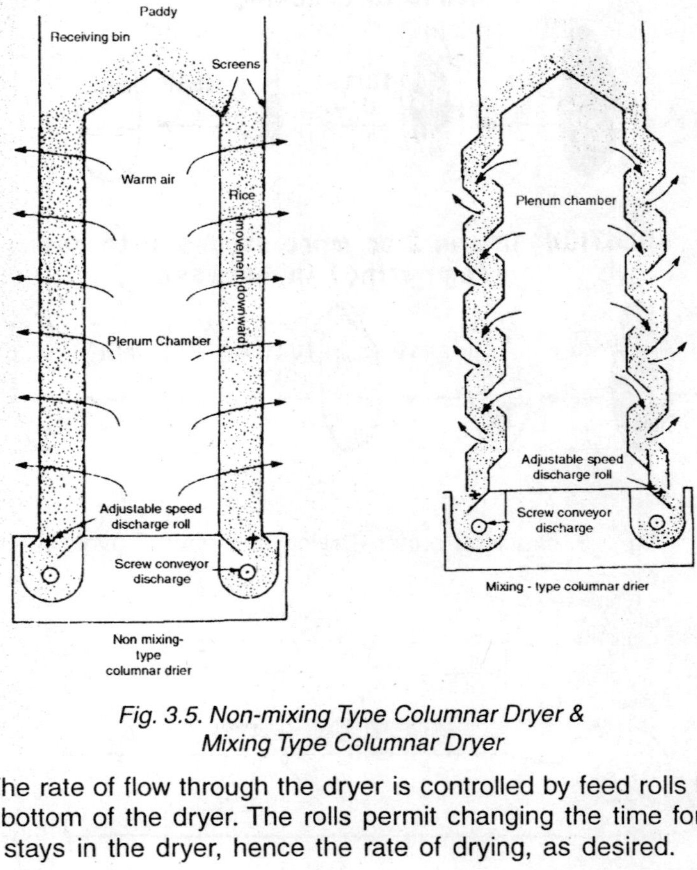

Fig. 3.5. Non-mixing Type Columnar Dryer & Mixing Type Columnar Dryer

The rate of flow through the dryer is controlled by feed rolls located at the bottom of the dryer. The rolls permit changing the time for which paddy stays in the dryer, hence the rate of drying, as desired.

To avoid the cracking of grains, the intermittent system of drying is to be used. If the intake paddy has a moisture content of not more than 18-20%, drying may be accomplished in two drying stages (or passes) with one tempering in between. If the moisture content is over 20%, three or even four passes of drying with rest in between each successive two passes are necessary. An air temperature of 60-70°C is most commonly used for drying raw paddy.

Fuel for drying

Paddy husk is the most common fuel used for drying paddy. The hot flue gases coming out from husk-fired cyclone furnaces are mixed with ordinary air to reduce temperature to the appropriate level and the mixture is blown through the paddy. The combustion process must be carefully controlled to ensure clean and complete burning. Where the flue gases are not clean or in the case of parboiled paddy which has a slight opening of husk, drying is generally done by heating air through a heat exchanger. The heat exchanger may be steam-to-air or gas-to-air type.

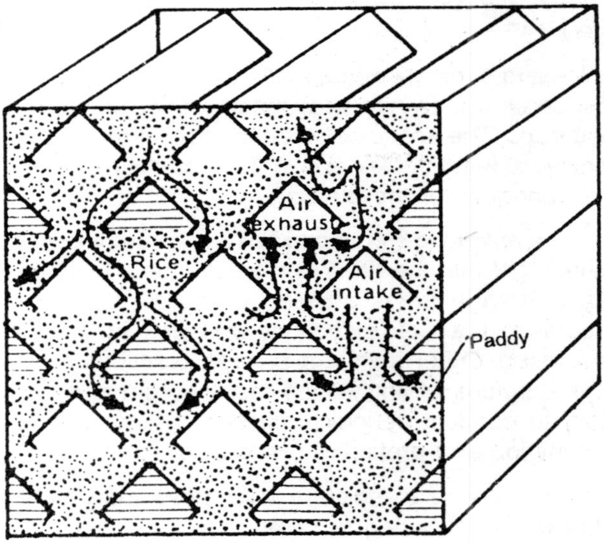

Pattern of air and rice flow in LSU-type

Fig. 3.6. LSU Type Dryer

Large commercial paddy drying installations consists essentially of: (i) dryers, (ii) heating facility (combustion furnace with or without heat exchangers), (iii) conveying equipments, and (iv) tempering bins.

Storage

Paddy is harvested twice or thrice a year. But rice is consumed throughout the year. Therefore, paddy is stored to supply the need between harvests.

Storage must keep the paddy safe and also maintain its quality. It should provide protection against weather, insects, rats, birds, micro-organisms, moisture and any type of contamination. Care should be taken to store different varieties of paddy separately to avoid mix up.

Conditions for safe storage

Paddy should be clean and dry before storage. Impurities cause rapid deterioration in quality and quantity. High moisture content is the greatest enemy of good storage. Wet paddy is easily attacked by moulds as well as insects. This causes hot spots to develop, which further helps mould and insect attack, leading to rapid deterioration. High temperature also promotes deterioration by moisture migration within the storage structure, especially in silos. Hot paddy obtained after drying should not therefore be immediately.

Rats, mice and birds are serious pests of stored paddy. Rodents and birds may be controlled by physical means, good sanitation practices, chemicals and traps. The easiest method to prevent rodents is to build the storage premises 0.9-1.0 meter above the ground and provide ledges. Then rodents cannot enter the building.

Insects are a hazard to stored paddy. They contaminate and consume the grain. Insects get into the grain in the field, bins, bags or at any time during storage. Storage areas should be kept clean. They should be constructed so as to keep *out* insects as well as keep *in* fumigant gases when they are used. Other standard storage practices are to clean the storage premises before refilling, as left-over stocks may infect new paddy. It is necessary to conduct periodical checks. Insects should be kept in control by fumigation and protective insecticidal sprays.

Paddy dried to a safe moisture level (less than 14%) should be maintained dry and cool during storage.

The grains on receipt into godowns should be sampled properly and examined for live infestation, condition and quality of the grains. In case of infestation, they should be fumigated immediately to prevent cross infestation to other stocks in the godown.

As the period of storage increases, it is likely that food grains tend to deteriorate in condition. Therefore, on the basis of condition, quality, age and other connected aspects, the stock should be released for processing or disposal.

Storage facilities

Paddy can be stored in bags or in bulk. The choice between the two systems depends on a number of local factors including cost of local construction, bags, operating and handling equipment, transport system, labour and management. Either method can provide safe storage as long as scientific storage practices are observed. Storage containers may be made of steel or concrete.

Bagged paddy or rice should always be stacked on wooden dunnage to prevent moisture absorption and to permit good sanitation practices. Dunnage materials should be cleaned thoroughly and disinfested before use, in order to ensure that they are not a source of infestation to the grain stored over them. Bags should be stored in easily accessible stacks with adequate walking space around each stack. Paddy bags are stacked 16-bag high. Rice bags are stacked 12-bag high. Common capacity of warehouses are 200, 500 and 1000 tonne units. About 0.8 m^2 of floor space is needed for each tonne of storage capacity.

All buildings used for bag storage should

1. be protected against sun, rain and water;
2. not allow the entry of rodents or birds;
3. have smooth walls and floors that can be easily cleaned;
4. be built 0.9-1.0 meter above ground to permit easy unloading or loading, as well as to prevent rats from entering;
5. have wide doors for easy access;
6. have no inside pillars that restrict stacking arrangements, reduce capacity or make .pest control difficult;
7. be located on a good, well drained, safe site with good road access; and
8. permit good ventilation for working conditions.

During emergency, bags can also be put outside for temporary outdoor storage. Bags are stacked on good dunnage as usual. The stacks are covered with plastic sheets or tarpaulins. This system offers economical, safe, temporary storage.

Milling of Rice

Unlike other food grains, rice is mostly cooked and consumed in whole form. Milling technology is therefore geared to obtain maximum outturn of milled rice and to reduce breakage to the minimum.

Before the paddy is kept ready for milling operation, it is necessary to bring all the grains preferably to a uniform moisture content which may vary from 10% to 14% for optimal milling yields and avoid excessive breakage.

Rice milling systems range from the home-scale to the large, complex modern rice-processing installations. They include hand-pounding equipment, single hullers, battery of hullers, emery sheller-cum-huller mills, emery sheller-cum-cone polisher mills and the modern rubber-roller rice mills. As on 1994, in India there are 90,091 huller mills, 8,362 sheller-cum-huller mills, 4,237 sheller-cum-cone polisher mills, 33,557 modern/ modernised mills, totalling 1,36,247. Unfortunately the number is too large, and most mills operate only one-third to half their capacity.

The single huller mills are by and large located in villages or in localities where paddy is custom milled for producers. Their capacity ranges from 250-500 Kg per hour and they still handle bulk of the country's production. The large-capacity rice mills located in urban or semi urban areas for commercial milling are of 1 to 4 tonnes per hour capacity and handle the rest of the paddy milled. Some battery of hullers are still in operation as large commercial mills, specially for milling parboiled paddy.

Types of Rice Mill

Huller mill

The huller mill combines both dehusking and polishing processes in one operation. Therefore the by-products, husk and bran, are mixed together. The average milled rice recovery in the case of raw rice is low -65% or less - breakage is high. Besides, it has a larger power requirement per tonne of paddy milled than other type of rice mills.

Battery of hullers

These mills consist of a battery of hullers. In addition, sieves for cleaning the "paddy, reciprocating sieves for removing brokens, aspirator to remove the husk and bran, etc., are added. The hullers generally work in parallel simply to increase the capacity. Sometimes two hullers may be operated in sequence to perform the milling in sequence,whereby somewhat better yield and separation of by-products are achieved. As yield from huller is poor with raw paddy, these commercial mills are mostly found in areas where parboiled rice is eaten.

Sheller-cum-huller mill

Here a disc sheller (emery sheller, emery dehusker) is used for dehusking and the huller is used for. polishing the dehusked (brown) rice. After cleaning paddy in a sifter, the cleaned paddy is dehusked in a disc sheller and the husk is aspirated. The stock from the sheller is fed to hullers for polishing, often with a screen type paddy separator in between. The mixture is then sifted and aspirated to remove bran and small brokens from head rice. The outurn of rice from this mill is higher by 1-2% over the huller mill for raw paddy.

Sheller-cum-cone polisher mill

The disc sheller-cum-cone polisher mill consists of a cleaner, disc sheller, husk aspirator, paddy separator, cone polisher and broken rice separator. This mill gives more outturn of rice than hullers by atleast 3% (for raw rice). In addition, the head rice yield is higher, for breakage is reduced, bran and husk are separated, the rice is clean and free from paddy, and the degree of polishing can be easily controlled.

Modern rice mill

Modern mills mean many things to many persons. When one speaks of a modern rice mill complex, one has in mind a fairly big industrial factory. It has a modern efficient rice mill, in addition to a paddy receiving-cleaning-drying section, huge godowns or silos, parboiling-drying system, a huge husk furnace-cum-boiler, ash handling section, bran-handling-processing section, etc.

A modern rice mill as such is a much simpler affair. It is basically a sheller mill, but the shelter is not an emery-disc sheller but a rubber roll sheller. And it has all the other secondary systems needed for good rice milling.

As the name implies, what was modern yesterday is not modern today, and what is modern today will not be modern tomorrow. Therefore, it should be understood that what is called modern mill today is nothing but a mill which incorporates a rubber-roll sheller along with the full combination of a paddy separator, efficient polishers, grader, etc. It should also be noted that disc shelter mills also usually incorporate all these combinations. In such case, these mills approach a so-called modern mill. But they may not have all the secondary systems, in which case, they are different from a modern mill. On the other hand, a rubber-roll sheller is not enough to call a mill a modern mill. If it does not have all the secondary systems, it is surely not a modern mill.

Why a modern mill? It has been found that modern rice mills yield more rice not only as compared to hullers but also as compared to disc sheller-cum-cone polisher combinations, particularly for raw paddy. The extra yield obtained by processing in modern mills is atleast 2% in case of raw paddy and about 0.5-1% in case of parboiled paddy as compared to disc sheller-cum-cone polisher mills. Head rice yield in the modern mills average about 5% more than those in sheller mills and 10-15% more than in huller mills.

The results of a study undertaken by CFTRI in late 60's on the performance of different imported mill types versus traditional commercial mills - shellers and hullers, showed that the modern mill gave about 2.5% and 6.6% higher yields of total milled rice for raw paddy and 0.8% and 1.6% for parboiled paddy in comparison to sheller and huller mills respectively. Increase in head rice yields were 6.1% and 15.1% for raw paddy and 1.3% and 4.1% for parboiled paddy respectively. Modern rice mills gave relatively pure by-products also.

Modem rice milling process : Operations and Equipments

The purpose of rice milling is essentially to remove the husk and bran from the dried paddy to produce polished rice. Overall milling operation in a modern rice mill involves handling of the paddy coming from the storage end and turning it into polished rice. The unit-operations are cleaning, dehusking, husk separation, paddy-brown rice separation, polishing, grading, weighing and bagging. Transfer of products from one machine to another for each successive operation is done by elevators.

A flow chart of important operations, followed in sequence, for milling of rice in a modern rice mill is shown (figure 3.7). The operations are as follows:

Cleaning	Removes foreign matter, such as sand, stones, straw, seeds and pieces of iron from paddy.
Dehusking	Removes husk from the paddy with a minimum of damage to the grain.
Husk separation	Removes the husk from the mixture obtained after dehusking.
Paddy separation	Separates brown rice from remaining unhusked paddy, the paddy being returned for dehusking.
Polishing	Removes all or part of the bran layer from the brown rice to produce polished rice.
Grading	Separates brokens from whole rice. The brokens are separated into different sizes.

Bucket elevators are used to move the grain from one machine to the next for continuous operation. Conveying, bagging, weighing and other associated operations are also done as needed.

In brief rice milling process is as follows:

The paddy is first cleaned in the cleaner to remove foreign material. The cleaned paddy is dehusked in the sheller. The product of the shelter -mixture of brown rice, unshelled paddy and husk is passed through the husk separator. The resultant mixture of brown rice and paddy is conveyed to the paddy separator. The paddy separated in the separator is sent back to the return paddy sheller set aside for this purpose. Brown rice from the separator is conveyed to the rice polishers to produce polished rice.

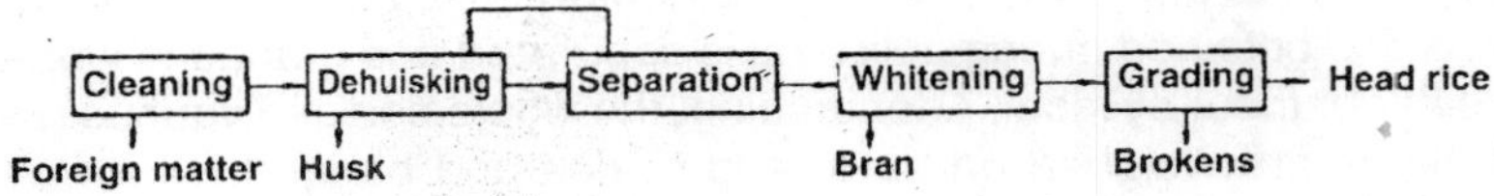

Block Diagram

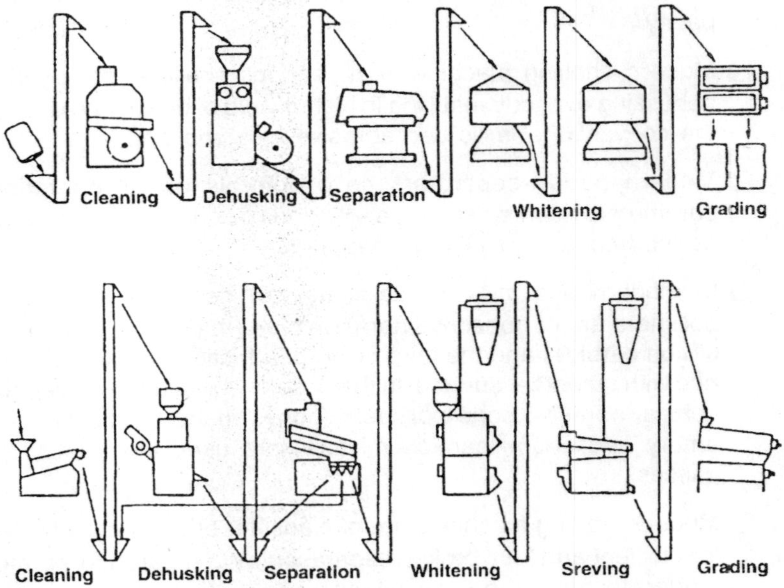

Process Flow Chart

Fig. 3.7. Flow Chart of Rice Milling Process

Generally, brown rice is not polished in a single pass through a polisher but through three or four polishers (abrasive or combination of abrasive and friction type polishers) in series. Three or four passes are superior to one or two passes in removing same amount of bran to get less brokens in rice. As the bran of parboiled rice is very sticky, about 2-3% of paddy husk is continuously added to the brown rice before it enters the first polisher. The husk acts as an abrasive and a scavenger for the sticking bran. It prevents caking of the bran and thus avoids clogging of screens, thereby facilitates polishing. Choking can also be prevented by increasing the quantity of air blown into polishers. When parboiled rice is polished, the cones are usually made to run at 10% higher rpm than that for raw rice. The friction type polisher is frequently used in the last pass of polishing for raw as well as parboiled rice to impart smooth surface to the rice. The milled rice is aspirated to remove loose bran. The mixture of whole and broken rice obtained during polishing is separated and graded in vibratory/ plansifter or trieur cylinder. After grading, the whole rice and various grades of brokens are weighed on automatic scales and bagged.

Commercial rice mills are classified as conventional and modern mills. The differences between modern and commercial mills are :

- Modern cleaning machines have provision to remove immature paddy.
- Modern shelling machines - rubber roll shellers, are used for dehusking of paddy resulting in higher yield of brown rice whereas the conventional mills use abrasive disc shellers.
- Modern paddy separators have controls on all operational parameters such as speed, angle and oscillation of deck as well as feed control for efficient separation.
- In modern rice mills for polishing raw rice, first and second polishers are of horizontal abrasive type (rotors made of fine grit silicon carbide) and the third being of a friction type to get milled rice with smoother surface. In the case of polishing parboiled rice, vertical abrasive cone polishers (cones made of coarse grit of emery and silicon carbide mixture) are used in three or four passes.
- Modern grading machines are of plansifter or trieur cylinder type for efficient and total broken separation as compared to vibratory graders used in the conventional mills.

A short description of the different steps and machines used for each step in milling is given below.

Cleaning

Cleaning is the first step in modern rice milling. It not only enables the production of clean rice but also protects other milling machinery and increases milling capacity.

Impuritites that are lighter than paddy are removed by an aspirator. This prevents spreading of dust inside the building and creates hygienic conditions. Metallic (iron) impurities are removed by the use of a magnet. Impurities larger or smaller in size than paddy are removed by sieves. Vibrating or rotating sieves or a combination of both are used. Impurities that have the same size as paddy but are heavier than paddy are removed by specific gravity separators, namely, destoners.

Intake paddy is often subjected to a preliminary partial cleaning (scalping) prior to storage and prior to the main cleaning in the mill.

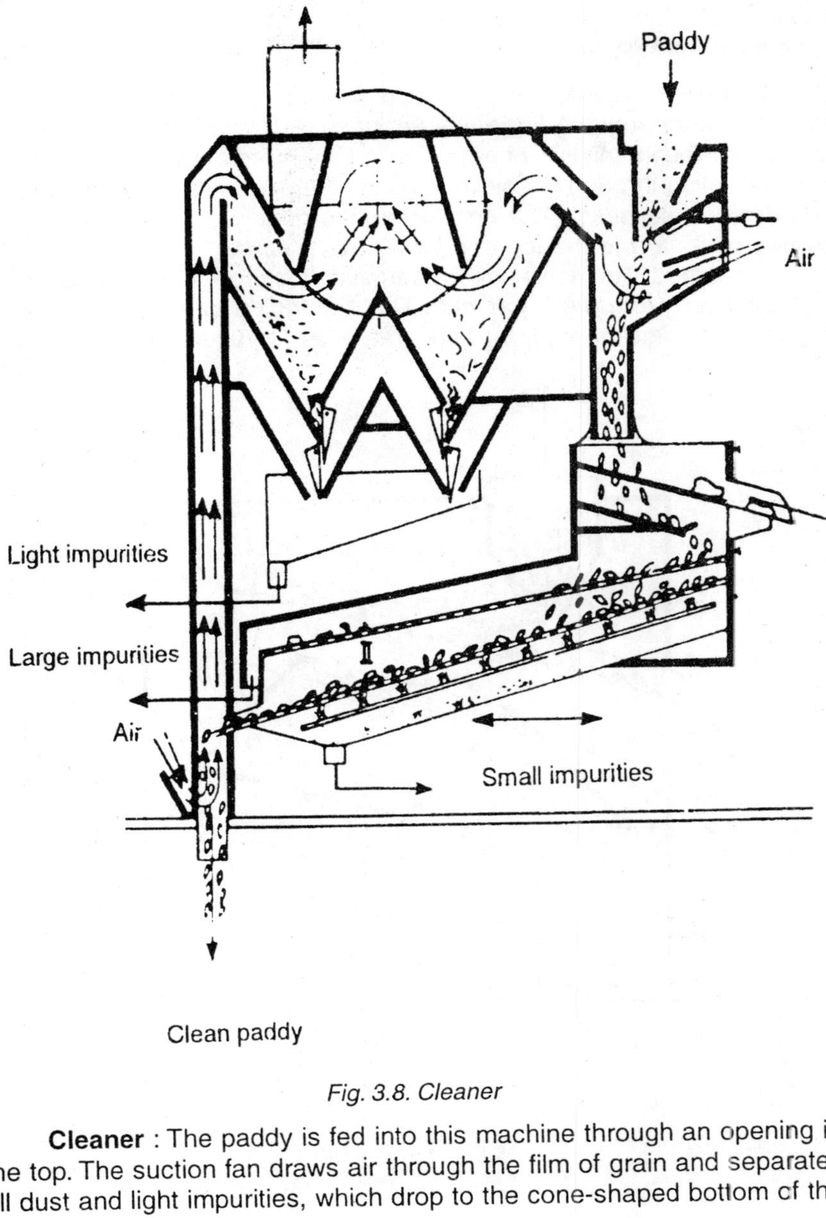

Fig. 3.8. Cleaner

Cleaner : The paddy is fed into this machine through an opening in the top. The suction fan draws air through the film of grain and separates all dust and light impurities, which drop to the cone-shaped bottom of the aspiration housing for automatic discharge. The paddy falls on a vibrating sieve with large perforations which removes large impurities such as straws, big stones, etc. The paddy with remaining small impurities then fall onto the bottom vibrating sieve with small perforations, which removes small impurities. The overflow from this sieve is again subjected to strong aspiration to remove the last traces of light impurities (figure 3.8).

Destoner : The destoner consists of a reciprocating perforated deck mounted at an angle. A large amount of air is blown from below through the sieve. When a mixture of paddy and stone is fed at the top of the sieve, the air coming through the sieve stratifies the materials according to their density (or heaviness). The heavier stones remain on the deck and are carried backward to the top end by the reciprocating motion of the deck and discharged. The lighter paddy remains floating and slides down and is discharged from the lower end. The separation can be controlled by adjusting the rate of feed, air flow and sieve tilt (figure 3.9).

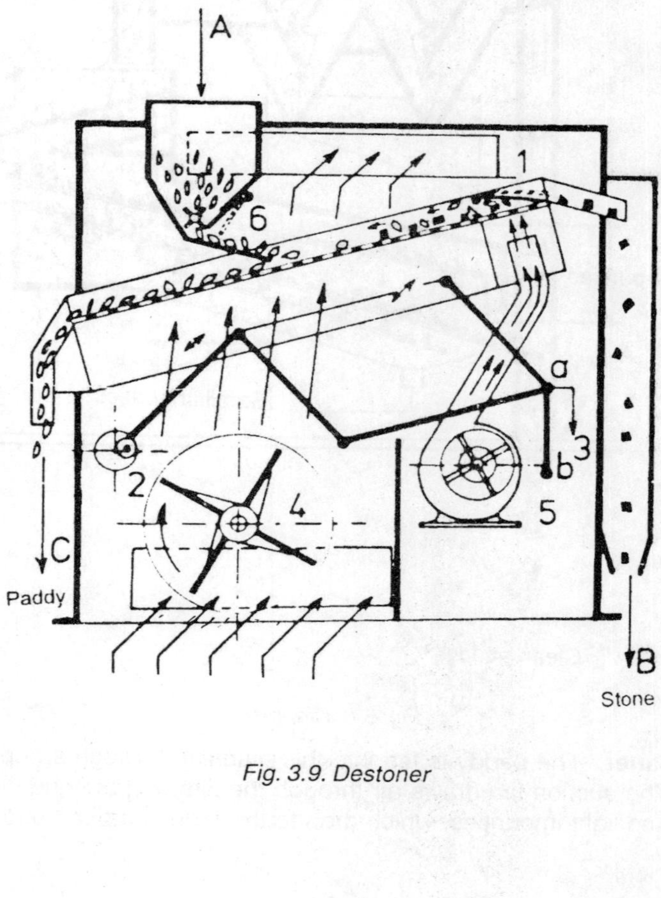

Fig. 3.9. Destoner

Magnetic separator : Type A (see figure) is a permanent magnet located in such a way that when unclean paddy moves across it, the iron particles are collected by it. The particles are later cleared by hand. Type B is cleaned automatically. The rotating cylinder is turned by the free-flowing paddy. Under the cylinder, there is a half-round magnet. As the paddy passes over the cylinder, iron particles are held by the cylinder's magnetic attraction. As the cylinder continues to rotate, when the cylinder is not moving over the magnet, the iron particles are automatically released and discharged separately (figure 3.10).

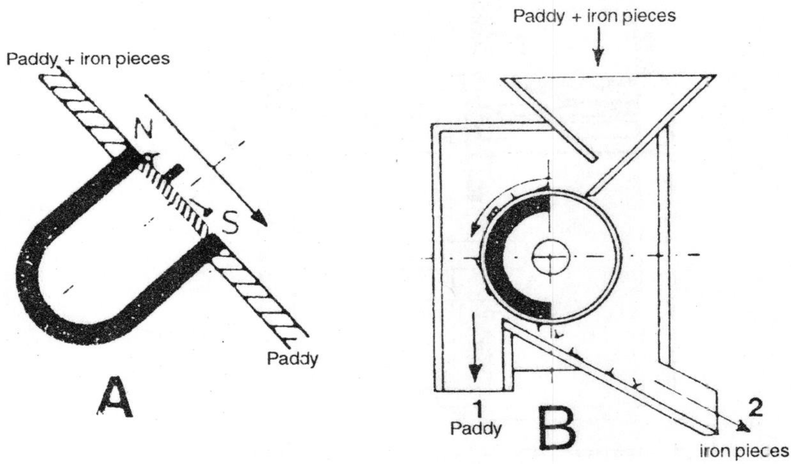

Fig. 3.10. Magnetic Separator

Dehusking (shelling)

The object of dehusking is to remove the husk from the paddy with minimum damage to the bran layer and without breaking the brown rice grain.

Disc sheller : It consists of two horizontal iron discs coated with emery. The top disc is fixed to the frame housing, and the bottom disc rotates. The rotating disc can be moved vertically up or down to adjust the clearance between the two discs. The clearance is thus adjusted to the size of the paddy grain (figure 3.11).

Paddy is fed into the centre of the machine. As it reaches the rotating disc, it moves outward by centrifugal force. During its travel outward, whenever it is up-ended, it is caught between the top (stationary) and bottom (rotating) discs and is dehusked by the shearing action. The clearance between the two discs is critical to avoid excessive breakage.

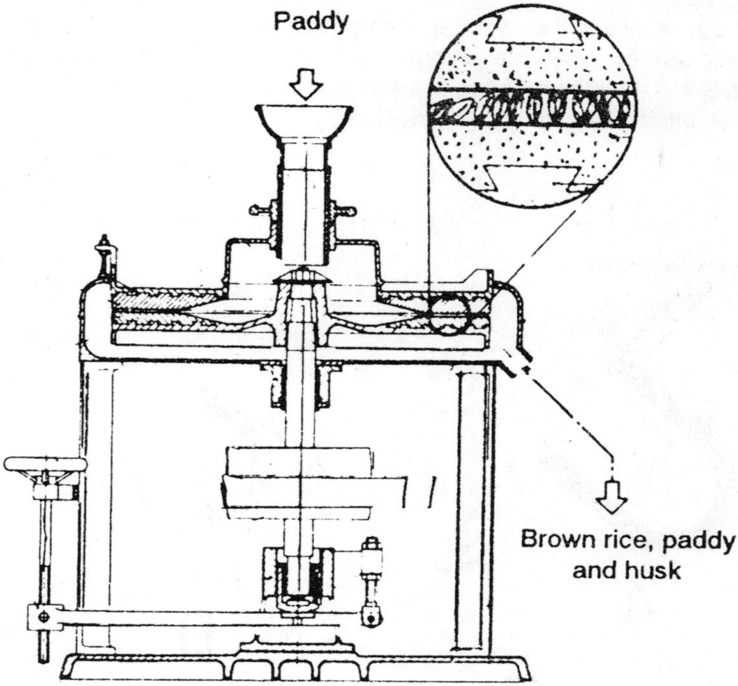

Fig. 3.11. Disc Sheller

Quite often, the effective width of the emery coating is made too large causing unnecessary breakage of the grain. The width should be l/6th to l/7th of the disc diameter.

As the grain has to travel across the entire radius of the disc, some rice breakage does occur in this machine. Some polishing also takes place for the same reason.

Rubber-roll sheller : The rubber-roll sheller consists of two rubber rollers rotating in opposite directions at different speeds. Both rolls have the same diameter, but one roll moves about 25% faster than the other. The difference in peripheral speeds subjects the paddy grains falling between the rolls to a shearing action that strips off the husk. One roller is fixed in position and the other is adjustable laterally in order to increase or decrease the clearance between the two rolls (figure 3.12). Rolls are cooled by blowing air on the roll surface. The shelling (i.e. dehusking) rate is generally maintained at about 85%.

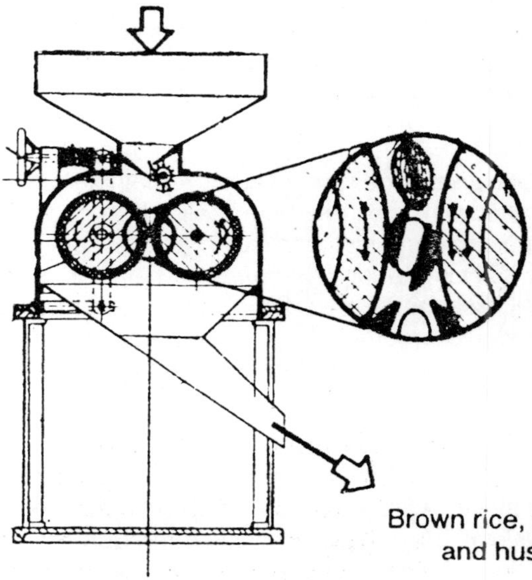

Fig. 3.12. Rubber-roll Sheller

For operation, at no time should there be a rubber to rubber contact. Otherwise, there would be excessive heat, excessive wear and tear of the rolls as well as discolouring of the grains.

The durability or capacity of the rubber rolls varies with cleanliness of paddy, moisture content, pressure applied to the rolls, heating of rolls, the paddy variety (abrasiveness of the husk, short or long grain) as well as the quality of the rolls. Hardness of rubber should be 90 Shore number. A pair of good quality rolls has an average capacity of about 100 tonnes for raw paddy and 200 tonnes for parboiled paddy. The optimum age for rubber rolls begins 2-3 months after manufacture and decreases rapidly when the rubber is 6-9 months old. Therefore, rubber rolls should not be stored for longtime.

To obtain more operational life per pair of rubber rolls, they should be frequently interchanged to ensure uniform wear. It is best to interchange rolls for every 2-3 mm of wear. Uneven wear of roll changes the relative peripheral speed and reduces hulling capacity.

Compared with the disc sheller, the rubber-roll sheller has the advantage of giving negligible breakage and causes no polish. In disc shelling, some breakage invariably occurs and the fine brokens may be blown off along with the husk. Shelling percent with the rubber rolls can be raised to about 85% without fear of grain breakage, whereas the disc sheller can be operated at no more than 60-70% degree of shelling to keep breakage at a low level. However, the rubber rolls wear out fast and have to be replaced often. This is undoubtedly a disadvantage. But this is offset by the reduction in breakage and increased total rice outturn.

Husk separation

A mixture of dehusked rice (brown rice), remaining unshelled paddy, some broken rice and husk that has been split off the paddy comes out of the sheller. This mixture is subjected to sieving-cum-aspiration to separate brokens and husk. Sieving prior to aspiration helps in separating and recovering the small brokens formed during shelling, particularly from the disc shellers which would be otherwise carried away along with the husk. Light weight paddy husk is separated from the heavier paddy and rice by aspiration.

Husk separator : The mixture of paddy, brown rice, brokens and husk are fed at the top of a vibrating sieve. The brokens pass through the perforations of the sieve. As the mixture of husk, paddy and brown rice overflows from the sieve, air is blown or sucked through the mixture. Husk is carried away by the air. The paddy and brown rice mixture is collected separately (figure 3.13 & 3.14).

Paddy separation

Shelling is never done to the level of 100% to avoid rice breakage. The grains also differ in size, so that the smaller grains remain unshelled. Therefore a paddy separator is used to separate the remaining unhusked paddy from brown rice. The separated paddy is returned to the dehusker for dehusking while the brown rice is carried forward to the polisher. The separation is accomplished in the separator by taking advantage of the difference in physical density (heaviness), size and surface smoothness (or roughness) of paddy and brown rice.

Compartment-type separator : The oscillating table is divided into zig zag channels and is inclined from one side to the other along the zig zag channels. The surface of the table is of smooth steel. The table oscillates crosswise, i.e., perpendicular to the direction of the grain flow. The mixture of paddy and brown rice is fed from the hopper to the centre of the channels. The impact of the grains on the sides of each channel causes the unhusked paddy grains to move up the inclined slope toward high side of the table. The dehusked brown rice slides down the slope to the lower side of the table. The slope and stroke of the table are adjusted to meet the needs of paddy of different size or condition, to ensure complete separation (figure 3.15). Usually there are several decks one above the other to increase capacity.

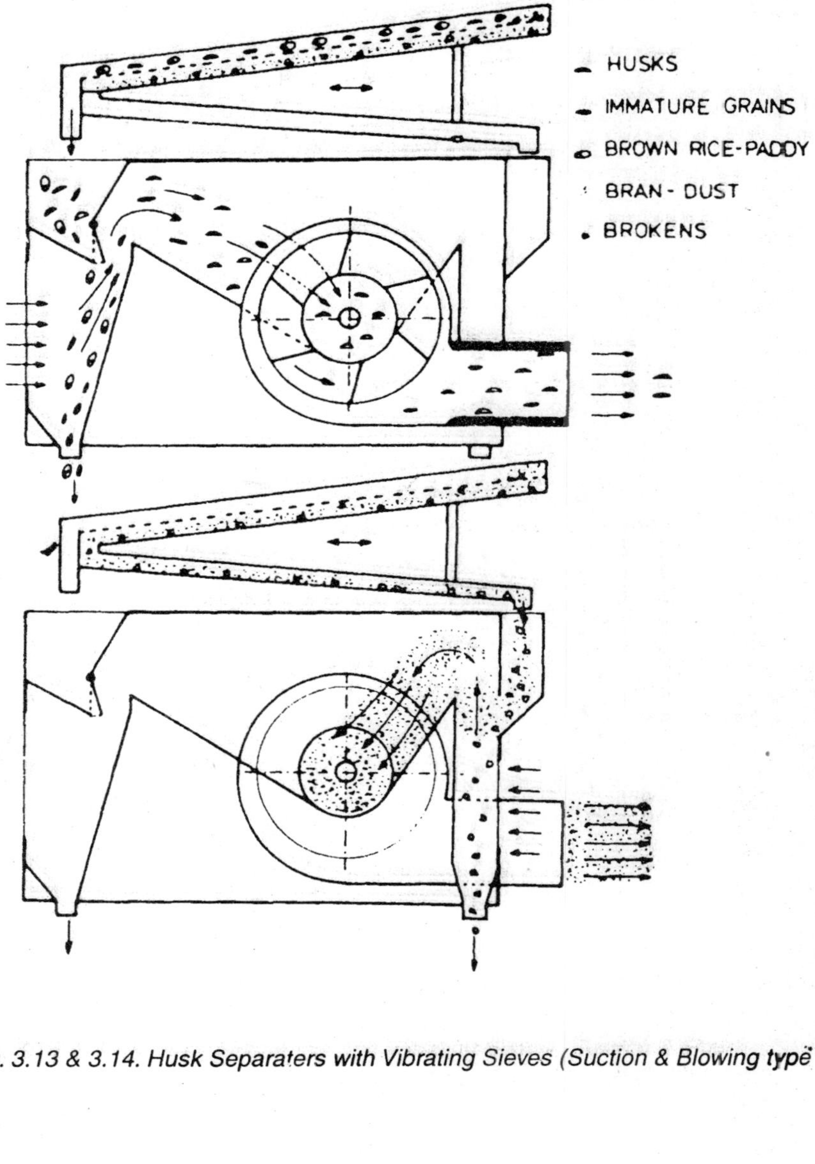

Fig. 3.13 & 3.14. Husk Separaters with Vibrating Sieves (Suction & Blowing type

Tray separator : It consists of several indented trays (i.e., trays having a large number of depressions) mounted one above the other, all attached to an oscillating frame. The tray section moves up and forward, making a slight jumping movement.

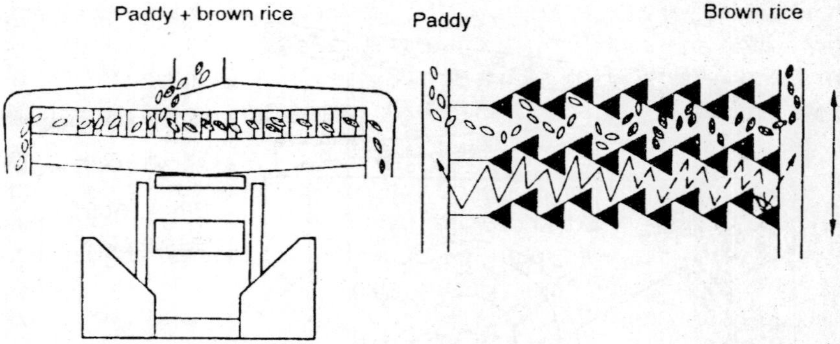

Fig. 3.15. Paddy Separator – Compartment Type.

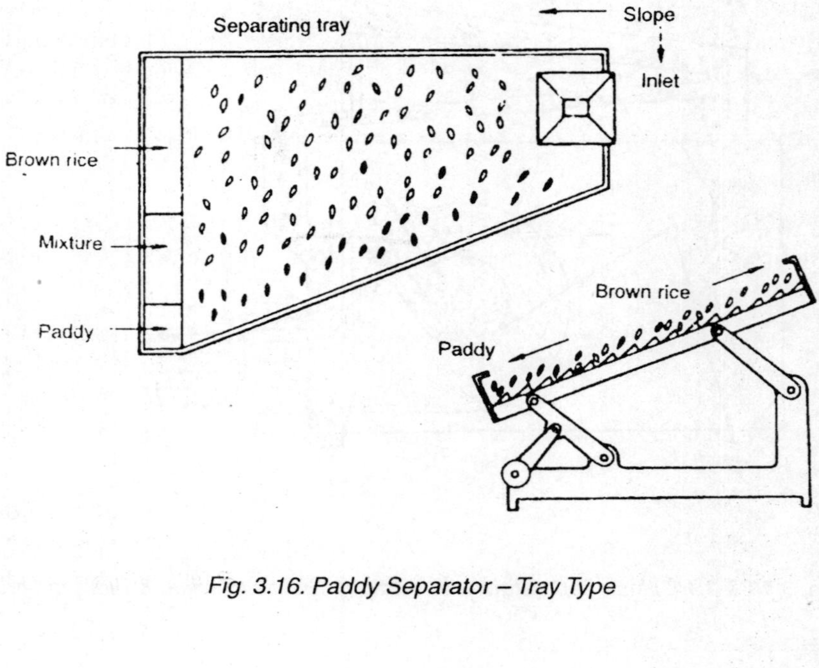

Fig. 3.16. Paddy Separator – Tray Type

The mixture falls on each tray at the top corner from the inlet hopper. The smooth, smaller and denser brown rice tends to go below and rough, bigger and lighter paddy to float up due to the motion of the tray. Further, the brown rice, being smaller, is caught in the indentations (depressions) and moves upward along with each jump of the tray. Thus it is carried to the upper side of the tray and is discharged there. The floating paddy slides downwards and is discharged there. Unseparated paddy and brown rice remaining in the middle portion are discharged in between and are returned to the hopper for recirculation. The table inclination is adjustable to meet different grain sizes and conditions (figure 3.16).

Operation: For efficient paddy separation, feed rate, speed, stroke and table inclination should be carefully set. Improper setting would result in brown rice going with return paddy or return paddy going with brown rice, or both, affecting capacity of the plant and the yield and quality of milled rice.

Shelling of return paddy

Paddy collected from the separator is called return paddy, for it has to be returned to the sheller. The return paddy grains are shorter (if in disc sheller) or thinner (if in rubber roll sheller) than normal paddy. Hence, it is preferable to collect the return paddy in a bin and shell it at the end with closer clearance between the discs or rolls. Alternately, the return paddy can be shelled in a separate, small sheller. This will increase the efficiency of the plant. If return paddy is returned to the original sheller with same setting, it will simply go on circulating, thus lowering the capacity.

Polishing

The brown rice is next polished to remove the bran layers. Some amount of polishing is essential for easy cooking and storage, although excessive polishing reduces the nutritive value of rice.

There are two types of polishers, one of emery and other of metal. The emery polishers (called whiteners) polish the grains by abrasion with emery while the metal polishers (called pearler) polish by friction between the rice grains. The abrasive polishers are again of two types - vertical (cone polisher) and horizontal.

Cone polisher : It consists of a vertical truncated cone, covered with emery, which rotates inside a wire screen/perforated sheet. The clearance between the cone and screen can be adjusted by raising or lowering the cone. At regular intervals around the cone, the wire screen is divided into segments by adjustable vertical rubber brakes.

The brown rice enters at the top centre and moves outward by centrifugal force to the edge of the cone. As the brown rice rotates around

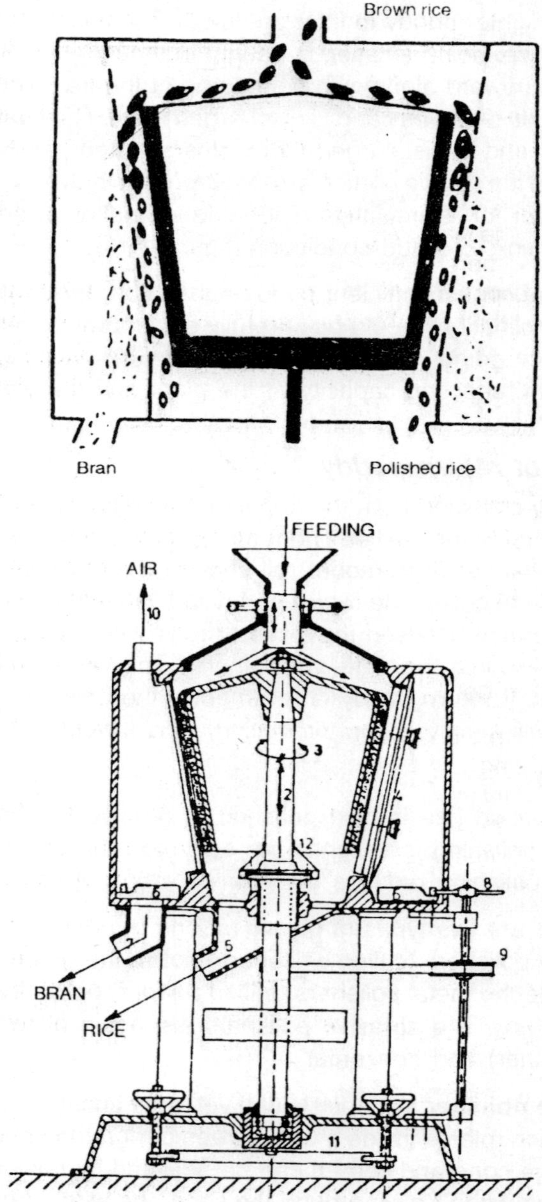

Fig. 3.17. Cone Polishers (Principle & Sectional View)

the cone and moves down between the cone and the screen, the abrasive action of the emery peels the bran off the grains. The bran goes out through the screen and is collected separately. The polished rice is discharged at the bottom (figure 3.17).

Horizontal abrasive polisher : The unit consists of an abrasive (carborundum) roll/discs attached to a steel shaft (solid/hollow) rotating in a cylindrical, perforated metallic screen mounted horizontally. Brown rice enters at one end, and moves around the abrasive roll and discharged at end. The pressure on the grain is controlled by hanging different weights on the discharge gate. As the grain passes through the space between the roll and the perforated screen, the bran layers are peeled off from the grain. The bran passes out through the perforated screen and polished rice is discharged through the outlet. On the disc type abrasive polisher a strong stream of air is blown through the hollow shaft and small gap between the discs. The air helps in separating the bran and removes the heat generated during polishing (figure 3.18).

Horizontal friction polisher : The unit consists of a cylindrical steel roller rotating inside a hexagonal perforated screen. The cylinder has a long slit along its length and a hollow shaft for passing air. The pressure on the rice is controlled by hanging weights on the discharge gate. The clearance between the screen and cylinder is adjustable by opening or closing the screen. A strong stream of air is blown by a centrifugal blower through the hollow shaft and long slit of the cylinder. The air helps in separating the bran and removing the heat generated by the friction between rice and rice (figure 3.19).

Operation : Stepwise polishing in several polishers gives minimum breakage during milling, thus increasing total and head rice recovery. Keeping the uniformity and balancing of abrasive roller, reduces grain breakage. When parboiled rice is milled, the bran tends to stick to the screens. In this case, the quantity of aspirated air is increased to overcome choking of the screens. The bran coming out of the polisher should be checked often to make sure that it does not contain broken rice, not to speak of head rice, i.e. to detect any damage to the polisher screen.

Aspiration of air through the polisher prevents heating, thus reducing the breakage, and keeps dust out of the mill.

Recent trends : Humidified polishing techniques give better appearance to the milled rice. Before polishing, brown rice is conditioned with humidified air using air coolers and humidifiers. In 'water milling', a requisite quantity of atomised water is passed through the hollow shaft of the final friction polisher. This softens the kernel surface rendering easy bran removal.

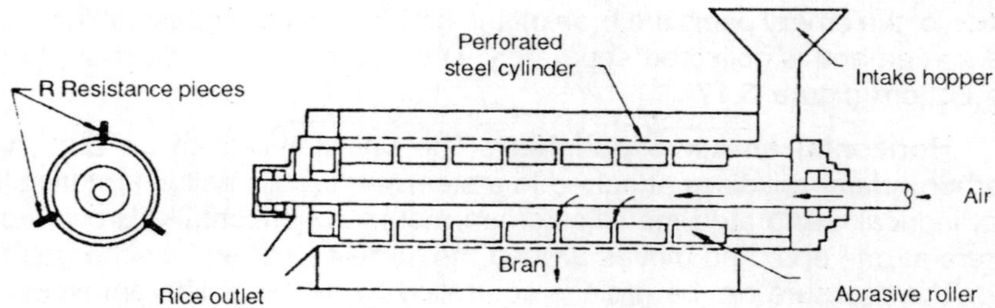

Fig. 3.18. Horizontal Emery Polisher

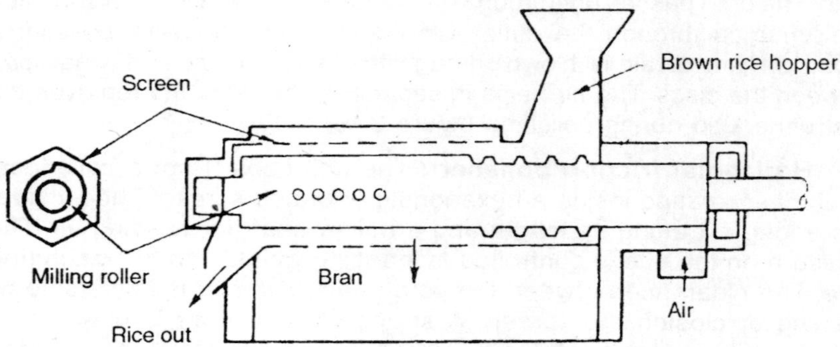

Fig. 3.19. Horizontal Friction Polisher

Air conditioning system with temperature and humidity controls are being employed in some rice mills for efficient performance. Automation of rice mills with computer or microprocessor controls is also possible.

Pneumatic bran separator : Bran obtained from polishers is sieved in a vibratory sitter. This bran is now passed through pneumatic bran separator. This equipment separates rice germs and brokens from. bran and also conveys the bran pneumatically (i.e. by air). It consists of a powerful centrifugal fan which aspirates the bran from the polisher and delivers it to a cyclone. A blower and an auxiliary cyclone aspirates the bran from the outlet of the main cyclone. Thus fine bran is separated from coarse meterials (germs and broken?) (figure 3.20).

Grading

After polishing operation, the milled rice contains, in addition to whole grains, broken grains of different sizes as well as some bran and dust. Separation of these materials, termed 'grading', must now be done. Bran and dust particles are removed by aspiration. Brokens may be separated either by a plansifter or by a 'trieur'.

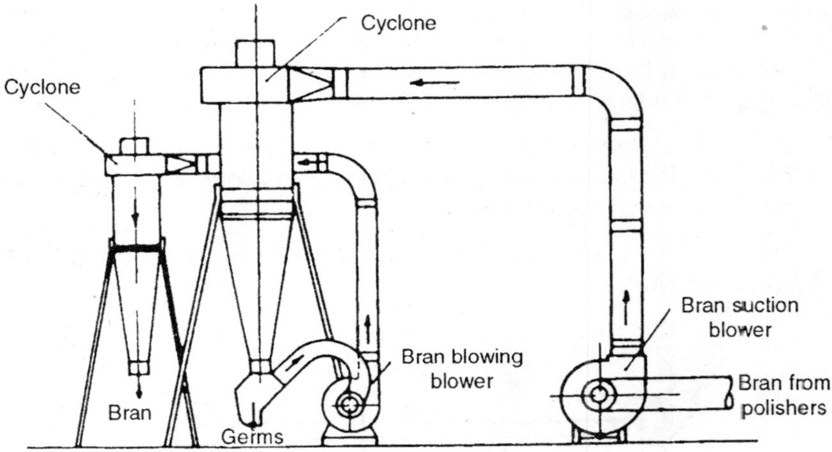

Fig. 3.20. Pneumatic Bran Separator

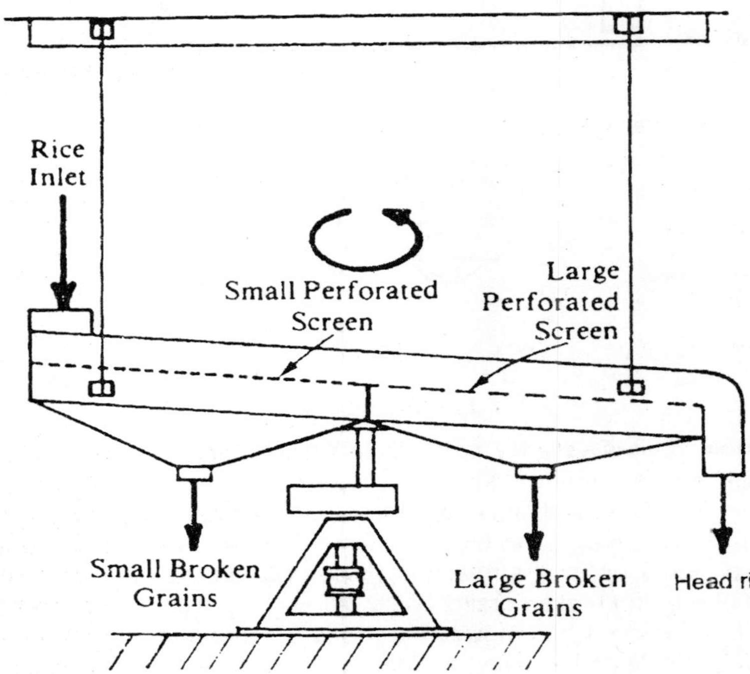

Fig. 3.21. Plansifter

Plansifter : It is a single or double decked sieve which is given a swinging motion produced by an eccentric drive. It consists of two sheet? of different perforations (first small and then large) to separate two grades of brokens from the polished rice. The grain moves across the swinging sieve in a continuous spiral path (figure 21).

A plansifter, being of sieve type, cannot separate ali broken grains from head rice. Big brokens remain alongwith head rice, while small brokens (less than half size) are removed.

Sieves of the grader should be kept free from clogging for maximum removal of brokens.

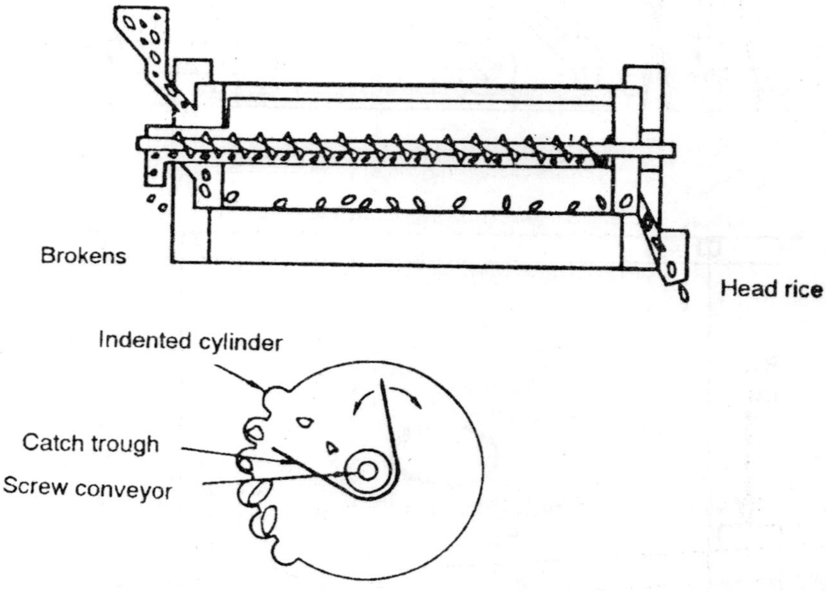

Fig. 3.22. Trieur Cylinder

Trieur : This is a slightly inclined rotating cylinder having indentations, like small pockets, all along its inner body. The mixed (head and broken) rice is fed into the raised end of the cylinder. As the rice passes along the slowly rotating cylinder, the broken grains sit nicely in pockets and are therefore picked up by the rotating cylinder. But as the cylinder rotates upward, the sitting broken grains finally fall out at a higher point and are caught by a collector trough fixed inside the cylinder and are discharged separately. Whole grains, being too long, cannot sit into the small pockets. Hence they move down the cylinder undisturbed as it rotates. Whole and broken grains are thus separated into two streams (figure 3.22). By adjusting the size of the indentations and the position of the trough, broken rice of different sizes can be separated.

Broken grains of half the length or more are later combined with whole rice in specific proportions to suit market requirements.

As big size broken rice is permitted in market rice in India, Indian mills generally use only plansifters and not trieurs.

Circular purifier : It is used for removing pieces of husk, bran and dust particles that remain adhering to milled rice after grading. Rice grains are kept suspended in a strong stream of air, when adhering particles are sucked away. Often purifiers are installed also to cool the rice between polishing passes.

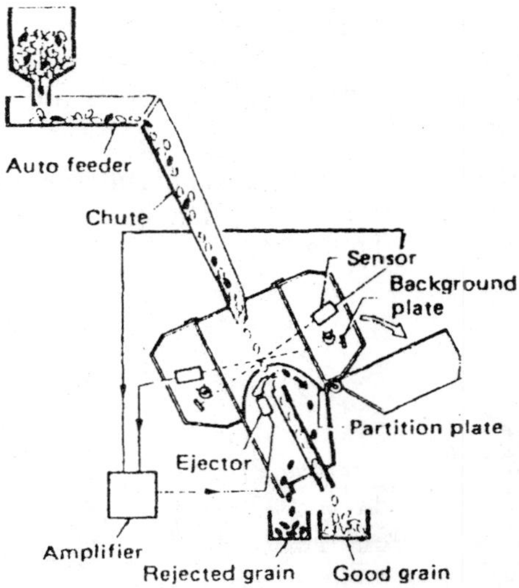

Fig. 3.23. Colour Grader/Sorter

Colour grader/sorter: It is used for sorting out discoloured grains from the lot. Optical sensors are adopted here to compare the colour of the individual grains. The discoloured grains are blown out of the main stream (figure 3.23).

Presently, these are only adopted in rice mills exporting basmathi rice to meet stringent quality specifications.

Weighing and bagging

Automatic intake weigher : Its function is to receive paddy in a continuous flow and release it in exact predetermined quantities by weight. At the same time, the number of weighments made is recorded by an automatic counter, thus giving an accurate record of the total weight of material processed in the mill.

Automatic bagging scale : It ensures dust free bagging of the finished products and records the number of weighments made, by an automatic counter.

Small Capacity Rice Mills

Paddy produced in Asian countries is still largely consumed by the farmers themselves. For this reason, there is still heavy demand in Asia for a small capacity mill, where small quantities of customer's paddy can be milled.

Engelberg huller

The Engelberg huller is the most widely used rice mill for this purpose. It is called by different names in different countries, e.g., Kiskisan mill in the Philippines. Hundreds of thousands of hullers are strewn all over the rice producing countries of Asia.

The huller consists of an iron ribbed cylinder mounted on a rotating shaft and fitted in a cylindrical housing. The bottom half of the housing is fitted with a slotted sheet (figure 24).

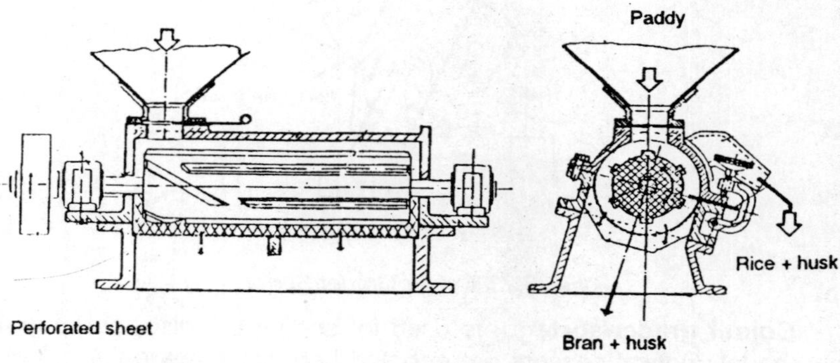

Fig. 3.24. Huller, Sectional View

Paddy fed from the hopper is forced to move around the cylinder towards the outlet because of a spiral at the inlet on the revolving cylinder. Friction between the grains and steel parts of the huller causes husk and bran to be scraped off in one operation. In the process, the husk and bran are ground into small pieces and are pushed through the perforated screen. Some husk and bran which are discharged with the polished rice are aspirated.

Mini rice mill

As already explained earlier, the huller has many defects. The rice outturn is low, breakage is high, a high degree of polish has to be given to remove all the unmilled paddy, thus reducing the yield further. Also, the husk and bran are mixed together, thus lowering the value of the bran. Its power requirement per quintal of paddy is also high.

Yet there is a great demand for a small capacity rice mill to do custom milling and for rural areas. As a result much effort is being made in recent years to design efficient but small capacity mills, generally called 'mini rice mills'.

The most important feature of the mini rice mill is that the shelling and polishing are kept separate. However, as the huller is widely available and is inexpensive, a huller is most commonly used as a polisher. For maximum advantage, it is necessary also to use a paddy separator, whereby need for high polish can be avoided, thus avoiding unnecessary loss of rice.

A woven wire vibrating table type paddy separator designed in CFTRI is most convenient to use. It is somewhat similar to the tray type paddy separator mentioned earlier but there are no indentations except the roughness caused by the mesh. It is inclined from feed to discharge for the material to flow down, and it is vibrated in a direction perpendicular to grain flow. Good separation of paddy and brown rice is obtained by adjusting feed rate, deck inclination and speed, while in action.

In addition, a mini rice mill should preferably contain a small cleaner.

Thus a cleaner, a centrifugal sheller/rubber roll sheller, a husk aspirator, a paddy separator and a rice polisher (generally a huller) arranged in a sequence give a good mini rice mill. Gravity is made use of for flow of material. Centrifugal sheller is found economical for parboiled paddy and rubber roll sheller for raw paddy. Thus, either of shellers can be easily fitted in the mini rice mill as desired (figure 3.25).

Such a mini rice mill gives at least 2-3% extra yield of rice over the huller. It also yields good bran, free from husk particles. Further, the degree of polish can be adjusted as desired. Cost of the unit is also not very high for a throughput of about 400-500 kg/hr. One advantage of the mini rice mill over the large mills is that the hold up of rice in it is very small, while in the large mill the hold up is very high.

But other combinations can also be used depending on convenience. For example, a centrifugal sheller plus a huller will give the simplest mini mill, which will still be better than a huller alone.

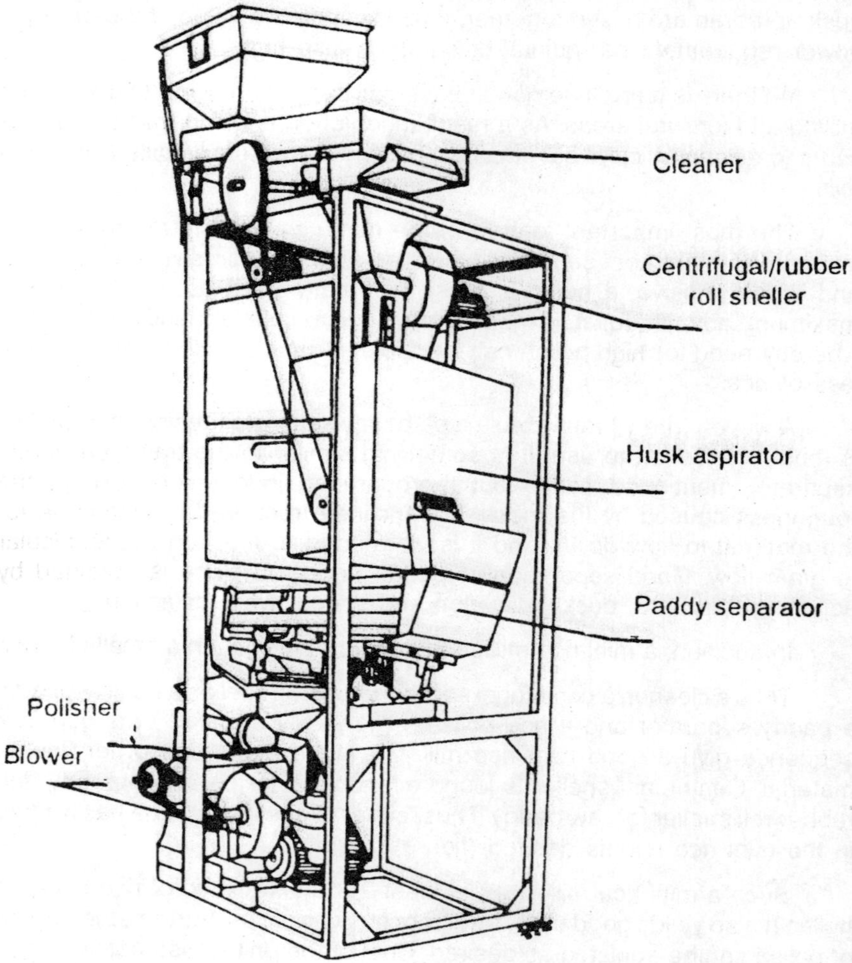

Single Pass Modern Mini Rice Mill

Fig. 3.25. Mini Rice Mill

Centrifugal shelter

It consists of a high-speed rotating disc surrounded by a stationary rubber rim. The paddy is fed on to the disc rotating at a very high rpm, which throws the grains against the rubber rim with much force. The husk gets cracked by impact, thus the paddy is shelled (figure 26). Some breakage does occur, but the performance is good enough for a mini mill.

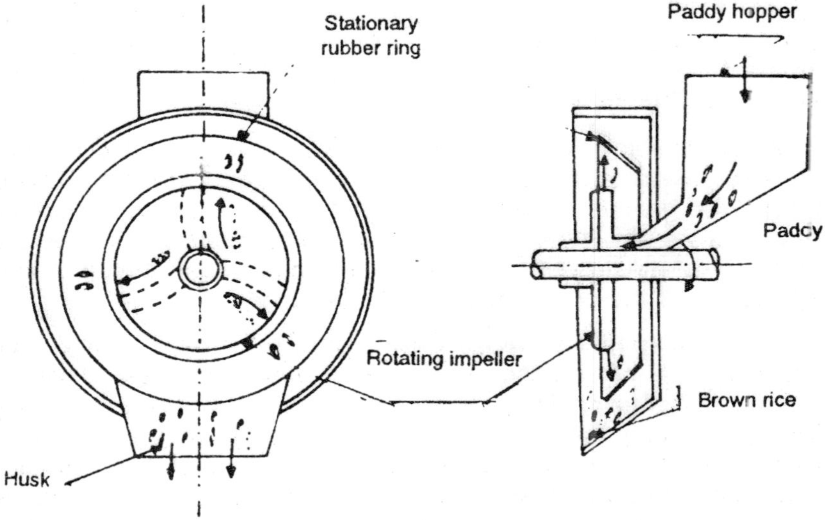

Fig. 3.26. Centrifugal Sheller

Factors That Affect Rice Outturn During Milling

Outturn of rice from paddy after milling differs from sample to sample. This difference arises from three overall factors.

Amount of husk in paddy

First, rice outturn depends on the husk content of paddy. More the husk, less is the rice and less the husk, more is the rice. On an average the husk content of paddy is in the range 20-22%. But there are varieties which have as high as 26% husk and there are others which have as low as 15% husk. Clearly husk content makes a big difference in rice outturn.

Degree of milling

Second, rice outturn depends on the degree of milling. The more brown rice is polished, less is the rice outturn and the less brown rice is polished, more is the outturn. By law in India the degree of milling is fixed at 5%. But in practice rice is milled as low as 1-2% ("Government Polish") and as high as 8-10%. This practice therefore strongly influences rice outturn.

Breakage of rice

Third, and by far of greatest importance, is the breakage of rice during milling. As rice is consumed in whole grains form, there is a preference for whole grains, and broken rice reduces the value of rice. But more importantly, whenever rice breaks, some fine brokens are also produced. These fine brokens may get lost either during sieving or during aspiration. So breakage reduces not only value but also outturn of rice. Therefore grain breakage is the biggest problem in rice milling.

Why does some rice break during milling? Some people feel that rice grain is very delicate and so it breaks from the stress of milling. This is not true. Rice grain is actually very tough and can easily withstand the stress of milling. But it breaks if it is already weakened by some defect. In other words, milling alone does not cause rice to break. Milling causes breakage only if the grain was originally damaged.

Damaged grains : Cracks in rice grain are the most harmful type of grain defect. Cracks arise in rice due to very quick loss or gain of moisture, in other words by quick drying or wetting. If paddy is dried very quickly for too long, then rice cracks. The reasons have been explained earlier. For similar reasons, if paddy is wetted with water, then also rice cracks. Also, delayed harvesting causes cracks in paddy. When mature grains remain standing in the field, they undergo drying in day time and wetting in night every day, and thereby get cracked (figure 27). Therefore harvesting should be done a little early when the grains are still slightly greenish at the panicle bottom. If proper care is taken in harvesting and drying and if grain is protected from wetting, there will be no cracks and the outturn will be high.

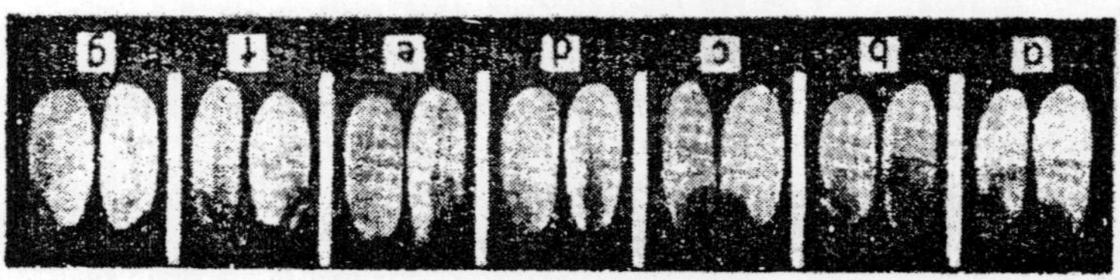

Fig. 3.27. Racks in Paddy

Another cause of breakage is immature grains. If the paddy is harvested too early, there will be more immature grains. These are soft and so break during milling. For best results paddy should be harvested in a moisture range of 20-24%. Then both cracked and immature grains will be minimum and grain breakage will be low.

Paddy damaged by insects and moulds during storage is also weakened. These too tend to break during milling.

Thus breakage of rice invariably originates only from cracked, immature and other damaged grains. Sound grains almost never break.

Other factors : Does it then mean that all defective or damaged paddy grains will break during milling? No, that is also not true. Here comes the importance of other factors, namely, (a) mill type, (b) size and shape of the variety, and (c) moisture content.

(a) Practically no type of mill breaks a sound rice grain, as already mentioned. But that does not mean that the type of mill is not important. Some types break more of the damaged grains while some can protect them well. For example, most damaged rice grains are well protected by a rubber-roll sheller but less so by a disc sheller and very much less by a centrifugal sheller. Similarly, more of the damaged grains are broken in a metal polisher (like huller) than in an emery polisher. So when the paddy to be milled contains much damaged grains, different mill types give quite different breakage. That is why rubber roll sheller-emery polisher mills are so much better. In addition, as mentioned earlier, gradual step by step polishing protects many damaged grains from breaking.

(b) Size and shape of the variety also influence breakage. More of the damaged grains break in long and slender varieties than in short and round varieties. So we generally find more breakage in fine than in coarse varieties.

(c) Again, too much moisture in rice makes it soft. So if paddy contains too much moisture during milling, more of the damaged grains break and outturn becomes low. As a matter of fact if moisture is too high, not only damaged but even some sound grains may start breaking. And too low moisture in rice makes it brittle which leads to breakage.

So we see that the ultimate cause of rice breakage during milling is the defects in grain. Maintaining good grain quality by proper harvesting, drying and storage practices is therefore of greatest importance for reducing rice breakage. But the type of mill, the moisture content and the grain size and shape are also of secondary importance, for how much of the defective grains do actually break depend on these factors.

By-Products of Rice Milling

Paddy when milled usually yields, apart from marketable rice (head rice + medium and big brokens), 21-24% husk, 3-7% bran and 0.2-2% small brokens and germ, which are the three important by-products of rice milling.

The economic utilisation of the by-products, which constitute nearly 30% by weight of paddy processed, is essential for proper viability of the industry. The potential uses of the by-products are given below.

Husk

One-fifth to one-fourth the weight of paddy consists of husk, which makes up the largest milling by-product of rice . It has a high ash content, about 20%, the major portion of which (over 90%) consists of silica. It is not edible, even by animals. It is voluminous and its transportation out of the mill complex is expensive.

Husk has many possible uses. But at the moment its most practical, profitable use is as fuel, particularly in the rice mill. A rice mill needs energy for many purposes. First, energy is needed to run the mill. In olden times many mills used to be run by a steam engine using husk. These steam engines were replaced by electrical motors after electricity became available in plenty. Now again electricity is in short supply and there is scope for use of other sources of energy. Second, rice mills need energy for parboiling and drying of paddy. Third, energy is needed for lighting.

Much of this energy need can be met by burning husk. Husk has a calorific value of about 3000 kcal/kg (nearly one-third of that of mineral oil and half that of coal). So far grate type furnaces have been used to burn the husk. Efficiency of such furnaces is not high, even though their design has been recently improved. Recently, fluidised bed combustion/ cyclone-type furnaces have become available. Their efficiency is much higher. Gassification of husk is being introduced now in some countries. especially China. In this system energy utilisation is the highest. It is said that by proper utilisation of its husk, a rice mill can become completely independent of external supply of energy.

At the moment, ail rice mills doing parboiling raise steam in a boiler by burning husk. The steam is used for parboiling and often also for drying through a steam heat exchanger. Alternatively, drying can be done directly from the husk furnace by direct flue gases or through an air heat exchanger.

Husk is also used as fuel in the household and in small hotel establishments. For ease of transportation and storage for such purposes, briquetting machines are available. Special stoves which make use of the husk as fuel have been developed for use in kitchens.

Fully burnt white ash of husk contains 95% silica and can be used for manufacturing Sodium silicate, silica gel, insulating bricks, etc. If husk is incompletely burnt, the ash can be used as diluent for manure. The ash is also used to increase the bulk of industrial cleaning compositions.

Other applications of husk are as loose insulating material in building and cold storages, in shipping as packing material, etc.

Bran

Rice bran is the most valuable by-product of rice milling industry. It contains 12-15% protein, 14-20% oil if the paddy is raw and 18-25% if parboiled, and is a rich source of B-group vitamins.

Bran can be utilised in various ways. It is being used as feed for animals. However, it is a valuable source of vegetable oil and should best be first solvent-extracted to recover the oil. The extracted bran is used as animal feed. The crude oil extracted is used for the manufacture of soap and fatty acids. Edible grade oil is produced by refining the crude bran oil having low free fatty acids (not more than 8%).

At present about 27 lakh tonnes of bran is being processed in India by solvent extraction industry to produce about 4 lakh tonnes rice bran oil. Nearly 57% of this oil is of edible grade.

A peculiar feature of rice bran is its poor keeping quality. It becomes rancid due to hydrolytic damage of the oil by an active enzyme (lipase) present in the bran. High proportions of free fatty acids (FFA) in the extracted oil make refining uneconomical. The damage due to activation of the enzyme starts soon after milling.

Stabilisation of bran inactivates the enzyme and extends the storage period of bran without any appreciable change in FFA content. It should be done at the mill site soon after milling.

There are three methods of bran stabilisation: (i) dry-heat treatment; (ii) wet-heat treatment; and (iii) mineral acid treatment. Practicability for use at the mill site, convenience and economics would decide the choice of the method.

The dry-heat or mineral acid treatment could be adopted by rice mills where steaming facilities are not available. The wet-heat treatment is most convenient to adopt in rice mills where steaming facilities are available.

Where parboiling is practiced, there is no problem of development of FFA in bran provided sufficient steaming time is allowed in the process and the parboiled paddy is properly dried. For additional precaution, the bran obtained during milling should be dried to a moisture content less than 8-9%.

Broken rice

Although 5-50% of the rice grains may break during milling, the medium and large brokens as per usual Indian marketing tradition can be mixed with head rice, unless of course the breakage is excessive. Therefore, it is only the very small brokens that are separated during grading of milled rice.

Under normal milling practice, where the stones are not completely removed, the small stones and mud particles collect mainly along with the small brokens. Such small brokens are difficult to use as food and are often used as poultry feed. But when paddy is rigorously cleaned before milling, brokens can be used in the form of semolina or flour with blackgram in preparation of breakfast foods such as *Idli* and *Dosa*. A number of deep-fried products are also prepared traditionally using rice flour.

Quality Control Laboratory

During procurement of paddy, it is desirable to determine the variety, moisture, dockage, milling yield, etc. of representative samples. The rice output and bran also need analysis. Test equipments are available to evaluate paddy, rice and bran samples.

To determine the potential milling yield of paddy, the paddy sample is first put through a dockage tester to remove the impurities. Next the sample goes through the dehusker to remove the husk. Polishing to remove the bran follows. Finally, a grader separates the brokens from the head rice.

Grain characteristics can be tested for variety, size, shape, uniformity, damage, chalkiness, odour and admixture of other seeds. All these characteristics determine the quality of the sample and how the sample stands against certain grades or standards.

Sample preparation

Bulk samples should be collected from the procured lot, mill streams or other stock using appropriate tools (such as sample probe). The bulk sample is divided using a "sample divider" to reduce the sample size to about 1 kg for various tests. The test sample is thoroughly mixed in a sample mixer to get a uniform homogeneous sample.

Removal of dockage

Impurities of various types present in the sample are determined by a dockage tester using aspiration and suitable screens and riddles. Chaff, immature grains, other seeds, sand, stones or other trash particles are thus determined. Hand sorting is done when necessary.

Moisture content

Moisture content has a marked influence on all aspects of paddy and rice quality. Most important is on the keeping quality of grain during storage. Milling quality is also greatly influenced by the moisture content of the paddy at harvest time, during drying and storage, and while milling. The moisture content of paddy is also of direct economic importance during purchasing. Purchased paddy containing more than 14% moisture will have drying losses plus higher drying cost.

Several methods are available for determining the moisture content of paddy and rice. Accuracy combined with rapidity are the most important points.

Thermostatic ovens are essential in any laboratory to check and calibrate rapid-type moisture testers.

Commonly available rapid moisture meters work either on the principle of conductivity or of dielectric property of the grain which varies with the moisture. But all moisture meters must be periodically calibrated against moisture estimated by the oven-drying method.

Test Milling

Preparation for test milling : If the paddy sample has more than 14% moisture, it should be dried before a milling analysis is made. Damp paddy cannot be milled with reliable results. The simplest method is to dry the sample in a tray in the room for about a day. Finally, it should be thoroughly mixed.

Dehusking : The clean paddy sample is weighed before putting into the dehusker. The dehusker consists of two rubber rolls (or fluted metal roll and rubber roll) where dehusking takes place. The brown rice and husk fall through an air stream that permits the brown rice to drop through, while the air picks up the immature grains and husk. The immature grains drop out separately for collection and husk is collected in the attached cyclone. The residual paddy should be separated and reshelled. The brown rice (including the brokens, if any) is carefully collected and weighed to give the brown rice yield.

Polishing : The brown rice is now milled in a polisher. Vertical and horizontal abrasive polishers and horizontal friction polishers are available. The milling conditions (load applied, time of milling, aperture clearance, etc.) are adjusted to get the required degree of polish. The total amount of bran removed during milling is first sieved in an 18-mesh sieve and then weighed, from which the degree of milling is calculated. The exact adjustment required for each paddy variety can only be determined by experiments on that variety in the laboratory. All the milled rice, including the brokens recovered from the bran, is carefully collected and weighed to obtain the total rice yield.

Grading : After polishing, the sieved milled rice is graded in a sizing device to determine the amount of head rice and brokens. Any grain which is three-fourths the kernel size or longer, is termed head rice. Pieces smaller than that are termed brokens. This gives the head rice yield.

Laboratory equipments

The following is a complete list of laboratory equipments required in a rice quality control laboratory.

1. Sampling probes
2. Sample pans
3. Sample divider
4. Sample mixer
5. Sample containers
6. Scale for weighing samples
7. Analytical balance
8. Thermometers
9. Electrical air oven, desiccator, moisture cups
10. White enamelled plate, scoops and tweezers for examining grains
11. Gauge for measuring length, breadth and thickness of grains
12. Hand sieves
13. Screen perforation measuring guage
14. Magnifying glass
15. Dockage tester
16. Rapid moisture tester
17. Apparatus for determining weight per volume (density) of grains
18. Measuring jar to determine volume of grain
19. Grain counting device
20. Paddy viability tester
21. Paddy crack detector
22. Microbiological colony counter to examine cracks in brown rice or paddy crack detector
23. Hand device for rough milling of paddy
24. Laboratory Satake rubber-roll sheller or McGill sheller
25. Laboratory cone polisher or Satake horizontal abrasive polisher or McGill miller
26. Indented plates or sizing device or laboratory trieur cylinder for separating broken rice.
27. Laboratory grain aspirator
28. Laboratory paddy separator
29. Laboratory brushing unit.
30. Wet and dry bulb thermometers or humidity meter

4

Modern Conventional Milling

A modem rice mill is an elaborate assembly of devices for handling the rough grain as it comes from the warehouse end and turning it into finished white rice, sacked and ready for market, using a minimum of labor. All operations are mechanically performed, including transfer of rice from one machine to another for each successive operation. Descriptions of rice milling and processing equipment have been published by the Food and Agriculture Organization of the United Nations.

According to van Ruiten, modem commercial mills can be categorized as conventional and Japanese style. He differentiates these styles as follows:

(1) Japanese pre-cleaning machines include provisions to remove immature rough rice, but many conventional mills do not.

(2) Conventional mills use abrasive disk hullers for both initial and return hulling. All Japanese rice mills use rubber-roll hullers.

(3) Conventional rice mills use a compartment-type rough rice separator which produces two fractions—rough rice, which is returned to the dehulling section for reprocessing, and brown rice, which is conveyed directly to the whitening section. Japanese rice mills, however, use a multitray type of rough rice separator which produces three fractions—rough rice which is returned to the rubber-roll huller, brown rice which is sent to the whitening section, and a mixture of rough and brown rice which is immediately recirculated over the rough rice separator.

(4) In conventional rice mills, abrasive whitening cones are used, frequently in a multi-pass configuration. The abrasive coating is coarse, normally being made of emery grit or a mixture of emery

grit and silicon carbide. Japanese use a multipass system, with the first and second whiteners being of the abrasive type and the third being of a friction design. This causes the milled rice to have a smoother surface. For the abrasive surfaces, a relatively fine silicon carbide grit is used.

Equipment for milling rice is fairly well standardized in the U. S. Rough rice is delivered to the mill from the drier or warehouse. It contains various types of debris which have not been removed by preceding cleaning operations. Among these are straw, loose hulls, bran, weed seeds, pebbles, and granules or balls of dirt. There will also be some broken rice present. This mixture must first be cleaned with shaker screens to remove small and large heavy impurities and then aspirated to get rid of hulls and other low density chaff. An example of a cleaning machine is shown in the diagram presented here as Figure 4.1.

In this cleaner, rice is fed into the machine at "A", and distributed over the upper shaker screen. Coarse material (scalpings) is carried downward on the surface of the upper screen past a slow-travel retarder, "B." Rice falls through the upper screen and is discharged at "C." The rice stream is deflected at "D" against an air current entering at "E," and then discharged

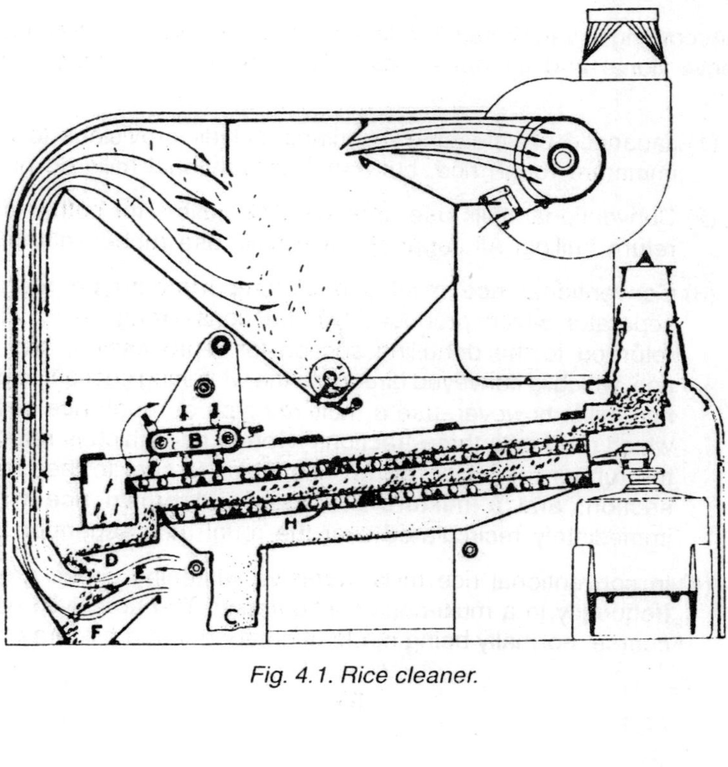

Fig. 4.1. Rice cleaner.

at "F." Air currents aspirate the dust and chaff out of the rice and carries it to a settling chamber through "G." Bouncing rubber balls, "H," impart a vertical vibration to the screens so as to keep them from clogging. The cleaned rice is then dehulled in a shelling device.

There are several types of dehullers, but the one most commonly used is the stone sheller, which consists of two horizontally-aligned disks separated by about the length of a rice grain. More recent practice is based on findings that optimum huller efficiency is obtained when the clearance is slightly more than half the length of the grain. The apposed surfaces are coated with an abrasive emery-cement mixture. When it is in operation, the upper stone remains stationary while the lower stone revolves. A stream of rice is fed through the opening in the center of the upper stone. Centrifugal force causes the rice to move outward from the center of the stones and, as the grain continues on this path to the periphery of the mill, it tumbles end-over-end, allowing the tips of the hulls to be cracked and abraded by the surface of the stones. The rice grain then falls away from the loosened hulls, and the comparatively light fragments of the hulls can be removed from the shelled grain when the mixture is aspirated through a cyclone separator.

The hull aspiration system will often be a double air-trap aspirator, in which the hull is partially removed by air currents as rice passes over a coarse bran sieve, and the remainder is taken off by an air-trap system placed above the rough rice separator.

The brown rice produced in the shelling process includes some small unshelled rice grains which must be removed. This operation is performed in a device known as a paddy separator, which consists of flat bins divided into three tiers of irregular compartments. The compartments are tilted in such a way that, when they are rapidly shuttled, the lighter, bulkier, rough rice (paddy) is concentrated at the raised side while the heavier brown rice migrates to the lower opposite side. The process is continuous, and streams of brown and rough rice are removed simultaneously. The unshelled paddy is then fed into another pair of shelling stones set closer together than the first set, and the above process of shelling, aspiration, and separation is repeated. Adjustments which can be made in this machine include feed rate, input to each compartment individually and collectively, angle of the table, frequency of the stroke, and stroke length.

Rough rice can also be shelled between rubber rolls or with a rubber belt operating against a ribbed steel roll. These devices are quite effective, but the abrasive hulls wear down the rubber, which must be replaced after a time. They are less bruising on the bran layers of the brown rice than shelling stones are, however, and so the brown rice produced in rubber shelling devices is more resistant to fatty acid development in the oil fraction. A diagram of a rubber belt sheller will be found in Figure 4.2.

The legend for this diagram is as follows: (1) Feed hopper; (2) Feed plate; (3) Feed roller; (4) Stationary roll; (5) Belt tension roll; (6) Rubber hulling belt; (7) Ribbed steel hulling cylinder; (8) Discharge for hulls and hulled rice; (9) Inspection doors; and (10) Housing and frame.

Whether produced by stone or rubber shellers, the brown rice is now ready for milling. Brown rice is first milled to remove the coarse outer layers of bran and germ, later it will be polished. The most common device for milling is often, erroneously, called a huller because it was adapted from a machine used for hulling coffee. Strictly speaking, in this application it is not a huller (or de-huller) because the rice entering it has already been deprived of its hull. It would be more appropriate to call it a milling machine. Unlike the milling of wheat flour in which fine particle size is desired in the product, rice milling must be conducted so as to break as few kernels as

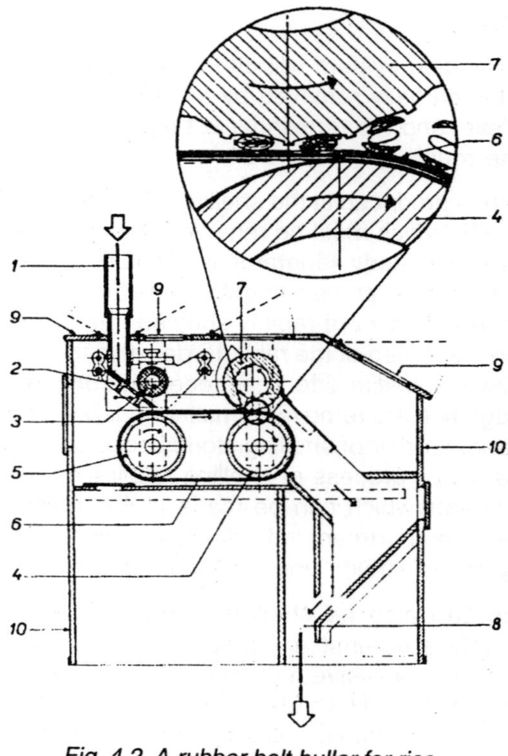

Fig. 4.2. A rubber belt huller for rice.

possible because whole grains (head rice) are of greater commercial value than broken grains. The price differential may be several cents per pound, depending on the market.

Brown rice can be converted into milled rice by use of "whitening cones" in single or multi-pass operations. These machines consist essentially of a cast-iron, cone-shaped rotatable cylinder coated with an abrasive material and mounted inside a perforated screen (or wire mesh) conforming to the shape of the cone (really, a truncated cone with the small diameter on the bottom). Clearance between the cone and the screen can be adjusted by lifting or lowering the shaft of the rotatable cone, and it is this clearance which is the principal factor controlling residence time of the grain in the mill. Adjustable rubber "brakes" or ridges are fitted on the cone, running from top to bottom.

Two views of another type of milling machine can be found in Figure 4.3. The legend is as follows: (1) Feed hopper; (2) Hopper seat; (3) Feed regulation gate; (4) Cover; (5) Shaft; (6) Ribbed rotor; (7) Slotted screen;

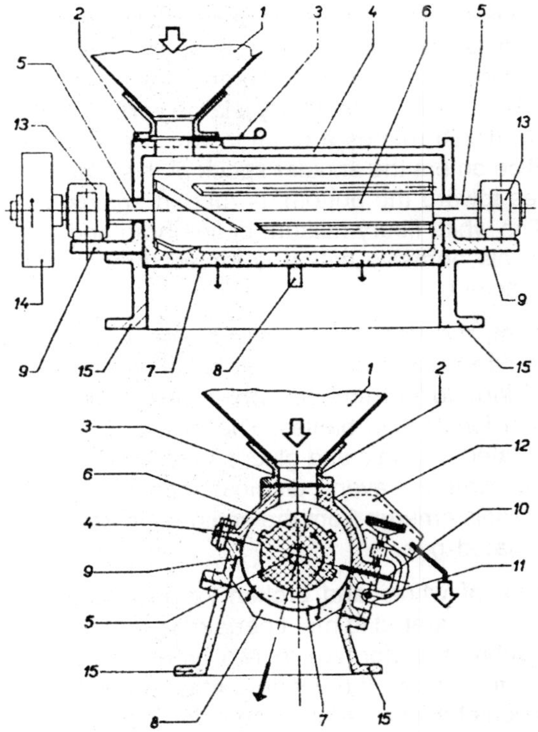

Fig. 4.3. A rice milling machine.

(8) Screen holder; (9) Upper frame; (10) Blade; (11) Cover clamp; (12) Discharge; (13) Bearings; (14) Drive pulley; and (15) Lower frame. The outer part of this device consists of a hollow horizontal cylinder, the lower half of which is slotted. The upper half contains an adjustable longitudinal blade. Inside the outer shell is a ribbed steel rotor. The blade is adjusted so as to force grains of rice against the rotating ribs. Brown rice is fed into the top of the milling machine until the annular space is filled. The grains are rubbed by the ribbed rotor and by each other to remove bran and germ which are forced through the slots by internal pressure. There is always a certain amount of breakage in this process, and the finer bits of broken endosperm pass out of the mill along with the bran and germ. The milled rice is removed after it has been carried through the machine by the spiral action of the ribs.

Milling may be accomplished in one or two "breaks." That is, by a single pass through a mill or by consecutive passages through two mills, depending on plant practice. In some plants, as many as four breaks have been used.

After the rice is milled, it consists of almost white whole kernels mixed with broken kernels of different sizes. It is now ready for the brush—a device for removing the white inner bran layers and the proteinaceous aleurone layer. The brush is essentially a large vertical stationary cylindrical screen inside of which rotates a drum to which are attached overlapping leather flaps. Rice enters the annular space of this machine at the top and, as it progresses toward the bottom, is rubbed against the screen by the leather flaps. The white floury mixture of fine bran and aleurone layer that is removed by this abrasive action is forced through the screen and is collected and sacked.

At this point, the rice is fully milled. Some trade outlets, however, require that the rice kernels have a high luster, so they are polished. This operation is performed in trumbols, which are large, horizontal, rotating drums fitted with lengthwise baffles. The milled rice is charged into the trumbols and treated with talc and glucose solution while the trumbols are rotated. After the coating is evenly distributed on the kernels and dried with warm air, the kernels emerge from the equipment with a smooth glistening luster. This is coated rice.

The mixture of whole and broken kernels obtained in the milling process is usually separated to meet certain grade requirements for milled rice. This operation is performed in two types of equipment. One is a rotating horizontal cylinder, the inside surface of which contains closely spaced depressions having a shape and a depth that allows broken grains to lodge in the cavities. When the cylinders are rotated, broken grains are carried upward until they reach a point where the shift in their center of gravity causes them to fall out of the depressions. They are collected in a chute or discharge device which carries them out of the cylinder. Unbroken grains are too long to lodge in the depressions, so they move along the lowest part of the cylinder and discharge at the end opposite the point of loading. The reader will recognize similarities between this separator and various cleaning devices used for wheat, rye, corn, etc.

In recent years, the indented cylinder has been replaced in many plants by the disk separator. This machine also has the outward form of a drum or horizontal cylinder, but within it revolves a series of parallel indented disks. The indentations are designed with one deep side and one shallow side. As the disks rotate through the bed of rice which is moving along the bottom part of the cylinder, broken grains lodge against the deep side of the indentations and are carried upward. They fall out at, or slightly beyond, the zenith of rotation. Like the indented shell type of separator, the operation of this device is continuous. By proper choice of conditions such as rate of feed and speed of rotation of the disks, an almost complete separation of broken grains from head rice can be achieved. These machines are provided with sets of disks having depressions of different sizes for use on different kinds of rice. Disks designed for short grain rice, for example, would not be suitable for long grain types.

Although different nulling processes will yield different percentages of finished products, the ranges shown in Table 4.1 can be considered representative of modern milling results.

Table 4.1

***Ranges of Product Yields in Rice Milling*[1]**

Product or by-product	Yield range, lb
Hulls	17.0 - 21.0
Bran	8.0 - 14.0
Polish	1.8 - 4.0
Head rice	37.0 - 65.00
Second heads	2.6 - 11.7
Screenings	3.1 - 11.0
Brewers' rice	2.0 - 4.9
Loss and discards	1.2 - 3.0

[1] *Starting with 100 lbs of rough rice.*

Abrasive Milling of Rice

It has been shown that the composition of samples taken from a rice kernel varies with the distance of the sample from the exterior surface of the kernel. When samples of powder are collected and analyzed as the whole kernel is ground smaller and smaller, the fractions will be found to differ in their percentage contents of protein, fat, starch, and other components. No commercial use has yet been made of this finding, so far as is known.

Investigators have shown that the outside layers of milled rice contain more protein, calcium, phosphorus, thiamin, niacin, riboflavin, and lipids than do layers nearer the center. Starch content of the samples becomes greater as the layers approach the center. Flours containing as much as 20 to 21% protein were obtained from kernels having an average protein content of not more than 8%. The amino acid composition of the proteins obtained from the various layers was substantially the same. Differences in mineral and vitamin content are very striking. Calcium is as much as 20 times higher in the outer layer than in the whole kernel; phosphorus 10 times higher; the vitamins were 4 to 8 times higher. The lipid content was 5.8% compared with 0.2% in the original milled kernel.

If the flour removal is held to about 8%, the remaining grain does not suffer in appearance and its cooking quality is close to that of the original rice. The flour contributes unusual viscosity effects to pastes and in this application behayes more like pregelatinized rice flour than it does unheated rice flour. These pastes show very little viscosity when tested in the Brabender viscometer. A commercial rice whitening machine has been used to prepare pilot plant quantities of the "peripheral flour" of Deobald.

Lye-peeling

The so-called WURLD process for lye-peeling of cereal grains has been applied to bran removal from rice. Hot sodium hydroxide solution is sprayed on the grain, allowed to stand a short time, and then washed away, carrying with it the loosened bran layers. In the laboratory procedure described by USDA workers, brown rice is first soaked in water that is gradually heated almost to boiling. The soaked rice is then transferred to a rotating drum, and hot 2 to 5% lye solution is sprayed on it. After the treated mass has been tumbled for about three minutes, it is dumped into water to remove the excess lye and to commence the washing process. The grain is next passed through a device in which it is subjected to an intense turbulence and whirling in additional water. This removes the loosened bran and further washes the peeled kernels, which are then rinsed in a dilute acid to neutralize any remaining alkali, and dried.

The yield of head rice by the lye-peeling process can be higher than from the usual dry milling methods if conditions are optimal; it may approach 100% of the total rice yield. The aleurone layer and germ remain on the kernel, which is duller or yellower in appearance than conventionally milled rice. This process would be more expensive to apply than dry milling and thus would have little to recommend it unless the yield of head rice was sufficiently increased to compensate for the extra cost. It is not clear that the equipment cost would be less for the lye-peeling method and there are some questions about pollution or waste-disposal problems. There is also the need to fully evaluate the effect of this process on nutrient composition.

Turbo-milling

Attempts were made by some USDA laboratories to devise an air-classification method which would permit the separation of finely ground rice flour into protein-enriched and carbohydrate-enriched fractions, analogous to the turbomilling processes so successfully applied to wheat flours. Because rice starch granules are tenaciously embedded in the protein matrix and are also much smaller than the granules of other cereals, separation of protein-rich from protein-poor material proved to be very difficult. The equipment used consisted of impact or turbulence grinders for reducing the rice flour to about the size of single starch granules, and air-classifiers to separate the fine powders into fractions based on particle size. So far as can be determined, no commercial installations exist for air-classifying rice flour.

Extractive Milling

When clean hulled brown rice is soaked in certain oily or aqueous liquids under carefully controlled conditions, the bran coats are softened while the endosperm retains its initial properties. As a result, certain efficiencies can be achieved in the subsequent processing and improvements made in the final product. This observation forms the basis of a milling technique used for large scale production of milled rice.

The patent of Wayne describes the salient features ot this procedure and lists many examples of bran-softening agents, including oils (both mineral and vegetable), soaps and esters of fatty acids, glycols, aqueous solutions of certain alkalies and salts, and acids. The essential steps are: (1) apply softening agent to hulled rice; (2) allow the treated rice to stand until the bran layers are penetrated by the liquid; (3) pass the rice through milling machines; (4) separate the bran; (5); remove the solvent; (6) grade and size the product. The bran goes through a "desolventizer" which removes the oil mixed in with the solvent and then through two centrifuges. In the second centrifuge, the bran is washed with hexane to remove most of the remaining oil. Finally, the bran goes through another desolventizer and a cooler. The oil is passed through a solvent recovery system.

The softening agent used in the commercial process is a mixture of rice oil and hexane. Since both of these substances will be present in the system in any event, use of the combination avoids the introduction of a third component which would have to be removed later. Furthermore, rice oil-hexane rapidly and completely penetrates the bran layers while rice oil alone, in the proportion of 1.5% of the finished rice, may require 6 hrs to exert its maximum softening action.

The softening agents are used in amounts varying from 0.25 to 5% of the rice weight, and the time of contact is adjusted so that the bran is thoroughly penetrated but the endosperm is not much affected. According to the inventor, a sufficient degree of softening of the bran coat is indicated when it may be easily removed from the brown rice kernel by scraping with a fingernail. The softened bran coat is easily removed, exposing the white endosperm. The milling action in the process equipment need not be more severe than the fingernail scraping test.

For the most part, conventional equipment is being used for dehulling and the actual milling steps. Because of the softened condition of the bran, however, the removal or detachment of the pericarp is carried out under conditions giving far less severe impact, mechanical, and abrasion effects and thermal stresses than when using conventional dry-milling hullers. The major economic advantage which results from these changes is an increase in yield of head rice of up to 10%

Rice prepared by this process contains less fat than white rice milled by conventional methods, but otherwise it is nutritionally similar to ordinary milled rice. The bran is creamy white and contains 17 to 20% protein but less than 1.5% fat. It has been recommended for use in dietetic foods and snacks by manufacturer. It is obvious, though, that the savings in caloric content would be of very little importance in the average diet or, perhaps, in any diet. For each barrel of wet-milled rice, about 2.5 lb of oil is obtained, and this is more than the yield when bran obtained from the conventional milling process is extracted.

The patent claims that a rice product superior to brown rice in color, stability, and cooking response can be made if the processing is conducted in a manner designed to retain most of the bran layers.

Rice Flour

There is a fairly good market for rice flour for use as a food ingredient. Its principal value is connected with the starch component, which consists of very small granules, about 3 to 10 microns in the largest dimension.

Different rices have different starch properties, based on their relative content of amylose and amylopectin, and, of course, these properties are reflected in the characteristics of rice flour. Most rice flour is ground second head rice, the larger broken kernels resulting from rice milling. The ground product may be used as it comes from the grinder or it may be sifted to obtain fractions with specific particle size distributions.

There is a demand for a simulated bread which does not include wheat flour, since some people are allergic to wheat. Rice is one of the obvious candidates for a replacement cereal, and it has been shown that a kind of yeast-leavened loaf can be made from rice flour if the formula includes the gum hydroxypropylmethylcellulose to act as a gas-retaining film. In a study of rice flours ground on various mills (roller, burr, pin, hammer, and turbo) and used as 100% of the cereal ingredient in a yeast-leavened bread, Bean showed that the roller, burr, and pin mill flours produced a loaf but the much finer hammer and turbo milled flours did not. The failure of the last two was attributed to the heavy starch damage created by the rigorous action of the two mills.

Waxy rice flour has been recommended as an ingredient in puddings which are to be frozen, since the finished product is damaged much less by numerous freeze-thaw cycles. When substituted for wheat flour, 10 to 15% waxy rice flour imparted a desirable soft and crispy texture to waffles, a texture which was retained after freezing, thawing, and reheating in a toaster.

Further Processing of Rice

A fairly large percentage of the rice used in the U.S. is processed into prepared foods of various kinds, such as parboiled, quick-cooking, enriched, and canned rice, canned soups, canned rice and vegetable mixtures, dry soup mixes, breakfast cereals, baby foods, and frozen dishes. When ground into flour, rice is sometimes used as a thickening agent in canned foods because of the smooth texture of its pastes and its bland flavor. Rice flour is also used occasionally in commercial bakeries for dusting loaves of bread before they go into the oven. Because rice is lacking in gluten, it cannot be used by itself to make the type of bread desired by the average U.S. consumer, but some types of imitation bread have been made with rice as the major component, in order to meet the needs of those persons who are allergic to wheat. Broken rice is frequently used as a source of carbohydrates in beer brewing.

Various additives can be added to rice to correct some of the problems which the grain presents when processed in normal ways. The natural antioxidants found in rice are usually destroyed in processing, so the small amount of fat which is not removed by the usual manufacturing operations may cause flavor deterioration during storage. Antioxidants, such as BHA and BHT, may be added for delaying rancidity development. The natural nutritional deficiencies of milled rice may be still further increased by certain types of processing but may be partially remedied by adding to the products vitamins, iron salts, and protein supplements containing essential amino acids.

Boiling and Steaming

Cooking of rice, whether in the home kitchen or in the factory steam kettle, is a simple process but requires a certain amount of care if a food of optimum texture is to be obtained. The Rice Council for Market Development has published a collection of directions for cooking rice which can be considered authoritative. Comments in the following paragraphs are modified and paraphrased versions of the Rice Council's directions.

The general rule is to use one part by volume of rice to two parts by volume of liquid. Add the desired amounts of salt and fat. For drier, fluffier rice, the liquid should be decreased by about 10%. Combine the rice, liquid, salt, and fat in a cooking container about 8 to 10 times the volume of the dried rice kernels. Heat the liquid to boiling, stir once or twice, and decrease the heat to simmer. Cover the container with a tight fitting lid, and cook 15 minutes for regular rice, 20 to 25 minutes for parboiled rice, or 45 minutes for brown rice. If, at the end of this time, the rice is not quite tender throughout the kernels, or if the liquid is not fully absorbed, replace the lid and cook 2 to 4 minutes longer.

Rice can be prepared by microwave cooking. Use two parts by volume of liquid for one part by volume of raw rice. Combine all ingredients in a microwave-safe baking dish. Cover and cook on high power for five minutes, or until the liquid boils. Reduce setting to 50% power and cook 15 min for regular rice; for brown rice, reduce setting to 30% power and cook 45 min. Separate and fluff the rice kernels with a fork.

Acid liquids such as tomato juice, fruit juices, and wines have a tendency to make the rice grain cook firmer and to lengthen the cooking time. These effects can be ameliorated by diluting acid liquids with equal parts of water. Milk has a tendency to lengthen the cooking time. Fat is often added to the cooking liquid to help keep the grains separate. When raw rice grains are sauteed in fat, the fat coats the rice to keep the grain better separated; the hot fat also has a tendency to break down the starch on the surface of the rice. This results in a final cooked product that has a slightly mealy texture and splayed ends on the grains. Sugar in the cooking liquid, especially in high concentrations, will result in firmer rice grains. Using a U.S. medium or short grain rice will reduce the firming effect of the sugar.

Parboiling

Traditional methods—Parboiling of rice is a term that encompasses quite a variety of different processes, some of them quite primitive technologically, others quite advanced. The basic or essential features are that rough rice is first wetted, then heated, and finally dried. Many changes occur in the rice kernel as a result of this treatment. Of particular importance are the translocation of some nutrients from the outer layers to inner layers and the gelatinization of the starch. Subsequently, the rice is milled and, of course, it must be cooked in water before consumption.

It is said that parboiling was first developed in India as a method for facilitating removal of the hulls from the rice kernel. In its earliest forms, parboiling consisted of soaking rough rice (paddy) in warm water overnight and then drying the grain in the sun. The rice hulls split open and were easily removed from the kernel. Later, it was learned that parboiling provides nutritional benefits, since thiamin and other essential nutrients which are normally present in fairly high concentrations in the bran (but at low concentrations in the kernel) migrate to the endosperm during the water soaking step. Since nearly all rice is milled to remove the bran, parboiling preserves more of the nutritional values contained in the whole grain. When hot water is used, the starch in the rice endosperm is changed into a condition which causes the kernel to be more resistant to breakage and thus gives a greater yield of whole kernels after milling.

Rough rice can be parboiled by soaking in water and then pressure-cooking to gelatinize the starch completely. The rice is then dried and milled to remove the outer layers. Conditions used in the soaking and cooking steps are critical with respect to the properties of the milled product, particularly for its appearance and the yield of head rice.

The soaking step is carried out in warm water. In one variation, rice is elevated from storage bins to an automatic scale hopper which weighs and dumps the rice into a accumulating hopper. When rice sufficient to make a batch has been collected, it is dumped into a steeping tank. This vessel is connected to a vacuum system, a water system, and a compressed air system. When the batch of rice is dropped into it, the tank is evacuated to remove air from the grain. Then, sufficient water at a temperature of about 200°F is introduced to cover the rice. The tank is pressurized to about 100 psi and the rice is steeped about 190 min. Temperature and time may be varied somewhat depending on the specific characteristics of the rice used, its moisture content, time in storage, etc. During the steeping operation, water soluble B-vitamin components and minerals are infused into the endosperm from the bran, germ, and hull. At the end of this step, water is drained off and the rice is discharged into a jacketed rotating vacuum drier equipped with steam tubes.

Variations in properties of different lots of rough rice may affect their response to soaking conditions, although acceptable products may be obtained over a wide range of conditions. Poor results are obtained at soaking temperatures above the gelatinization temperature of the starch. Incomplete soaking or tempering is reflected in excessive breakage of kernels when the rice is cooked, dried, and milled. For example, Calrose rice soaked at 150°F for two hours followed by one hour of tempering before it was cooked and dried yielded more than 30% broken kernels in the standard milling test.

In the drier, the soaked rice is vacuumized and heated with steam to remove excess moisture. Dry steam is then injected to gelatinize the starch in the grains, after which the vessel is vented and evacuated until the moisture of the rice becomes low enough to permit it to be milled successfully. The dried rice is conveyed to bins where it is cooled by drawing air through it, and tempered to equalize the moisture content of the batch. Finally, the rice is milled to remove the hull, bran, and germ. Examples of conditions which have proved to be successful for cooking are steam pressures of 20 psi for 5 to 8 minutes. Then, drying could be conducted at 120°F in a crossflow air drier.

In another process, cleaned rice is steeped in two parts of water at 130° to 150°F in open steel tanks for 9 to 12 hr until the rice has absorbed 30 to 35% moisture on the wet basis. The soaked rice is transferred continuously to a vertical pressure vessel equipped with rotary valves on the inlet and discharge openings. There it is steamed at 230 to 245° F for 8 to 20 minutes, depending on the degree of parboiling and the cooking quality and color desired in the end product. Shorter cooking times result in rice of lighter color. Little additional water is absorbed in the steaming process, and the rice is discharged with a moisture content of about 35%. It is dried in a steam tube drier and a series of hot air driers to 11 to 13% moisture, then milled in conventional equipment. Yields are from 66 to 71 lb of total milled rice and 58 to 67 lb of whole grains per 100 lb of the original rough rice. The product is said to contain 2.0 mg of thiamin, 0.40 mg of riboflavin, and 44.0 mg of niacin per kg of dry material. Its useful storage life is about 2 to 3 years. Milling by-products are disposed of in regular commercial channels for these materials. The waste water from the steeping process is generally not utilized; although it could be dried to yield a material having some nutritional value for feed, this would not be an economically viable operation.

A third process is similar to the second in general principles, except that both the soaking and steaming steps are performed in rotating cylinders.

Another variant of the parboiling process consists of the following steps. Rice is tempered in hot or cold water, depending on the variety, and is then conveyed to soaking tanks each of which hold 15,000 lb of rice. Hot (100° to 200°F) water is added and the rice allowed to soak for 1 to 10 hr, depending on the variety. After soaking, the rice is transferred through a rotary valve to a screw conveyor passing through a pressure vessel. Here the grain is cooked at 15 to 100 psi steam pressure for 10 sec to 3 min. Cooked kernels exit through another valve, and are cooled and dried before milling.

Modern commercial parboiling processes generally include the steps of: (1) soaking the rough rice in 50° to 70°C water for 3 to 4 hours to yield a rough rice having 30% moisture content; (2) draining the free water from the soaked rough rice; (3) applying steam heat under pressure for 15 to 20 minutes to gelatinize the starch and to raise the water content to about 35%; and (4) drying the steamed rice with hot air to reduce its moisture content to about 14%. The dried rice is then milled.

Properties—Milling yield is higher after parboiling and there are fewer broken grains, i.e., there is a greater percentage of head rice. The grain structure becomes compact, translucent, and shiny. Germination is no longer possible, so some storage problems are alleviated. The endosperm is denser, making it more resistant to insect attack, and the grains remain firmer during cooking and are less sticky.

According to Luh and Mickus, the most important changes occurring in parboiling processes are:

(1) The water-soluble vitamins and mineral salts are spread throughout the grain, thus altering their distribution and concentration among its various parts. The riboflavin and thiamin contents are four times higher and the niacin level is eight times greater in parboiled rice than in whole rice. Thiamin is more evenly distributed in the parboiled rice.

(2) Moisture content is reduced to 10 to 11%.

(3) The starch grains imbedded in a proteinaceous matrix are gelatinized and expanded until they fill up the surrounding air spaces.

(4) The protein substances are separated and sink into the compact mass of gelatinized starch, becoming less susceptible to extraction.

(5) Enzymes present in the kernel are partially or entirely inactivated.

(6) Microorganisms and insect forms are either killed or greatly reduced in number.

Parboiled rice has a somewhat elastic texture, and for that reason resists breakage when it is milled. The better head rice yields obtained from the milling of parboiled rice, as compared to raw rice, defrays to a considerable extent the cost of parboiling so that the parboiled product generally does not sell for much more than white rice.

Although parboiled rice is not quick cooking, it has certain advantages over raw rice. It is more resistant to insect infestations and it does not break up as much when used in canned formulations such as soups and puddings. When overcooked, it does not become as mushy as raw rice. Parboiled rice is darker than raw milled rice and has a slightly different flavor, but it is widely accepted and is often preferred to white rice. In some rice-eating areas of the world, however, attempts to introduce it have not been successful. Its color, which is usually a light tan, is probably an adverse factor for consumers who look upon extreme whiteness as a indication of high quality.

Some variant methods—A patent obtained by Veluppillai *et al.* improved the parboiling process by making use of microwave heating. In its essentials, the new technique consists of the following steps: (1) soaking rough rice in water at about 55°C until it reaches about 29% moisture content; (2) subjecting the soaked rice to microwave energy to partially gelatinize the starch and to raise the water content of the rough rice to about 36%; (3) draining free water from the heated and soaked rice; (4) subjecting the drained grain to a second dose of microwave energy to cause substantially complete gelatinization of the starch and to lower the moisture content of the rice to about 27%; and (5) drying the parboiled rice to 14% moisture content.

Acid parboiling is a method developed in Japan for increasing the transfer of thiamin from the bran and embryo to the endosperm. In the original method, polished rice was soaked in a 1% aqueous solution of acetic acid to which thiamin had been added. The resulting enriched rice was then drained, steamed, and dried. A disadvantage of this method was that cracks in the kernels appear, leading to an unsatisfactory appearance, and nutrients are more readily lost in soaking. To correct these deficiencies, thiamin derivatives which are soluble in organic liquids but not in water are dissolved in acetone, ethanol, and chloroform and applied to the kernels. Rice treated in this manner does not exhibit excessive cracking.

Converted rice is made by a modification of the parboiling process. Rough rice is placed in an autoclave and deaerated under vacuum. Hot water is then introduced into the autoclave and compressed air used to force the water into the kernels. This is followed by steaming in continuous flow pressure steamers, then hot air drying is done in two stages separated by a tempering period. In a previous process, soaked rice was steamed under pressure in a rotary autoclave and then partially dried (in the same pressure vessel) by applying a vacuum and heating the rice by contact with hot surfaces. Drying was completed in rotary driers with medium-hot air. The Malek process is similar. Rough rice is soaked in hot water for 3 to 6 hr, then steamed in vertical autoclaves. Partial drying is done in steam-heated, rotating cylindrical driers at a high temperature. Final drying is in a columnar drier with medium-hot air.

Storage changes—When parboiled rice is stored, rancidity occurs following an induction period. This effect is accompanied by a rise in fat acidity and in monocarbonyl and peroxide values. Both monocarbonyls and peroxides rise to a maximum, then decrease, and simultaneously the rancid odors begin to subside and ultimately disappear. Fatty acids continue to rise during storage, but the rate of increase diminishes as storage continues.

The behavior of the fat fraction in Pearl and Patna parboiled rice, with respect to development of oxidation products and free fatty acids, was experimentally studied by various investigators under a variety of conditions including dark and light storage, closed and open containers, and several temperatures. When in open containers which were stored in the dark, both rices exhibited the development of maximum carbonyl in about al year at 77°F, in about a month at 100ºF, and in about a week at 180°F.

In closed containers held at 77° and 100ºF, peroxide and monocarbonyl changes were similar to those for open storage, but induction periods were longer. At 140°F, no significant rise of either function was observed. It was found that light accelerated rancidification of parboiled rice held at 77°F.

The effect of storage on color changes in parboiled rice at different temperatures has also been measured. For both rice of the Pearl and Patna varieties, color changes were negligible for about a year at 77°F in either open or sealed containers. At 100° and 140°F, color changes were observed after 3 to 4 months due to nonenzymatic browning and they were accompanied by losses of reducing sugars. Amino nitrogen and free amino acids were also reduced in amount. Sulfur dioxide added during processing inhibited browning of parboiled rice but did not delay rancidification.

As parboiled rice is frequently sold in small permeable packages and moves from factory to consumer rather rapidly, little difficulty is experienced with rancidity in products held on retail store shelves. But when stored in bulk, this product frequently "goes off' in large quantities, and manufacturers of parboiled rice now stabilize it with antioxidants, which have proved quite effective. Close milling of the rice to reduce its fat content is also practiced, but always a few tenths of a percent of fat remains and this is enough to cause trouble unless rancidity develpment is hindered in some way.

Expanded parboiled rice—Parboiled rice expands to a light porous product when rapidly heated to fairly high temperatures in hot air or oil. Roberts *et al.* made an intensive study of the influence of parboiling conditions on various properties of rice, including its color, the solubility of the amylose fraction, and the extent of expansion upon heating under controlled conditions. The steaming step of parboiling had a particularly great influence on these properties. The expansibility of the grains, depth of color, and starch solubility in the final product increased decidedly with the severity of the treatment. According to Bhattacharya, the expansion capability of parboiled rice is a consequence of gelatinization, and the degree of expansion increases with increases in the temperature of steaming during parboiling, up to about 130°C. Dry-heat parboiled rice gives a still higher expansion, which observation was interpreted as an indication of the inhibitory effect of starch retrogradation on heat expansion. Addition of common salt increases expansion. Maximum expansion is given by varieties having 27% total amylose or 13.5% hot-water-insoluble amylose, or both.

Expanded parboiled rice is usable as a dry breakfast cereal but for that purpose its comparatively bland flavor should be enhanced with other ingredients such as honey, malt syrup, salt, etc. Precooked brown rice expanded by toasting and then ground to farina size was patented as an instant-cooking breakfast cereal.

Quick-cooking Rice

Obviously, the relatively long cooking time of raw rice, and the quality problems that may develop if the cooking conditions are not controlled within a fairly narrow range, do not fit the modern American housewife's need for foodstuffs that can be prepared quickly, with a minimum of utensils, and with low risk of failure. Quick cooking rice has been developed to meet this need.

Parboiled rice, though fully precooked, cannot be prepared "instantly" because the grains are quite dense and therefore do not take up water readily. Puffed rice, such as is used in breakfast cereals, takes up hot water extremely fast, but the finished food is unacceptable because of its mushy texture and collapsed, limp appearance. What is needed is a fully cooked grain that is quite porous, so that it rapidly absorbs hot water, but which has a finished texture resembling that of rice cooked from the raw grain. Various approaches to this problem have been made, with varying degrees of success. Some of the work is summarized below.

In one commercial method, the cooking time of both brown and white rice is shortened by heating the dry grains in a current of air at elevated temperatures. The kernels are so modified by fissuring of the surface layers, by dextrinization, and, in the case of brown rice, by loosening of the bran layers, that the cooking time in the home is reduced to about one-third that of raw rice. This represents an extremely important saving of cooking time and energy, especially for brown rice which, when not so treated, requires 30 to 45 minutes of cooking to make it soft enough to eat. Heat-processed brown rice is improved nutritionally by coating it with thiamin, riboflavin, and iron phosphate, and it is stabilized against rancidification by adding an antioxidant. These various substances are applied all at one time using a vegetable oil-water emulsion. Unlike fortified or enriched raw rice, enriched heat-processed rice is not coated with a protective film and it should not be rinsed before being cooked for serving.

Other forms of quick-cooking rice are made by precooking white rice and either rapidly drying the cooked product in a current of hot air or drying it slowly followed by expansion of the dried grains with heat. A large number of patents have been taken out to cover different variations of the wet process for making quick-cooking rice.

One widely sold form of enriched quick-cooking rice can be prepared for serving in about five minutes. Methods for making this product probably follow the general procedures outlined above. In the original form of this process, the rice was gelatinized in one step, by completely cooking it in water. This procedure resulted in extensive losses due to overcooking of the surface layers of the grains, which dispersed into the cooking water. In one modification, the soaked rice is steamed under pressure to partially gelatinize the grains, which are then slightly compressed. They are retreated with hot water to enlarge the grains and complete the gelatinization process. After these treatments the rice is dried under conditions which produce a slight puffing effect.

Quick-cooking rice may also be made by first heating the raw grains in hot air or by infrared radiation, then gelatinizing them with moisture and heat, followed by quick drying to set the grains in their enlarged porous condition. In another patented process, cooked rice is expanded by heating it under pressure and then suddenly releasing it into a vacuum chamber. Still another process consists of soaking and cooking rice, then freezing, thawing, and dehydrating it. The product can be home-prepared in about five minutes.

Presence of oxidizable iron in the cooking system results in the development of grayness in the final product. It has been proposed to eliminate this problem by adding a chelating agent such as sodium acid pyrophosphate to the water. Starch complexing agents such as monoglycerides of fatty acids can be added to the cooking water to prevent matting and adhesion of the rice during drying.

In a recent patent, the manufacture of a readily reconstitutable cooked rice by a somewhat different method is described. The consumer can prepare the product for the table, or as an ingredient for casseroles and the like, by adding boiling water and allowing the mixture to stand for about 9 or 10 minutes. An example relates the following conditions. A kilogram of parboiled rice was boiled for 15 minutes in water of pH 7.0. The cooked rice was rinsed in cold water and drained to arrive at a total weight of 2.84 kg and a moisture content of 68.5%. The rice was then placed in a layer 5 mm thick on a hot air belt dryer and subjected for 12 minutes to hot air having a velocity of 12 meters per minute and a temperature of 175°C. This treatment reduced the moisture content to 32%, so that the rice grains did not stick together. These kernels were then placed in a vibrating fluid bed dryer and dried at 175°C for one minute, after which they had reached a moisture content of 8 to 10%. The dehydrated rice had a bulk density of 40 grams per 100 cc. When 180 grams of this rice product was prepared for consumption by adding to 500 cc boiled water and allowed to stand for ten minutes, it was found that 376 grams of water had been absorbed and the product had a good, tender, firm, even, texture. The improvement in texture appears to be due to the applying of a slighter than normal puffing effect to the fully cooked rice.

Microwave heating can be used to achieve the degree of starch gelatinization essential for a rapidly rehydratable convenience product. After raw rice has been soaked in water until it reaches a moisture content of about 35%, it is passed through a microwave oven to cook it rapidly and completely. Some rices require a second soaking and cooking treatment for optimum results. After cooking has been completed, the grain is again immersed in excess water to allow it to come to 68% moisture content, about equal to that of normal cooked rice. Because of the method of heating, the outer surfaces of the kernels are not overcooked and not extremely sticky and loose as is often the case with steam cooked rice. Therefore, the rice can be dried in such a fashion as to leave the desired degree of porosity and fissurring, in the finished product. Additional advantages of the microwave process are that washing and leaching losses of solids can be kept low and the original flavor of the rice can be rather well maintained. Furthermore, the reduction in gumminess and stickiness minimizes mechanical losses due to clumping and breaking during processing.

The property possessed by dried gelatinized rice of expanding under heat treatment is most advantageous in the preparation of quick-cooking rice products. The degree of expansion in hot air may be as high as fourfold when proper conditions are used. The grains retain their normal shape after expansion, but are crisp and porous. Addition of boiling water causes them to shrink to about the size of boiled white rice grains. The texture is not the same as for rice cooked in the usual manner, however.

Packaging of quick cooking rice in plastic trays, often with added condiments, provides a product which can be rapidly prepared in a microwave after the consumer adds a measured amount of water to the tray. The trays currently being used for "microwave rice" do not appear to contain susceptors, that is, special areas designed to enhance the evolution of heat.

Shelf-stable Cooked Rice

The convenience of a retail package of fully cooked rice, which needs only to be heated, either by immersing a plastic bag in hot water, heating to serving temperature in a pan on a stove burner, or in the original container in a microwave, has suggested several lines of approach. The most obvious, of course, is the conventional canning process. Other approaches include the reduction of A_w of the cooked product to the point where microbiological growth is greatly inhibited.

Cseri *et al.* concluded that an A_w of 0.88 or lower would be satisfactory. They invented a product which achieved this level by using polyhydric alcohols as part of the ingredients. This product, however, was not fully hydrated, but had to be immersed in excess water at a temperature above 160°F for at least five minutes in order to prepare it for serving.

Table 4.2 represents one of their test formulas and the calculation used to insure that the finished product will be at an A_w of 0.837. After an initial cooking stage, the rice is drained and soaked in an infusion solution. Then, the excess solution is removed and the rice dried in heated air until the grains are free-flowing and have a moisture content of about 35%.

There are few, if any, products of the preceding type on the commercial market today, though the convenience feature seems good. Canned rice is probably more convenient and need not have the taste problems which might be associated with the additives specified in the Cseri *et al.* patent.

Canned rice—Canned cooked rice may also be considered a form of quick-cooking or convenience rice. In its earliest versions, canned rice was made almost exclusively from parboiled rice because this form does not disintegrate as much as white rice when the cans are retorted. Roberts was among the first to suggest that the problem with white rice could be alleviated by limiting the moisture content of the finished product to 55%.

Table 4.2
Shelf-Stable Fully Cooked Rice Product[1]

Component	Infusion solution	Final product	Lowering effect on water activity	Before drying
	%	%		%
Rice solids	-	62.7	-	30.00
Water	91.50	25.0	-	11.90
Salt	3.44	5.0	0.110	2.40
Glycerol	3.44	5.0	0.035	2.40
Propylene glycol	1.42	2.0	0.015	1.00
Potassium sorbate	0.20	0.3	0.003	0.14
Totals	100.00	100.0	0.163	47.84
			Water to be removed	52.16

[1] *According to the patent o-f Cseri* et al.

Briefly, this process consists of: (1) soaking the rice to its equilibrium moisture content of about 30 to 35% water; (2) cooking the rice for 4 to 5 minutes in excess water; (3) draining and packing the rice into cans; and (4) vacuum sealing and retorting. When the ultimate user removes the rice from its can, it can be prepared for serving by adding a small amount of additional water and heating for about two minutes until the added water is absorbed. The critical points of this process are: (1) holding the moisture content within the prescribed limits; (2) adjusting the pH of the product to about 5.5 to 6.0 before canning; (3) packing in C-enamel cans or glass jars with C-enameled lids; and (4) sealing under at least 26 inches of vacuum.

It is important that the moisture content of the white rice as cooked for canning be in the range of 50 to 55%. If the moisture content is below 50%, the rice will be too dry to quickly absorb additional water. Moisture contents higher than 55% cause the rice to become pasty during canning and retorting. There are significant variations between different varieties of rice in their resistance to breakdown or disintegration as the result of heat processing received during canning. These variations are related, at least in part, to the amylose content of the starch. Rice with low amylose content will always have poor stability, but, on the other hand, not all rice with high amylose content will have good resistance to breakdown. Some varieties of rice, such as Jojulta, become extremely firm. Some varieties with good potential for retaining form and texture under retort conditions are Belle, Patna, Bluebelle, and Dawn. Other commercially produced long grain varieties have not been found to be as suitable for canning.

Other methods which have been suggested for improving the canning behavior of plain white rice include adding a small amount of oil to the cooking water, using salts to control water absorption, soaking the rice in acidified water, and chemically treating the rice to cause cross-linking of the starch molecules. Burns and Gerdes say these methods do not work well and recommend their own patented discovery which involves using instant parboiled rice and a cold water quench following blanching to elminate product sticking and clumping.

The Roberts process, and some variants of it, are designed for the canning of plain, unseasoned rice, having little or no free liquid present in the container. For products such as soups, e.g., chicken and rice soup, the texture and appearance of individual rice grains is not nearly as important. Also, in products where there is much excess fluid and the can contents can be agitated during retorting, the opportunity for clumping is much less and the problem is basically one of preventing rice kernel disintegration. If the mixture contains a substantial amount of an acidic ingredient—tomato and rice soup would be an example—the potential exists for treating the product as a high acid food and canning it by the hot-fill method, which much reduces the total heat damage undergone by the rice.

There has also been a lot of interest in canning finished recipe items which are viscous and contain a high proportion of rice. Examples are Spanish rice and rice pudding. These pose additional problems and yet offer some consumer advantages as compared with the basic commodity. Regular white rice, with its near-neutral pH, is considered a low-acid product which must be retorted after the can is sealed. This inevitably means that the product will be subject to intense thermal shock, which limits the type of mixture which can be successfully canned. There are at least two ways of resolving these problems: (1) aseptic canning, which demands a very high temperature, very short time sterilization procedure under relatively turbulent conditions before the product is filled into a sterile can and (2) bringing the pH of the product to a level, say 4.5, which will allow hot-fill techniques that avoid retorting. There are problems with both these techniques. In aseptic canning, the presence of granules which must be heated to their center dictates special treatment. On the other hand, not all recipes can be adapted to high acid conditions—Spanish rice might be suitable, for example, but rice pudding is more doubtful.

Aseptic canning has been successfully applied for processing some commercial rice products. The first approach was the separate sterilization of the rice kernels, in a minimum amount of liquid, and the "sauce" portion of the pack. These two components are then combined as they go into the can. Separation of the rice and the sauce is necessary because of the different sterilization conditions required by the two components. The liquid or sauce portion can be rapidly sterilized by several convenient mean—swept wall heat exchangers, Spiratherms, Uperizers, or triple-tube heat exchangers—while requirements for sterilization of the rice are much more stringent due to the necessity for allowing heat to thoroughly penetrate all parts of the kernels. If the combined product is heat treated sufficiently to sterilize the rice, there is a tendency for the sauce to become overheated with excess browning and the development of off-flavors.

Some data on the acidification of rice mixtures with citric acid to reduce the amount of heat treatment needed for conventional canning procedures (retorting or hot-fill) were published by Sharp *et al.* As previously stated, this strategy is more adaptable for formulated items than for plain white rice. Many consumers do not want their plain rice to have a tart, acidic taste, and washing the canned rice to remove part of the acid (some will remain inside the kernels) will not be sufficient to restore the original and expected taste.

Frozen cooked rice—Boiled and steamed white and brown rice which have been frozen and reheated are virtually indistinguishable from their unfrozen counterparts. Frozen storage for up to about one year appears to have no deleterious effects on quality. In fact, white rice actually seems to improve in some respects with frozen storage, according to the verdict of a taste panel.

There are many frozen rice products of excellent quality in the marketplace today. The majority of these are combination dishes which can be reheated by the boil-in-bag method or by microwave heating. Evidently, the sticking together which created problems in earlier versions has been prevented by quick freezing of the individual grains together with the inclusion of oily type sauces.

An early reference for commercially processing small lots of frozen cooked rice included the following steps:

(1) Place rice in an excess of water at to which has been added enough citric acid to give a pH in the range of 4.0 to 5.5. Enough water should be used to cover the rice after it has soaked for two hours. The water should be at a temperature between 130° and 140°F.

(2) After two hours, drain off the soak water and rinse with more of the same pH-adjusted water to remove fines.

(3) Drain thoroughly, tapping the screen to shake loose the adhering water, or blow the rice layer with air.

(4) Meanwhile, place a small volume of water in the bottom of a pressure cooker and heat to boiling with the cover on. When the apparatus has heated up, place the soaked drained rice in layers two inches deep, or less, on screens which are supported above the water in the vessel. Close the vessel and heat with the vent open until steam is emitted, then close the vent and raise the pressure to 12 to 15 psi and hold for 12 to 15 min. Then blow off steam gradually to prevent violent boiling and flashing of the hot water.

(5) Remove the hot, steamed rice. It should have a rubbery texture. Place it in an excess of hot water at 200° to 210°F and without stirring let it imbibe water until the grains are large, tender, and separate. Stirring will cause the rice to become sticky. The rice should be held in a perforated vessel so that water may circulate freely through it. Do not boil the rice.

(6) Cooking should require only 10 to 15 minutes following the step described in (4). Drain off the hot water, rinse twice with cool or cold water having the pH adjustment described in (1) above.

(7) Tap and shake to remove free water; or better still have the equipment suck away the free water over a vacuum filter.

(8) Convey the cooked rice on a stainless steel mesh belt through an air-blast cooler to reduce it to approximately room temperature, then package it in cartons. Freeze in air-blast freezers or by other appropriate means.

Although freezing stops starch retrogradation and the accompanying textural changes affecting cooked rice stored at temperatures which allow liquid water to exist, consideration must be given to the retrogradation which will occur as the rice is being frozen. Little change will take place if the freezing is very rapid, as when individual kernels are being frozen, but rice which is inclosed within layers of insulating packaging material or frozen under other conditions where the temperature change is relatively slow, may spend considerable time in the temperature range of maximum retrogradation rate, say around 40°F. Under the latter conditions, the kernels may acquire a tough texture which will be regarded as unpleasant by most consumers.

Freeze-drying has been suggested as a means of preserving rice. This procedure consists of removing moisture from frozen material by sublimation under high vacuum. Desirable volatile constituents which might be lost under high temperature drying are often retained under the conditions of freeze-drying. The finished material is generally much easier to rehydrate than conventional dried products, since the freeze-dried piece is usually not collapsed but retains very much of its original volume and is filled with open channels through which water can penetrate. This method has been applied to rice in laboratory tests and pilot plant processing, but evidently not in commercial factories.

Rice Cakes

Rice cakes, as defined here, are not layer cakes made with rice, but agglomerations of puffed and dried rice grains in a thick disc, the most common variety weighing about an ounce, although they are also being made in much smaller sizes. These products are offered in salted, sweetened, and seasoned forms, as well as plain. They are usually eaten like a cookie, as a snack, or, perhaps, as a substitute for bread. They are useful for people who are allergic to wheat products, those who believe rice has some special nutritional properties, or people who just like rice a lot.

Rice cakes are made by heating a predetermined quantity of rice grains in a hermetically sealed chamber at pressures considerably above atmospheric pressure, and then suddenly releasing the excess pressure so that the grains expand to fill the chamber. The size and shape of the chamber determine the size and shape of the rice cake, and the weight of rice determines the density and, to a considerable extent, the texture of the finished product. In a typical apparatus, a quantity of rice is mechanically fed onto a heated piston. The piston and its load of cereal grains are then hydraulically pushed into a heated mold to create a small hermetically-sealed chamber enclosing the rice. Heat and pressure are then applied to the chamber until the grain has been sufficiently cooked, using conditions experience has indicated are needed. Then the pressure is suddenly reduced by retracting the piston, which is held in a closed but vented position by a locking device. As the pressure abruptly drops, the rice kernels expand to fill the chamber. Because the grains are in a plastic state, and their surfaces are somewhat sticky, they bond together to form a small cake. The locking device is released and the piston is fully retracted to allow the cake to be removed by an automatic pusher.

The rice used in the process must be pretreated by putting it through washing and tempering steps. For example rice at a moisture content of about 15 to 16% is first cleaned by a rice washing machine and is then placed in a basket where the excess water is allowed to drain off for 15 to 20 minutes. Moisture content of the grain immediately after washing is typically 30%. After a predetermined amount of salt has been added to the rice, it is dried for a day, then further air-dried for 2 to 3 hours until it reaches a moisture content of 15 to 20%. It can then be loaded into the puffing equipment. As can be seen, the moisture content of the rice at the time it enters the puffing chamber is not much above that of commercial stored grain.

Rice cakes are quite fragile which leads to considerable breakage during packaging, distribution, and consumption. This fragility is a commercial disadvantage of considerable magnitude. A patented process disclosed by Wu is said to cause improved bonding of rice grains, and also to allow the formation of self-supporting cakes of other grains, which has evidently been impractical with previous processes. Wu's improvement consists primarily of an improved pre-treatment process for the grains. The moisture content of the kernels is first adjusted by adding the amount of water necessary to bring them to a moisture content between 12 and 18%. Steam is then applied to the grains in an unpressurized container until time and temperature conditions are sufficient to partially gelatinize the starch.

Exact time and temperature requirements are different for different grains, that is, wheat will require different conditions than barley, wheat, etc. The initial moisture content of the grain will also have an influence on the requirements. For example, wheat at a moisture content of 14% could be steamed at about 205° F for twenty minutes to condition the grain to later produce a highly expanded product. Following this gelatinization pretreatment, the grain is dried to a moisture content of less than 18% facilitate loading of the steamed cereal into the cake-forming apparatus.

A diagram of forming plant for rice cakes, according to Wu, is shown in Figure 4.4.

Rice Milk

A traditional Japanese non-alcoholic beverage, amazake, is prepared from steamed or cooked rice blended with koji. The koji provides saccharifying enzymes and other factors to the mixture, and is made by inoculating cooked rice with spores of the mold *Aspergillus oryzae* and cultivating the inoculated rice. After fermentation for about 4 to 48 hours, the saccharified blend is filtered. The filtrate is a white to beige colored slurry having a distinctly sweet, rice-like flavor. In some examples, a sour taste is also present. As a claimed improvement on the traditional process, Mitchell *et al.* disclosed a method involving the selection of whole grain rice, liquefying it with a-amylase then with glucosidase and/or a β-amylase. The quoted patent gives recipes for puddings, brownies, chocolate beverage, and other products made using the rice milk as an ingredient.

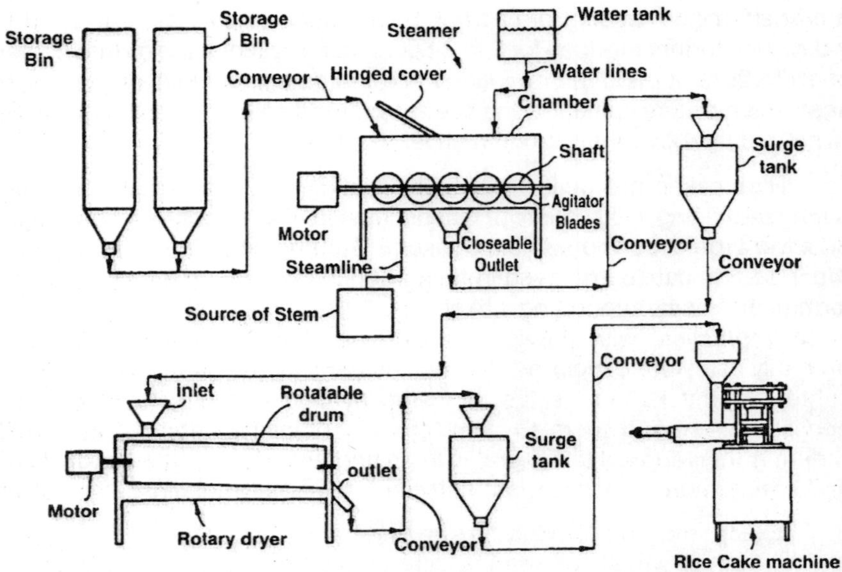

Fig. 4.4. A plant for making rice cakes by the method of Wu.

Enrichment

Vitamins and Minerals

The use of highly polished rice has been a public health problem in many places where rice is the main article of diet. A large percentage of the vitamins are removed with the bran and aleurone layers in preparing white rice. The situation is further complicated by the loss of nutrients during cooking. Studies have shown that cooking rice in eight volumes of water, the excess of which is then discarded, leads to loss of about one-third of the minerals and half of the vitamins. If the cooking water is alkaline, particularly large amounts of thiamin can be lost. Loss of carbon dioxide from bicarbonates during boiling can cause the pH of some waters to become as high as 10. Under these conditions, as much as 60 to 70% of the thiamin can be lost during cooking. If the water is acidified before cooking, the loss is reduced to 5 to 8%.

Beriberi or severe B-complex deficiency diseases can and do occur where these practices are common. Since these diseases are quite serious, disabling or killing the victims, much attention has been given to means of prevention and the usual approach has been to add vitamins to the rice as this seems to be simpler and much less expensive than trying to add vitamin-rich foods to the diet.

A test in the Bataan province of the Philippines from 1947 to 1950 demonstrated conclusively the value of rice enriched with thiamin, niacin, and iron for reducing the incidence of, and mortality from, beriberi. The results of this test were so dramatic that the Philippine government continued the enrichment of rice in Bataan and gradually extended it to other provinces.

In 1951, the Puerto Rican government enacted legislation requiring that all rice sold on the island be enriched. And in the U.S., South Carolina, which has a high per capita consumption of white rice, passed a law requiring that only enriched rice be sold within the state after July 1, 1956. Enriched rice has also been made available in many other countries throughout the world.

Approximately 80% of the thiamin, 56% of the riboflavin, 65% of the niacin, 60% of the pantothenic acid, and 55% of the pyridoxine are removed from brown rice when it is milled. Not all of these nutrients are retained in parboiled rice, so it must also be supplemented with small amounts of vitamins and iron if it is to approximate the nutrient composition of brown rice.

Rice can be enriched in several ways. The parboiling of rice is actually equivalent to an enrichment process because vitamins diffuse from the bran into the endosperm during the soaking and cooking steps. In areas where parboiled rice is consumed as the main form of this cereal, most of the population apparently receives a satisfactory dosage of these nutritional substances.

Some of the methods which have been used for adding dietary supplements to rice are:

(1) Mixing with the kernels a powder containing the vitamins and minerals. It is necessary, in this case, that the consumer be cautioned against washing the rice, for such an operation removes the enrichment.

(2) Supplying a wafer which must be added to the rice at the time it is cooked. The problems which would be involved in securing the cooperation of distributors and consumers in this procedure are rather obvious, but the method has been used successfully under military conditions.

(3) Adding a small percentage of rice grains which have been coated or impregnated with the enriching ingredients. This is the method most commonly used. It should be mentioned that many instances have been observed of consumers picking out and discarding the strange appearing grains under the impression they were damaged or contaminated.

The highly enriched grains described above, sometimes called the premix, can be made by at least two processes, which are somewhat similar.

In one of these, which is representative, a 2,150 lb lot of milled rice is deposited into a trumbol fitted with baffles. A vitamin solution made up ot 39.5 lb niacin, 6 lb thiamin, 21 lb sulfuric acid, and 58 lb water is fed into the trumbol by a perforated stainless steel pipe that extends the full length of the unit. In about ten minutes, the rice grains become uniformly coated with the liquid, and air is then blown into the trumbol to dry the coating so that the grains again become free-flowing. Next, half of an enrobing solution consisting of 13.75 lb of abietic acid, 16.25 lb of a solid fatty acid, 20.25 lb of zein, 18 gallons of isopropyl alcohol, and one gallon of water, is sprayed on the rice and the kernels are again dried. Open scoops containing 270 lb of dry ferric pyrophosphate with 405 lb of talc are then run into the trumbol and inverted. When the solid material is well dispersed over the rice, the second half of the enrobing solution is applied. With these proportions of ingredients, the final product has a content per pound of 440 mg thiamin, 3.2 gm niacin, and 2.6 gm iron. The premix is diluted incrementally with 60 lb quantities of untreated rice in the required 1:199 ratio by proportional weighing.

The quantities of enriching ingredients specified in the above description apply to one procedure commonly used in the U.S. In the Far East, different amounts of vitamins may be used, and the composition of the coating solution is modified to meet specific local needs, both nutritional and environmental.

The highly enriched kernels or premix can be artificially made from wheat dough (water, durum semolina, and enriching agents) by a process similar to that used for making macaroni products. In this method, the enriching ingredients are uniformly distributed throughout the imitation rice grain and cannot be removed by any amount of washing, and not much of it is removed by the cooking process if the premix is made of wheat flour. Fairly good replicas of the rice grain can be made if the extruding and finishing processes are sufficiently sophisticated; the reader who is familiar with Italian cuisine may have encountered a type of pasta made for adding to soups which has a superficial resemblance to rice. Even so, these miniature dough balls are hardly likely to deceive a suspicious consumer who suspects the vendor or the government is trying to put something over on him, and, of course, the cooked texture, flavor, and consistency of the pasta will not be the same as a cooked rice grain.

To give the grains of enriched rice a whiter appearance than they have after being treated by previous methods, and to permit addition of riboflavin to the enriching mixture, the protective coating may be supplemented with white pigments such as calcium phosphate, talc, and titanium dioxide. When riboflavin is included in the coating, its yellow color diffuses into the water when the coated kernels are boiled, causing unsightly blotches on the cooked rice.

A simpler one-step process of enriching rice is also practiced. In this process, the powdered fortifying agents are merely tumbled with the dry rice until they are uniformly distributed over the surface of the grains, to which they cling with considerable tenacity. Such a coating could not be expected to pass a washing test, as specified in Puerto Rico. In other localities where this form of enriched rice is sold, warnings against rinsing the rice before it is cooked appear on the package.

Amino Acids

The first limiting amino acids in rice are lysine and threonine. Several workers have attempted to develop methods to supplement the raw rice with these amino acids. Considerably larger percentages of additive are involved than when vitamins are added. The published material seems to deal exclusively with coating or infusion procedures although it would seem to be much simpler to use the simulated rice grain technique described above for these macrosupplementations.

Uses for By-Products

The most common application for rice bran is as a component of animal feeds. Its use in foods has been limited because rancidity develops rapidly once the bran is removed from the rice. Various methods have been suggested for "stabilizing" bran, that is, decreasing the rate of rancidity development. One obvious method is to remove the oil; this is effective, but rather expensive. Processing the bran through dry heat extrusion equipment to inactivate the lipase enzymes is a less expensive method which leaves the oil in place, a feature which has advantages for some purposes. Three types of stabilized rice bran are compared in Table 4.3.

Carroll discussed the use of heat-stabilized bran as a source of fiber for human food. The 25 to 30% fiber content of rice bran is about twice that of oat bran. Furthermore, this form of rice bran is relatively high in unsaturated oil and plant sterols which are said to have cholesterol-lowering effects. Carroll gave formulas for bread, muffins, and peanut butter cookies containing up to about 12% heat-stabilized rice bran. The formula for muffins is reproduced in Table 4.3.

In recent years, there have been many attempts to use rice byproducts as health food ingredients. Jodlbauer (1989) described the preparation of a fast-cooking granular rice product composed of husk flour, scouring flour, polishing flour, and broken rice. The ingredients are combined, heat-treated, and formed into granules in a cooking extruder.

Table 4.3.

Composition of Three Types of Rice Bran[1]

Component	Stabilized natural rice bran	Low-fat natural rice bran	Defatted rice bran
	%	%	%
Protein	13.0-16.0	15.0-18.0	16.0-20.0
Oil	18.0-22.0	6.0-9.0	0.5-1.5
Moisture	5.0-8.0	4.0-7.0	5.0-8.0
Ash	6.0-9.0	7.0-10.0	7.0-11.0
Crude fiber	6.0-9.0	7.0-10.0	7.0-11.0
Dietary fiber	25.0-30.0	27.5-37.5	30.0-40.0
Free fatty acids	1.5-3.5	1.5-2.5	1.5-2.5

[1] *Adapted from Carroll .*

Table 4.4.

Formula for Rice Bran Muffins[1]

Ingredient	Percent	Ingredient	Percent
Low-fat buttermilk	21.55	Fresh egg whites	4.58
Honey	14.95	Granulated sugar	4.30
Zucchini, grated	13.38	Vegetable oil	3.29
Rice bran	9.80	Baking soda	0.57
Whole wheat flour	9.00	Salt	0.43
Raisins	6.68	Vanilla	0.40
All-purpose flour	5.80	Allspice	0.08
Chopped pecans	5.19		

[1] *Adapted from Carroll.*

Note: Quantities are by weight, based on batch=100%.

5

Properties of Parboiled Rice

Advantages of Parboiling

Parboiled rice behaves in many respects quite differently from raw rice. As a result, parboiling has many great advantages, but also a few disadvantages. These can be listed as follows :

1. All cracks, chalkiness and other defects in rice grains, which cause grain breakage during milling, are healed during parboiling. As a result, if drying is done properly as explained earlier, there will be almost no breakage of parboiled rice during milling, no matter what the breakage was before parboiling. In fact even if paddy is intentionally damaged, say by over-drying or by wetting, as much as we wish, even that paddy will give nearly 100% whole-grain rice after parboiling. Therefore parboiled rice gives much better head rice yield and milling outurn than raw rice.

2. Vitamins and other micronutrients in rice are located mostly in the other layers. So these are lost in the bran during milling of raw rice. But these nutrients get fixed to the inner kernel during soaking and steaming. So these are no longer removed during milling. Hence milled parboiled rice is nutritionally very much superior to milled raw rice. Loss of nutrients during washing of rice is also lower in parboiled rice. In fact, in old days, eating polished raw rice used to cause beriberi disease, which used to be cured by parboiled rice.

3. Parboiled rice is harder and smoother than raw rice. Hence it is not so easily attacked by insects. For this reason, milled parboiled rice stores better than milled raw rice.

4. Oil in the rice grain is pushed outward by the heat during parboiling. Hence bran from parboiled rice contains much more oil than that

from raw rice and is a better raw material for oil extraction. Moreover the bran is already stabilised by heat. So FFA will not rise in oil if the paddy was fully dried.

5. Parboiled rice loses less solid matter (which is also food) into the gruel during cooking than raw rice. Hence it conserves food better.
6. Parboiled rice needs more time to cook than raw rice. So it needs more fuel and time. This is a disadvntage.
7. Parboiled rice is more separate, hard and chewy after cooking than raw rice. This is liked by some but disliked by others.
8. Parboiled rice, being harder, needs more time and energy to polish than raw rice. But with conventional parboiling, dehusking is easier than with raw paddy, for the husk is opened.

Utilities

The following are the requirements of various utilities for the CFTRI improved parboiling process for one tonne of paddy.

Steam

200 kg steam at a pressure of 7-9 kg per. sq. (KSC) (about 100-135 psi) is required for hot soaking and steaming operations. In addition, 400 kg steam at the same pressure is required to dry the parboiled paddy using steam-to-air heat exchanger.

Water

About 1200 litres of water is required for soaking. In addition 220 litres of water for parboiling and 440 litres of water for drying will be needed for the boiler.

Electricity

About 31 HP (23kW) of electricity is required for running motors for the parboiling and drying plants. In addition, 15 HP is required for the boiler.

For the dry-heat parboiled system, steam is not required, water requirement is same, and total power requirement is about 26 HP per tonne of paddy. The entire fuel requirement can be met by husk.

Cost

The following are the approximate costs of the process

Cleaning System

Comprising paddy cleaner, steel structure, elevator and sheet metal piping.

1 tonne per hour plant -	Rs. 1,20,000/-
2 tonne per hour plant -	Rs. 1,50,000/-
4 tonne per hour plant -	Rs. 3,00,000/-

Parboiling system (CFTRI process)

Comprising overhead paddy holding bin, parboiling tanks, hot water tank, water pump, elevator, steel structure, sheet metal piping, etc.

1 tonne per hour plant -	Rs. 4,70,000/-
2 tonne per hour plant -	Rs. 6,50,000/-
4 tonne per hour plant -	Rs. 11,50,000/-

Drying system

Comprising paddy dryer, blower, elevator, steel structure, sheet metal piping, etc.

	With steam heat exchanger (indirect heating system)	With husk-fired cyclone furnace (direct heating system)
1 tonne per hour plant -	Rs. 5,00,000/-	Rs. 6,40,000/-
2 tonne per hour plant -	Rs. 6,60,000/-	Rs. 8,00,000/-
4 tonne per hour plant-	Rs. 13,20,000/-	Rs. 15,20,000/-

Boiler with husk-fired cyclone furnace -

1 tonne per hour plant -	Rs. 12,00,000/-
2 tonne per hour plant -	Rs. 15,00,000/-
4 tonne per hour plant -	Rs. 18,00,000/-

Dry-heat parboiling system (500-750 kg/hour) -

Cleaner - destoner -	Rs. 1,00,000/-
Masonry soaking tank -	Rs. 40,000/-
Hot water boiler (husk-fired) -	Rs. 1,00,000/-
Continuous grain roaster -	Rs. 2,00,000/-
Dryer of simple design with husk-fired cyclone furnace -	Rs. 4,00,000/-

6

Huller Use for Milling Parboiled Rice is the Chief Obstacle

So, as things stand today, bran from parboiled paddy is largely unavailable for oil extraction. Since a little over 50% of paddy in India is parboiled, the enormous loss in terms of oil availability can be very well appreciated. Actually it is a triple loss, for it means:

(a) Considerable portion of the rice bran from parboiled paddy is not available for oil extraction.

(b) this bran (parboiled) contains more oil than raw rice bran, and

(c) the oil in this bran is relatively stable and does not develop FFA (see below)

The wide use of hullers for milling of parboiled paddy even for commercial purpose is thus the most serious obstacle to increasing bran oil production in India. The Government has been trying hard for a long time to persuade millers to replace their hullers, but without much success. It would seem from the above discussion that a more selective approach in this respect is called for.

Hullers can be divided for practical purposes into three groups:

(a) hullers doing custom milling in raw rice areas,

(b) hullers doing custom milling in parboiled rice areas, and

(c) hullers doing commercial milling of parboiled paddy.

Hullers under categories (a) and (b) above exist due to socio-economic problems and cannot be dealt with immediately and may be ignored for the time being. On the other hand hullers under category (c) are a serious social menace and all steps must be expeditiously taken to eradicate them.

Since over 50% of paddy in India is parboiled, at least a half of this quantity, that is, atleast a quarter of India's paddy production, may be considered to be milled in hullers for commercial purpose (the other half could be for custom milling, which we can ignore for the time being).

Therefore if hullers for commercial milling are eradicated, at least **1.2 million to mies of bran** will be immediately available for extraction. Since this parboiled bran contains about 20% oil, it will immediately yield about **2.40 lakh tonnes of oil**. Moreover this bran is largely stabilized and therefore the oil will be **edible**. This tremendous potential shows what we are now missing and what should be done.

Use of Modified Huller

During the intermediate period when the above suggested step is being taken, as well as for hullers doing custom milling, another solution may be applied in the short run. This is to use a mini rice mill or even a modified huller in place of the huller so as to obtain pure bran.

7

Technology of Basmati Rice Processing

Cultivation

The process of cultivation of basmati paddy involves intensive scientific agronomic practices. First of all seed is selected, graded and its purity detected. In many cases, well-trained and experienced staff of buyers (company) visits different basmati growing areas and meet farmers to discuss their plans for the upcoming crop. They distribute the selected healthy and pure seeds amongst farmers free of cost or with minimum cost to ensure a pure crop after harvesting. Literature in local language is also distributed amongst farmers, giving them specific instructions on aspects like use of fertilizers, pest-control, storage of paddy etc. Most buying companies remain in close contact with farmers right from the seedling to the final harvesting stage.

Basmati seed is kept in water for 24 hours before sowing. To sow these seeds, small patches of land are selected as nurseries. Rice seedlings are produced at these nurseries. After 25 days, these plants are ready to be shifted to main farms. During end-June or utmost by July-first half, when weather in basmati growing areas is too hot to bear, these sapplings are shifted from nurseries to water-flooded main fields. Transplanting is done manually one by one.

The crop from beginning to the end is nurtured by snow-fed waters of the Himalayas and the valley of Kashmir to ensure plentiful water resources is available to feed basmati crop. This water, climatic effect and soil properties impart unique characteristics to basmati for which it is known globally. After 120-130 days of this perspiring toil, the crop is ready to cut. The harvesting is again done manually.

Procurement:

After harvesting in October-November, farmers bring in their produce to rice mills for sale or to the purchase points established by millers in the heart of major basmati growing areas. Usually, the buyers purchase paddy at the beginning of rice season that effectively eliminates all chances of mixing inferior varieties/grades. On the other hand, semi-processed rice available with brokers during rest of the year remains prone to mixing that is often hard to detect. Hence, paddy procurement plays a vital role in maintaining quality and purity of basmati rice.

Before a particular lot of paddy is purchased, it is subjected to various tests like tests for moisture content, kett-test, field admixture etc. Samples are then processed in mini mill to determine yield, kett-test and after-cooking characteristics in some cases. A lot is purchased only when it meets the stringent quality requirements of the buyer. Preference is, however, given to farmers who coordinate with particular buyer from seedling to harvesting stage. Quality of final product largely depends upon the quality paddy procured. Many buyers avoid indulging in such a laborious process and purchase semi-processed rice from brokers instead of paddy from farmers, compromising on the quality of the produce.

Processing

Rice is a delicate grain; requires extra care in processing. Any rough handling during processing can cause the grains to break or develop cracks.

Phase I — Paddy Storage

Paddy procured is stored under fumigation control to prevent any insects or microbial problems. Fumigation is done from time to time during storage. Stored paddy is transferred to processing plant for further processing when needed.

Pre-Cleaning

Paddy is thoroughly screened to remove any type of foreign material like stalks, dust etc. There are automatic pre-cleaners, which are scientifically designed to cater to the pre-cleaning problems.

Drying

On determining humidity limits of paddy through moisture testers, drying is carried out slowly and uniformly by blowing warm air to reduce the moisture to required levels. During drying, paddy is constantly stirred

Fig 7.1 Different Types of Destoner

through automatic stirrers to keep the grains away from packing together and to allow more airflow through them. In traditional method, basmati paddy is allowed to slowly reduce its moisture by natural-sun-drying-method, to achieve optimum moisture content for husking. Paddy is spread over large fields during the day and left for drying in the sun. This gradual drying helps to avoid thermal cracks in rice grains, which would result in broken grains at later stages.

Second Pre-Cleaning

Dried paddy is again pre-cleaned to minimise any chances of the presence of foreign material. This basmati paddy is then used to produce raw or parboiled basmati rice.

Phase II — Producing Brown Basmati Rice

De-Husking

Husk of the paddy is removed by De-Husking machinery, working with fully automatic rubber roll control system, which effectively removes outer husks of paddy, leaving bran layer of rice intact. Rice so produced is called Brown Basmati Rice.

Fig. 7.2 Huller and Husk Aspirator

Fig 7.3 Paddy separator

Paddy Separation

The De-Husked quantity still contains about 10-15% of paddy grains. This mixture is fed to Paddy Separators consisting of separating trays. The mixture is given special side way motion, separating brown rice from paddy. Paddy is returned to de-husking again and brown rice goes for further processing.

In brown rice production from minimal processing of paddy, only the outer husk is removed, leaving the germ and bran layer intact with the rice kernel, retaining most of the nutritional value. Bran is rich in protein, fat and crude fibre. This minimal processing therefore produces rice that is healthier to eat. The brown rice, after grading, is transported to warehouse

Warehousing

One of the main peculiarities of basmati rice is enhancement in its taste and aroma when it is seasoned for eight-to-nine months. This makes warehousing one of the very important steps in the whole production process. Stocks of brown basmati rice are stored in well-ventilated and spacious warehouses. These stocks are kept in most hygienic conditions under constant observation. During the period, stocks in warehouses are subjected to regular inspection and fumigation from time-to-time against disease and insect infestations. Good basmati rice should be aged for at least one year. The stored rice eliminates moisture from the grain and enhances its texture and flavour. Ageing also contributes to better cooking results, elongating 2-3 times its original size when cooked.

Fig 7.4 Different Types of Polishers and Whitners

Phase III —Converting Brown Basmati to White and Parboiled Basmati

For processing of White and Parboiled basmati rice in double-polished forms, Brown Basmati rice is fed to fully automatic rice polishers.

Rice Polishing

Rice polishing is conducted without addition of any chemicals to keep rice free from health hazards. For this purpose, Rice Polishers are designed in such a way that brown rice is polished by its own mutual friction among rice grains in polishing chambers to perform the polishing effect. Bran layer of brown rice is removed, producing pearly white kernels of basmati. Bran wastage produced here is removed by automatic vacuum systems, leaving behind double polished rice. Number of passes depends upon the degree of whiteness required.

Phase IV — Giving Silky Touch

Water Polishing

Automatic water polishers are used to convert double polished rice into silky rice. This silky touch to rice is given with care and extra-vigilance to keep rice quality optimal.

Fig 7.5 Water Polisher

Rice entering Water Polishers is moved through mist formed by mixing filtered air and distilled water coming from condensing chamber. This movement of rice through mist gives clean and glossy white appearance to the kernels.

Phase V — Grading Basmati Kernels Thickness/Length Grading

Both- thickness and length of rice kernel are important in grading. Grading machines with multi-features have following capabilities-

1. Selecting uniform grains
2. Maintaining A.G.L. (Average Grain Length)
3. Removal of broken kernels
4. Rejection of short grains and shrivelled rice
5. Removal of any foreign material (if any)
6. Rejection oversized grains

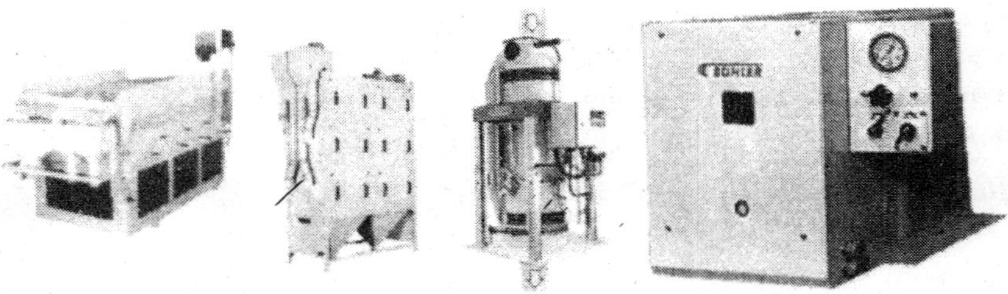

Fig 7.6 Gravity Separator, Drum Grader, Dump Weigher, Automatic Flow Balancer

Grading machinery has been manufactured on gravity classification and centrifugal principles, incorporating many excellent features with eminent abilities to grade and clean rice kernels. Uniform grain length renders nice appearance to the finished product and adds to the presentation (before and after cocking).

Phase VI — Adding Maximum Value to Basmati Colour Sorting and Grading

The final step in rice processing is colour sorting. This is aimed at removing discoloured grains from processed rice to give the final product a uniform-colour look. Colour sorting is an intricate computer-controlled process where CCD (Charge, Coupled Device) technology is used for performing high-resolution-optical inspection of each and every kernel. It removes the high concentration of predominantly chalky and discolored kernels to give final product a uniform appearance.

Fig 7.7 Different Types of Colour Sorters

Final Inspection

Basmati rice sorted is finally inspected by Quality Control department and is sent to packing section.

Packing

Processed basmati rice moves to specially designed packing bins where it is supplied to automatic packing machines, which pack rice on pre-set weighing scales. Modern electronic bagging scales have high degree of accuracy in weighing. Several kinds of packing material are used as per customer demand.

Electronic Weightment and Bagging

Storage system is designed to extend maximum flexibility, space, security and accessibility. Packed rice is directly loaded to containers, which carries the premium rice to the end users.

Fig 7.8 Electronic Weigher

General Flow Diagram of Basmati Rice Processing

8

Marketing of Basmati Rice

Marketing

Many small wholesale grain markets in India are characterized by large number of sellers and a relatively small number of buyers, thereby lending the price formation process open to manipulation through collusion. Government intervention limits the extent of such manipulation through the institution of regulated markets, where the rules of exchange are clearly spelled out and the price formation process is transparent.

Government procurement operations exclude basmati, and support prices for Grade-A varieties of paddy are too low to be relevant. Only private players participate in basmati paddy markets; the Government's role is limited to regulating the open auction.

Here is an illustration of the case of basmati rice marketing in Panipat mandi (Haryana).

Basmati Rice Marketing- Case of Panipat Mandi

Panipat mandi is a small (in terms of volume of transactions) regulated market situated in Panipat district in Haryana. The peak arrivals of basmati rice occurs during eight weeks- from late October to late December. Arrival pattern seem to mimic that of the harvest; farmers bring their grain to the market soon after harvesting the crop. 75% of the season's harvested produce reaches the mandi by end-November.

Players in the Market

The Sellers

Farmers do not directly sell their produce at the mandi, instead, a commission agent, or katcha artia undertakes to sell the grain. Katcha artias normally earn a commission of 3% of the total value of sales, which is paid by the buyer.

The Buyers

Pakka artias work as commission agents for the mills, undertaking to represent them at grain auctions and buy grain for them. Once a lot of grain is auctioned, the pakka artia with the winning bid owns the responsibility of storing the grain purchased from the mandi until it is transported to the mill. Miller typically picks up grain from several mandis, and usually appoints only one pakka artia as its agent at any mandi. However, it is possible for a pakka artia to act as the agent for more than one miller. Pakka artias earn normally a commission of 2% on the value of sales.

As commission agents for mills, pakka artias are generally given the price range in which he could buy grain of a given variety and quality of paddy. Some of them are in constant touch with their millers on cellular phones, even as auctioning takes place. Others also communicate with millers regularly over the course of the day; since millers, who pick up grain from several mandis constantly fine tune their purchase decisions across mandis. Constant communication between miller and pakka artia, and the fact that details of each auction including quantity sold, variety, and price get recorded in several places, enable the miller to monitor prices quite closely. Checks on quality, however, can only occur upon delivery. Given the multidimensional nature of quality and wide variation along each of these dimensions, some differences of perception between millers and their agents, about price-quality correspondence is likely to exist.

Buyers of basmati in Panipat may be categorized into three groups. The first group (Group A) of purchasers consists of representatives of local mills, who buy on their own account. Indeed, frequently, the owners themselves participate in the bidding. The second are pakka artias (Group B) who buy on behalf of one or more large mills, which are located relatively far away, and earn a commission on the value of the transaction. These mills buy in several markets (in 50-100 markets in Haryana and the neighboring States). The final group (Group C) consists of a large number of commission agents who buy primarily on their own account. Players in Groups A and B are 'large' and in Group C are 'small' players. Group A and B together command a market share of nearly 60%.

The significance of this classification of buyers lies in the incentives governing purchase decisions. Agents who represent mills and buy on commission (Group B), which depends on the sale value, have an incentive to try and raise the price so as to maximize their commission. However, the daily monitoring of purchase decisions means that too high a price may cause the millers to stop all purchases from this mandi. In contrast, local millers (Group A) clearly try to purchase grain at as low a price as possible. These differences in buyers have important consequences on price determination.

The Auctioneer

The market committee appoints an auctioneer who formally conducts the auction. The auctioneer receives 0.8% of the sale value of the lots sold; he thus has an incentive in raising the prices.

The Auction Process

Grains brought by farmers are displayed in lots by the katcha artia. The auctioneer starts the process of auctioning a lot by announcing a starting price, which he determines by reaching into the middle of a pile of grain, and inspecting a fistful for quality. Once assessed, it is rare for the lot to be unsold at the right price. Several players compete for the lot, and each makes independent assessments of quality by similarly examining the grain. Bidding proceeds as the auctioneer begins to raise the price; as the price rises, bidders may indicate that they have dropped out of the race by throwing down the fistful of grain that they drew out to examine. This process continues until all but one bidder have dropped out. The remaining bidder wins the lot at the price last announced. In this manner, the auctioneer proceeds from lot to lot until all the grain lots are sold.

Movement from Processor to Importer

Once paddy reaches the mill, based on the orders in hand, paddy is subjected to different processing by the miller. The produce is subjected to different processes like parboiling, dehusking and polishing. European markets prefer the dehusked or the brown rice, whereas the Middle East markets prefer parboiled rice. The white rice or the polished rice is for the domestic markets. Once the paddy is milled, it is stored in hygienic silos for ageing. The ageing ranges from six months to one year depending on the nature of orders. Aged rice fetches higher price, as the cooking quality is very good.

Based on the requirement of the importer, the rice is packed in different sizes of packs by the exporter. Utmost care has to be taken while packing regarding the broken rice percentage and markings on the bag. Any trace of marking ink on the rice may lead to rejection of entire consignment.

The consignments are then shipped to the respective destinations. The marketing of basmati rice abroad is mostly a relationship marketing wherein there is a close link between the exporter and the importer. Even in this closely knit network, the exporters take the help of the exporting agent, who liases with the importer and exporter to make the deal. The payment for the consignment is made once the product reaches the importer. Prior to the export deal all the terms and conditions are laid down on the letter of credit.

In the distribution channel, every player adds value in his own way. The miller adds value by milling and improving the quality when the final rice is consumed. The exporter adds value by making the product available to almost every nook and corner of the World in suitable packs. The export agent adds value by the services he provides in smooth closing of the deal between the exporter and the importer.

Packing

The basic functions of packaging are to protect and to contain the product. Packaging also makes product easier to handle and increase the products' life. Modern market, based on production and manufacturing, involves trade and transportation of goods at various stages before the ultimate consumer uses the final product. There is virtually no product or commodity that does not require packaging at various stages in one form or another.

Packaging is now a vehicle for product information, identification, measurement, presentation and distribution to ultimate consumer. It can no more be ignored.

Attractively packed rice is available in packs from 500 grams to 50 kilo grams (kg) in a variety of packaging in cardboard and laminated boxes, laminated poly pouches, white polyline cotton, natural jute, paper bags and polythene. Some companies also emphazise on tailor made rice packs to meet the specific requirements of individual customers.

Some of the widely used packaging material are-

1. Pouches
2. Cotton Bags
3. Jute Bags
4. Polypropylene Bags
5. Polyethylene Bags
5. Card Board
6. Plastic jars
7. Laminated paper bags etc.

Pouches are of three types-

(a) **Transparent**

(b) **Milky** - in which rice is not visible

(c) **Metallic**- these pouches have the advantage of nitrogen flushing, which keeps the rice fresh and free from insects.

The pouches are available in 1, 2, 5, 10 and 20 kg sizes either with or without zip.

Cotton Bags are multi-coloured bags available in all standard sizes upto 20 kg. Normally, these are preferred in 10 kg and 20 kg.

Jute Bags are environment friendly bags and are economical.

P.P. Bags are used as an economical option for bulk packaging, mostly for 50 kg packs.

Branding

Major Indian basmati rice based corporates are marketing their product in branded form both- in domestic as well as international markets. Taking cue from the big wigs, small-scale players are also venturing into creation of their own brands and marketing them abroad. Few exporters feel that the marketing of Indian brands in international market may not be successful, as the importer there would like to promote his own brand rather than promoting Indian brands. Marketing of home-brands abroad needs a well-orchestrated effort by exporters and the Government of India. This calls for availabilty of premium quality with reasonable price tag. The Government can add credibility to Indian basmati rice by monitoring the quality of the exportable product. The customer in the markets abroad is ready to pay a premium for quality basmati from India.

New technology of DNA fingerprinting will help to ascertain the quality of exported basmati. Private players are also coming into this area of evaluating the quality of basmati rice.

Promotion of a brand in markets abroad is a herculean task, yet many Indian exporters have accomplished it with ease. To promote a brand, one should establish his own distribution network or collaborate with the importer. Many trade fairs or melas are being conducted as a part of promotion campaign either by Indian Government or by corporate group initiatives. With such aggressive marketing activities, exporters are able to establish their brands in international markets. Innovative marketing attempts of the kind of the New Delhi-based KRBL, which made a big news by entering the Guinness Book of World Records by preparing the largest basmati rice dish, Kabsa during early

2002 in Bahrain as part of its aggressive marketing strategy for its Alwasim basmati rice brand, would go a long and large way in popularising the brands abroad. Though the purpose of KRBL was to create formidable brand presence in Saudi Arabian markets, the company and its brands gained huge mileage Worldover by way of extensive media coverge it recived for its unconventional marketing feat.

Coming home, the performance of the basmati brands in Indian markets has been commendable. Consumption pattern of rice consumers has changed to a great extent. The urban now prefer packaged rice to bulk rice. In this segment of packaged rice consumers, basmati occupies a prime position. Many exporters are trying to capture the mind space of the decision maker, the mistress of the family, in purchase of rice by sponsoring events relating to them. Worth mentioning here is the sponsoring of events like 'Gladrags Mrs. India' and 'Kohinoor of A Woman' contest by Satnam Overseas Limited, which owns the brand, 'Kohinoor.' Even the other big players are not leaving any stone unturned in this matter-may it be media campaign or promotions through trade fairs / melas.

Basmati Rice Export Zones

For diversifying from the rice-wheat cropping system, there is a suggestion for setting up an 'agri-export zone (AEZ)' for basmati rice in Punjab. However, some oppose the idea on the notion that even basmati rice should not be encouraged, as it is a water-intensive crop. It has to be realised that since this premium aromatic rice has a lot of export potential (if the produce can meet the desired quality standards), the creation of a distinct zone for its cultivation and export is a step in the right direction.

Diversion of some areas from non-basmati rice (grown during early June-October) to traditional aromatic basmati (grown during from July-October) in this zone could be expected to decrease groundwater use. In fact, due to favourable agro-climatic conditions (mainly low temperature during the ripening period) in northern parts of Punjab, this zone should have a focused agenda to produce export-quality aromatic basmati rice.

Management Ease Rendered by AEZ

In this basmati-specific zone, it will be possible to maintain quality of the produce by giving due consideration to- selection of an export-oriented basmati variety, suitable soil for basmati cultivation, quality irrigation water, pest (stem borer, foot rot smut, leaf miner, etc.) problems and their management, implementation of demand-driven quality control measures, remunerative marketing system (promotion, intelligence, favourable price structure), cost-effective and eco-friendly production for profit maximisation, conservation of the agro-ecosystem, etc. The involvement of public and private organisations will be essential.

To maintain purity/quality, it should be ensured that farmers in this zone grow only the identified (demand-driven) aromatic basmati rice and not any other variety. Separate zones may be created for different kinds of high-yielding non-aromatic varieties. The improved varieties viz. Pusa-basmati may give a higher yield but at the cost of the exquisite aroma of the traditional basmati-rice. Variety identity must be ensured even within different aromatic basmati varieties (e.g. Basmati-370, Basmati-217 etc.).

Quality (aroma in particular) of basmati rice has much to do with the soil and agro-climatic conditions of the zones under which the crop is grown. The fragrance in traditional basmati has been reported to be due to the presence of a large number of aromatic compounds (2-actyl-l-pyrroline dominates and many others), which are formed initially in the plant when it flowers, then gets transferred to the grains, where they remain preserved if temperatures remain cool during the ripening stage. The formation of aromatic compounds in basmati rice is controlled by a specific genetic (DNA) character, which gets expressed only under specific ago-climatic conditions.

Quality Ethics

Delineation of a geographical area (agro-climatic zone) for growing a specific basmati-rice variety and ethical processing and branding will prevent growers, traders and corporates from projecting other aromatic varieties as 'basmati rice.'

To achieve success in sustaining profitability from basmati, quality standards must be properly adopted by farmers, traders and all others at every stage from seeding, harvesting, post-harvest handling to the ultimate reach at the consumer hands. Foreign buyers will not be willing to shell out a huge premium for this unique rice without being certain that they will get what they pay for. Therefore, the Government policies concerning efficient production, marketing, quality control, etc. have to be modified, effectively implemented and rigorously monitored in the proposed zone at various stages of production till the product reaches the consumer.

Precise Specifications

Adulteration of grains of genuine basmati with non-basmati rice or other lower varieties is damaging the credibility of Punjab basmati. Aromatic rice should have about 7 milli meter (mm) length and 2.5 mm breadth; when cooked, the grains should elongate (70-120% over the pre-cooked grain); should not gel and amylose content should range between 24-32%. Traders, however, consider all varieties having grain length above 6 mm as typical basmati and pool grains of all such varieties, mill them together and market as single grade, which when exposed, creates a very bad impression of the supplier in the global market. In fact, the quality conscious global markets (UK in particular) are already carrying out DNA finger-printing to know the genuineness of the supplies. Hence, stakeholders of basmati rice industry must ensure that quality standards are not compromised at any stage.

Seed Purity

There are hardly any specific agencies in Punjab that produce and supply adequate quantities of good quality basmati seed. In general, the seed is spread predominantly through farmer-to-farmer movement, resulting in deterioration of purity. Government must ensure seed replacement at least once in three years by growers and breeders to identify and remove off-types to sustain seed quality. A regular basmati rice seed production and supply system should be developed in the identified zone.

Site-specific recommended soil-water-fertilizer-pest-crop management systems for basmati rice production must be effectively followed for obtaining high productivity and profitability. Effective use of fertilisers is crucial. Basmati is highly susceptible to stem borer and leaf folder, for the control of which soil or foliar (spray) application of highly toxic insecticides is essential. The effect of these insecticides (particularly when applied to soil) is always severe on the eco-system in the long run. Hence, plant breeders and entomologists have to play a significant role in recommending eco-efficient pest control technologies in the zone identified.

Markets

Saudi Arabia, UAE, European Union countries, USA etc. have been the traditional markets abroad for Indian basmati rice. India must explore additional overseas markets, especially in the light of the proposed new EU import regime for basmati rice imports under WTO and the re-emergence of Pakistan with 'quality' product.

Setting up state-of-the-art basmati-specific post-harvest handling, quality control and marketing systems including processing infrastructure (procurement, storage, transportation, drying, grading, packing, etc.) is a must in the proposed AEZ.

9

Speciality Rice

Different Types of Speciality Rice Based on its Physical Properties

Aromatic Rice : The first class of rice, which is classified as speciality rice is the aromatic rice. These contain a natural ingredient, 2-acetyl 1-pyroline, which is responsible for their fragrance, taste and aroma. The fragrance of aromatic rice can differ from one year's harvest to the next, like wine. The finest aromatic rice is aged to bring out a stronger aroma.

Coloured Rice : Some speciality rice are prized not for aroma, but for their colour, which is determined by levels of **anthocyanin** pigment in different layers of the pericarp, seed coat and outer grain layer. The endosperm colour of rice ranges from white to various shades of translucent to red, purple and black. In China, non-milled black rice is used as natural colourant in cakes, especially the New Year cakes and in black wine. It is also considered highly nutritious, rich in Vitamin B and many trace elements (e.g. bronze, manganese and calcium). The purplish-black Jieguno variety is said to strengthen the immune system and hasten the healing of bone fractures. Although China has released some 54 modern high yielding black varieties with good quality and multiple resistance, the area under this crop is less than 1.3% of the country's total rice acreage. Researchers say that red rice, most of which is processed into white milled rice for normal cooking and eating, has stronger tolerance to unfavourable environments, such as infertile soil and mountain areas.

Glutinous (Sticky or Sweet) Rice : Although called Glutinous, this rice is gluten free like all rice. The consistency of sticky rice is determined by two kinds of starch in kernels, **amylose** and **amylopectin**. More the **amylopectin**, greater will be the stickiness and the texture. Glutinous rice is easily distinguished from other varieties by its milky colour. Most widely consumed in areas where it is grown- mainly in dry areas of northern Thailand, Laos and Cambodia. It is often used as an ingredient in sweet dishes and snacks and for brewing beer. Laos is the largest producer and consumer of glutinous rice, which accounts for about 85% of its rice production. As compared to many other speciality rice varieties, sticky varieties bear lower yields. In Thailand, average yields of non-glutinous varieties are around 4 tons/ hectare, compared to 1.9 tons/hectare for glutinous types. But lower yield is compensated by good demand and higher prices. Export demand has been on the rise.

Boutique and Organic Rice : Combining glutinous and aromatic characters is the 'boutique' rice, which include many traditional Laos varieties and others grown and consumed mainly in Thailand and Cambodia. Boutique rice is considered to be the greatest potential for export markets. In China, for example, Scientists have developed **Shangnongxiangnuo** (from a local aromatic cultivar, **japonica waxy**), which yields an impressive 7.5 tons/hectare.

Meanwhile, many rice growers are switching over to cultivation of organic rice. While exact statistics are unavailable, surveys show that both developed and developing countries (mainly in Asia) are growing rice organically, hoping to enter the World's US$ 10,000 million commerce in organic foods. Growth in this rice type is slower due to higher costs, non-availability of inputs and technology, and limited participation of supermarkets and retail outlets.

Different types of Speciality Rice Based on Origin

1. Basmati Rice

A very long, slender grained aromatic rice grown mainly in the foothills of the Himalayas in India and Pakistan. It has a distinct flavour and aroma. The grains are separate and fluffy when cooked. In Indian recipes, it is often cooked with spices to enhance the grain's aromatic properties. Easy cook white basmati and brown rice basmati are also available. Brown basmati rice has a higher fibre content and has stronger aroma than white basmati.

2. Jasmine Rice (Thai Fragrant Rice)

This is another aromatic rice, whose flavour is slightly less pronounced than that of basmati. It originates from Thailand. The length and slenderness of the grains suggest that they should remain separate on cooking, but it differs from other long grain rice in that as it has a soft and slightly sticky texture when cooked. Good with Chinese and South East Asian food. Jasmine rice goes well with saffron and cardamom.

Jasmine rice is sold in both brown and white varieties. White rice sets off food flavours more distinctly, while brown rice has a higher fiber content and takes longer time to cook.

Jasmine rice is available year-round. As Jasmine rice was derived from traditional Thai rice variety, it can only be grown only during main season- from September to December. Jasmine rice is hand planted, Natural rain fed without plant protection chemicals so as to ensure complete organic rice.

Although Jasmine rice can be grown in any part of the World, that grown in north eastern region of Thailand gives the best quality rice- long grain, silky smooth, pure white, soft cooking and strong aroma. Currently, there are four sub-varieties of Jasmine rice viz. Kao Dok Mali, Go Ko 15, Klongluang and Suphan. All these sub varieties give very similar cooking rice.

3. American Aromatics

American rice industry has developed varieties of aromatic rice, which mimic both basmati and jasmine rice.

4. Japonica Rice

It is a short and medium grain rice, grown mainly in California in USA. It comes in a variety of colours including red, brown and black. It is used in Japanese and Caribbean cuisines due to its characteristic clingy moist and firm nature when cooked.

5. Risotto Rice (Aborio, Carnaroli, Vialone Nano)

It is an Italian rice used for cooking Italian dishes risotto (it also works well for paella). It is a starchy white rice, with an almost round grain. Risotto rice absorbs liquid as much as five times of its weight during cooking, whereas most rice absorbs up to three times of its actual weight. During the cooking process, starch is released to give the creamy texture characteristic of the classic Risotto, where the grains stick together.

6. Bahia Rice

This is a medium grain rice, originating from Spain, where it is used to make the Spanish national dish, paella. It is not as widely available as risotto.

7. Japanese Glutinous Rice

Its round, pearl-like grain, which is grown in Japan, turns sticky when cooked and tastes slightly sweet. Used by Japanese for sushi.

8. Chinese Glutinous Rice

Chinese rice is chalkier in colour than Japanese Glutinous rice. It is used mainly in the preparation of stuffings and puddings.

9. Thai Glutinous Rice

Available in white and black grains in Thailand, both are popular for Thai puddings. The grains are not as round in shape as the other glutinous rice.

10. Pudding Rice or Short Grain Rice

A short grain rice used for puddings and sweets, typically originating from Italy. Grains are tubby and chalky in appearance and cling together on cooking. Used mainly to make traditional rice puddings.

11. Wild Rice

Not a true rice, but an aquatic grass from a different genus that grows wild along side the waterways of North America, The grains are long and slim and range from dark brown to black in colour. It's grown in the USA and Canada, where it was the typical food of American Indians. It is often mixed with other types of rice, such as white or brown long grain and basmati for its visual appeal.

12. Wehani Rice

Wehani rice is produced in California. Wehani is another aromatic rice that is related to basmati rice. In uncooked form, it is light clay-coloured brown rice. When cooked, it splits lengthwise and resembles wild rice, and has a popcorn-like fragrance. Wehani rice is only available as brown rice. It is available all round the year.

13. Pecan Rice (Popcorn Rice)

This aromatic rice comes from Louisiana. Pecan rice has a rich, nutty flavour and a popcorn-like fragrance. This aromatic rice comes from Louisiana and is a basmati hybrid. Pecan rice is available in white and brown (unprocessed) forms. White rice sets off food flavours more distinctly, while brown rice has higher fiber content and takes longer time to cook. Pecan rice is available year-round.

14. Texmati and Kashmati

These American rice have a light, fluffy texture when cooked. Texmati rice is a cross between American long-grain rice and Indian basmati rice. As its name implies, it's grown primarily in Texas. It has distinctive aroma and flavour compared with American long-grain rice, but less than that of basmati rice, and has a light, fluffy texture when cooked.

Texmati rice is available in white and brown (unprocessed) forms. White rice sets off food flavours more distinctly, while brown rice has higher fiber content and takes longer time to cook. Texmati rice too is available year-round.

15. Calmati-201

This aromatic rice is produced in California. Calmati-201 is an early maturing, rough hulled, semi-dwarf, aromatic long-grain. Its pedigree includes germplasm from semidwarf and tall basmati rice varieties from Pakistan. Calmati-201 is suited only to warmer rice growing areas.

Identifying Pakistani Basmati Varieties

Fig 9.1 Identifying Different Pakistani Basmati Varieties

1. *Basmati Super Kernel (White Rice)*

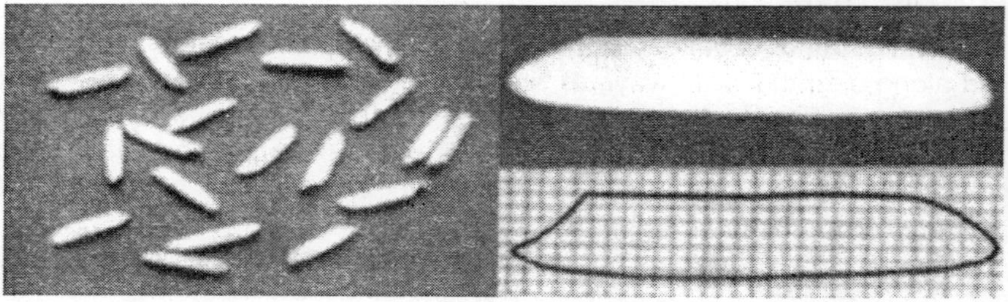

Length	:	7.45 mm
Grain Type	:	Extra Long
Width	:	1.62 mm
L/W Ratio	:	4.60
Thickness	:	1.51 mm
Shape	:	Slender

2. *Basmati Super Kernel 2000 (White Rice)*

Length	:	7.66 mm

Grain Type	:	Extra Long
Width	:	1.80 mm
L/W Ratio	:	4.25
Thickness	:	1.64 mm
Shape	:	Slender

3. ***Basmati PK-385 (White Rice)***

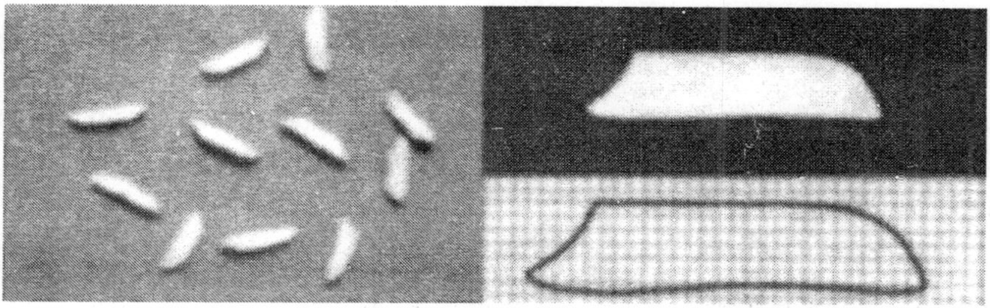

Length	:	6.73 mm
Grain Type	:	Long
Width	:	1.64 mm
L/W Ratio	:	4.10
Thickness	:	1.52 mm
Shape	:	Slender

Source: Rice Research Institute of Pakistan, Kala Shah Kaku, Pakistan

Brown Basmati

1. Basmati Super Kernel, Brown rice, (New Crop Only)
2. Basmati PK-385, Brown rice, (New Crop Only)

Supreme Quality, Colour Sorted, free from Paddy, Dust and any hazard materials, uniformly graded grains, nil broken specially prepared for European Rice Milling Units. Rich in aroma, taste and nutrition.

Silky Polished Parboiled Basmati

1. Super Kernel Basmati Rice, Aged (2 years old)

2 Super Kernel Basmati Rice, (New Crop)

3. Basmati PK-385 Rice, Aged (2 years old)
4. Basmati PK-385 Rice, (New Crop)

Extra Long Grain, Supreme Quality, Colour Sorted, Free from Paddy, Dust and any hazard materials, nil broken, uniformly graded grains. Rich in aroma, taste and nutrition, Best for cooking.

Silky Polished White Basmati

1. Super Kernel Basmati Rice, Aged (2 years old)
2. Super Kernel Basmati Rice, (New Crop)
3. Basmati PK-385 Rice, Aged (2 years old)
4. Basmati PK-385 Rice, (New Crop)

Extra Long Grain, Supreme Quality, Colour Sorted, Free from Paddy, Dust and any hazard materials, nil-broken, uniformly graded grains. Rich in aroma, taste and nutrition. Best for cooking.

Double Polished Basmati

1. Super Kernel Basmati Rice, Aged (2 years old)
2. Super Kernel Basmati Rice, (New Crop)
3. Basmati PK-385 Rice, Aged (2 years old)
4. Basmati PK-385 Rice, (New Crop)

Extra Long Grain, Supreme Quality, Colour Sorted, Free from Paddy, Dust and any hazard materials, nil broken, uniformly graded grains. Rich in aroma, taste and nutrition. Best for cooking.

The Speciality rices of the world see a rosy future for the sector. With growing prosperity, consumers are looking for better quality rice. Countries that could feed themselves with marginal quality but high yielding indica or hybrids, such as Republic of Korea, have switched almost entirely to low yielding but superior quality Japonica. Similarly, in India and Pakistan, demand for high quality Basmati has risen dramatically. Asians who migrate to Middle East, European and American countries can afford the best quality Basmati or Jasmine rice at higher price. Thus, the future of speciality rice is linked to the growing prosperity of people.

10

TRIPS and WTO

Introduction

India's biodiversity and its traditional knowledge continue to be increasingly patented in the United States (US). At present, nearly 48% of the 4000-odd plant patents granted by the United States Patent and Trademark Office (USPTO) in the recent past pertain to traditional knowledge from countries like India. In the wake of the problems with patents that India has experienced in recent years, it appears to have now realised the importance of enacting laws for conserving biodiversity and controlling piracy as well as intellectual protection legislation that conform to international laws.

Basmati rice is traditionally grown in India and Pakistan. Thus, granting patent on basmati rice in other country violated the Geographical Indications Act under the International Treaty on Trade Related Intellectual Property Rights (TRIPS). The TRIPS clause defines Geographical indication as "a good originating in the territory of a member, or a region or locality in that territory, where a given quality, reputation or other characteristic of the good is essentially attributable to its geographical origin." As a result, it is safe to say Basmati rice is as exclusively associated with India and Pakistan as Champagne is to France and Scotch Whiskey is to Scotland. Indians argued that just as the US can't label their wine as Champagne, they should not be able to label their rice as Basmati.

The Loophole

There is a widespread belief that Rice Tec Inc. took out a patent on basmati rice only because of weak, non-existent Indian laws and the Government's philosophical attitude that Natural products should not be patented. According to some Indian experts in the field of genetic wealth, India needs to formulate a long-term strategy to protect its bio-resources from future bio-piracy and/or theft.

The Case

In 1997, the USPTO accepted the Texas based Rice Tec Inc.'s application to patent basmati rice (patent # 5,663,484) obtained by crossbreeding two basmati rice varieties. This company insisted that it had 'invented' a 'novel' variety of basmati and has patented it as 'Basmati 867.' The Rice Tec patent covered any basmati variety crossed with a semi-dwarf strain grown anywhere in the Western Hemisphere.

Though Rice Tec claims that novelty Basmati-867 has been derived from Indian and Pakistani basmati rice lines crossed with semi-dwarf varieties, the basmati varieties used to invent it are actually farmers' varieties breed over centuries in South Asia.

International Support

India and Pakistan, who joined hands to tackle the crisis had a strong case against Rice Tec Inc. British traders supported India and Pakistan saying that "True Basmati can only be grown in India or Pakistan. We will support them in any way if the need arises."

The Middle East has also been supportive by only labeling Indian or Pakistani rice as Basmati. EU has launched an initiative in the World Trade Organisation (WTO) to protect products with unique geographical indications.

Plant varieties are not allowed Patent Protection in most countries (including India). However, US has been a strong proponent for Patent Protection of plant varieties. The WTO agreement does not require countries to provide Patent Protection to plant varieties- it only requires countries to legislate so that plant varieties are protected in some manner (not necessarily through Patents).

Crisis Management

The re-examination request filed with the USPTO by the Government of India (GoI) was done in the name of Agricultural and Processed Food Products Export Development Authority (APEDA). In April 2000, it challenged three claims related to rice grain (No. 15, 16 & 17), which in essence related to the grain quality like elongation on cooking and aroma of basmati grains, and no challenge was made to the remaining claims. The GoI, through APEDA, focussed only on protecting traders' interests, which was linked to grain, but not farmers rights, which are linked to seeds. In response to this, Rice Tec gave up four claims in September 2000.

The Unfinished Battle

Research Foundation for Science, Technology and Ecology, GoI continued its campaign for the defence of farmers' rights and basmati seed. It continued to call for the cancellation of false claims on invention related to basmati rice lines. Citizens across the World had been mobilised to defend farmers' rights. As a result of citizens pressure, USPTO cancelled claims 1 to 7, 10, 14 to 20, which were not challenged by the GoI though they are extremely broad in scope and had the potential to undermine the rights of farmers growing basmati.

The Patent Examiner also changed the title of the patent from 'Basmati Rice Lines and Grains' (covering a broad generic claim to invention of Basmati) to 'Rice Lines Bas-867, RT-1117, RT-1121', which are restricted to the specific breeding done by Rice Tec Inc. The new patent was not open-ended as the original patent was, which covered wide range of plant height, grain size, aromatic quality including the qualities of traditional basmati.

The patent abstract read- "The invention relates to novel Rice Lines-Bas-867, RT-1117 and RT-1121 and to plants and grains of these lines and to a method of breeding these lines. The invention also relates to the method of cooking and starch properties of rice grains and its use in identifying desirable lines. The novel rice lines are semi-dwarf in stature, substantially photoperiod insensitive and high yielding, and produce rice grains having characteristics similar or superior to those of good quality basmati rice. The 'starch index' of a rice grain can predict the grains' cooking and starch properties, to a method based thereon for identifying grains that can be cooked to the firmness of traditional basmati rice preparations."

The patent holder now cannot claim the unique qualities of basmati rice nor the unique name, 'Basmati'. The surviving claims- No. 8, 9, 11, 12 & 13 are narrow and related only to the varieties actually breed by Rice Tec Inc. These claims are 'deemed free of prior art'. The cancellation of other claims now prevents the potential use of basmati patent against growing traditional basmati.

Rice Tec was thus forced to give up the title of its patent, and give up 15 of its 20 claims, including those with the most far-reaching implications related to bio-piracy. Global citizen's campaign against bio-piracy, which was successful in getting the Neem Patent cancelled also succeeded in having the false and far-reaching claims in the basmati case cancelled.

The False Victory

USPTO very cleverly manipulated the patent claim to uphold Rice Tec's assertion that the company had produced rice with qualities that were equal or better than the traditional basmati varieties being grown in north-western India and Pakistan. It further stated that the company could sell its product in market as Bas-867, calling it a superior basmati grain. If the label says that the packet contains 'superior basmati rice', how is it a 'victory' for India?

India can thus legitimately argue that the granting of the Patent is an infringement of the 'Geographical Indications' clause in the TRIPS agreement under WTO. Regarding Geographical Indications, TRIPS requires all WTO members to provide the means by which the use of any indication, which would constitute an act of unfair competition, could be prevented. The TRIPS agreement says that member countries should provide improved protection for Geographical Indications of origin. However, India is still to pass the 'Geographical Indicators Bill' that could provide such protection.

The Right Path

It has been repeatedly voiced by experts that we should patent our plant varieties in order to prevent others from doing so. This betrays a shallow understanding of the patents issue. The developing World cannot fight the global patents regime by arguing for a more liberal patent's regime. This would be playing into the hands of the US and other developed countries, who are in a position to pledge enormous resources to mop up patents at a frenetic pace. Even the WTO agreement does not require us to patent plant varieties. Instead India should argue against the liberalised global patent regime, and particularly against patenting of life forms like plants.

Rice Tec has been granted what are called 'varietal' patents i.e. three strains developed by the company have been allowed protection. What is more important is that the company can label its strains as 'superior basmati rice'. It is difficult to argue that this will not constitute a threat to Indian exports of basmati rice. As a result of the varietal patent granted, not only will India lose out on the 45000 tons US market, which forms 10% of the total basmati rice exports, but also its premium position in vital markets like the EU and to some extent the Middle East.

If we accept that WTO is a reality today, unpleasant or otherwise, we need to work out means to increase our space for manoeuvrability within WTO. For that to happen, India must mobilise opinion among other Third World nations, who anyway constitute a majority within WTO. At the same time, we need to review existing laws, not because WTO wants us to do so, but in order to safeguard our own interests.

Concluding Remarks

The mere act of challenging the Basmati Patent in the US does not constitute enough strong action. The Basmati Patent application is not the first, and is by no means going to be the last of such applications that prey upon our traditional knowledge and our resources. Today, the World can be broadly divided into the 'biodiversity rich' nations of the Third World and the 'Patent rich' nations of Europe, North America and Japan. While the former is home to an overwhelming majority of species of living organisms, especially plant varieties, the latter hold over 99% of global patents! It is thus necessary to question the whole premise on which the Intellectual Protection Regime (IPR) is based. The developed countries are interested in monopolising their hegemony over the resources- both physical and intellectual of this planet; hence, the drive towards a stringent Patent Regime that can create monopolies for their Transnational Companies. The moot question really is what options do we have today? Instead of being frozen into a state of inactivity, India needs to play a greater pro-active role in protecting in rich Natural resource through Patents.

11

Details of Technology and Technology Providers

Buhler: The modern face of 'Basmati' Rice Milling

'Basmati' - a word that immediately fills the air with a mystic aroma and creates a picture of long, cooked and tasty grains of rice in 'pulao' or other mouth-watering rice dishes. Basmati is grown in the foothills of the 'Himalayas' and is native to India and Pakistan only. Though, many other countries have tried to genetically produce an equivalent of this, they have failed in getting the characteristics so typical of 'Basmati'.

Undoubtedly, 'Basmati' is one of India's largest exported commodities today. The unending demand from the various parts of the World like Europe, America and the Middle-Eastern countries has meant that the value of this rice has increased consistently in the global market.

Long, slender, brittle and fragile - each kernel of basmati is worth a lot and needs to be treated carefully and gently. The low bulk density and flowability of the basmati paddy as compared to the other varieties add to the complexities in processing the paddy in rice mills.

No doubt then that Buhler started its long association with the rice milling industry in India by providing value addition to the 'basmati' milling. The most difficult processing conditions and the high fragility of basmati kernels created an ideal situation for the

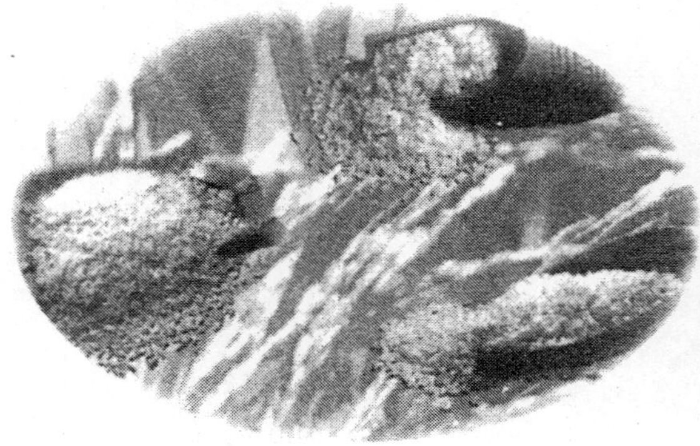

Buhler technologists to prove the prowess of their rice processing plant and equipment. Each grain of basmati saved for processors reflects directly in their profitability figures.

Buhler processing systems enable the yield of whole rice to be improved by several percentage points; each percentage point increase in the yield of whole rice saves up to US$ 180,000 a year in case of basmati rice. The price per metric ton of whole rice is US$ 600, the price per metric ton of brokens merely US$ 300. The difference for each percentage point gained is therefore US$ 300. In the case of a line with a capacity of 10 metric tons per hour and a typical annual capacity of 60,000 tons, it is therefore possible to gain up to US$ 180,000 for each percentage point of unbroken rice.

Today, due to the plain economic sense and higher yields provided by its rice milling equipment, Buhler has expanded its presence in Indian basmati rice processing field like nobody else. Amira Overseas, KRBL Limited, LT Overseas, Navbharat Exports, Picric Limited, REI Agro, Satnam Overseas, SSA International, Sunstar Overseas, etc. are some of the luminaries in this field who have had a long and mutually beneficial association with Buhler.

Buhler - Your technology partner

Buhler - a group with its parent company in Switzerland and World-wide activities in the field of plant and machine engineering - disposes of a comprehensive technological know-how and engineering. We are ranked among the international top plant constructors for more than 130 years focused on food, non-food and die-casting sectors. We are represented in more than 100 countries throughout the World. This proximity to the customer ensures prompt and perfect service. Buhler is famous for its long lasting and continuously developing relationship with the customers.

All machines are extremely sturdy and are of a proven design. This ensures years of trouble free operation, and the saving in down time is reflected as profits for the customer.

Further, the customer also benefits from the ongoing research and development process at Buhler during the entire lifetime of his plant.

In the field of rice processing Buhler stands for:

Local Manufacture: Buhler India's workshop has been laid out as per the World-wide Buhler standards. The machines manufactured here are exactly the same as those manufactured in Europe in terms of material, workmanship and efficiency. The key components are still imported from our principals.

Engineering: The most professional engineering staff works in close association with the customers as a team to ensure that their plant is built in the most economical manner.

Sortex: Sortex is a wholly owned subsidiary of the Buhler group with State-of-the-art Technology in the field of Automatic Colour Sorting. To our credit, we have in India over 400 satisfied and valued customers. Sortex being a part of the Buhler group, ensures that the customer gets a complete project from one supplier.

The turnkey concept: Buhler India is geared up to undertake food-processing plants on a turnkey basis. In India, we have successfully executed such projects in the fields of rice milling, spice processing, chocolate production, coffee processing and oil milling.

Services: Buhler's performance does not end with the delivery of machines, but also offers erection and commissioning by our own specialists. A dependable after-sales service and support is guaranteed over the years.

All these points add up to the most comprehensive package offered in the global market.

Buhler adds more value to each process in the area of rice milling. Some of these are highlighted below.

Cleaning: Thorough cleaning of the input ensures increased efficiency in the down side processes. Also, the life of the wear parts and key equipment largely depends on the efficiency of the cleaning process. Classifiers are used to remove straw, sand, stones, paper, etc. from the paddy; while destoners remove heavy impurities such as stones and glass. It is also essential to use magnets in various stages.

Hulling: This is an extremely important process since the long and slender kernels of basmati are highly fragile. The volume of husk is quite high. Hulling of basmati requires a completely automatic hulling machine, which can maintain a constant roll pressure throughout the process while adjusting the roll gap even with the reduction in roll diameters.

Thick Admixtures: Thick red grains of non-basmati called 'Choba' are found in basmati. These have to be separated using a drum grader prior to the whitening process.

Thin Admixtures: If the harvest is with a large percentage of immature paddy, the drum grader again helps in removing these immatures from brown rice for increasing the efficiency of the vertical whiteners.

The Art of Gentle Whitening and Polishing: The secret behind the better yield of whole rice is the gentle whitening and polishing of basmati rice by Buhler machinery. Minimising the pressure helps prevent breakage. In addition, the process ensures an excellent and uniform surface finish, giving the rice a nice and appetising appearance. This is an important sales proposition in countries where rice is a staple food.

The bran is scraped slowly and gradually. The slow and steady peripheral speed helps to achieve better whole kernel recovery.

The waterjet polisher provides a uniform, silky finish to rice kernels by gelatinising the outer layer. This improves the shelf appearance of the rice.

Colour Sorting

The new Z-series sorter from Sortex, which was launched recently, has also been assisting in the final processing of basmati. It is capable of detecting colour deviations in rice with an accuracy unknown up to now, allowing the defective kernels to be removed.

Automation - an additional advantage

The automation systems from Buhler help the customers meet the most rigorous quality standards and boost the efficiency of the rice mill. This in turn helps in cutting costs.

The electrical control panel is important for process plants, as it directly helps in safeguarding the machines. Automation reduces total labour cost and the use of variable frequency drives, soft starters, etc. considerably reduces power consumption.

An automated plant takes care of the bin filling and avoids overload of machines/ conveying elements by controlling the product flow in bins/ hoppers. The control system takes care of the automatic start & stop of sections, depending upon the product levels so that all sections are optimally utilised. This enhances the plant utilisation to the optimum capacity. The operators can concentrate on the machine setting and monitoring & control of the quality of the product at different stages.

As the market price for processed rice is controlled by various outside factors, the saving made in production costs is the key to better profits for Buhler's customers.

The automation needs to be easy to control and operate. This allows workers the ability to select the process flow based on raw material and finished products, track the process on a monitor, and dispense printed reports.

The customer can thus run the plant with fewer employees and at an optimum capacity with continuous production.

In case of any queries, please contact:

Buhler (India) Pvt. Ltd.
13-D, KIADB Industrial Area,
Attibele - 562 107,
Dist. Bangalore (India).
Phone: (080) 2782 0000;
Fax: (080) 2782 0001,
E-mail: buhler.bangalore@buhlergroup.com,
www.buhlergroup.com/rice

Schule Muhlenbau

Schule Muhlenbau has been in existence for 110 years and is focused purely on rice milling unlike other companies who have diverse interests. All Schule equipment therefore are specific to rice and do not have multiple applications, thus ensuring that they have a very high efficiency on rice.

Basmati rice is undoubtedly one area where India has distinct competitive advantages in the World market. Unfortunately, majority of basmati rice is processed using local equipment, which do not lend itself well to the production of quality rice.

The process of parboiling is generally gaining popularity, though, on Basmati it, has not become widespread because of the total lack of quality processing systems.

Schule is the only major rice mill machinery equipment manufacturer, who designs and build parboiling plants Worldover.

General process steps of Schule rice parboiling system: Schule plants are designed to process Long Grain Paddy (Basmati), which is a sound matured long Grain Paddy whose variety should be as pure as possible with a bulk density higher than 550 g / l

The importance of cleaning and destoning equipment is stressed, as these are required to remove impurities, and for the preparation of uniform paddy fraction for parboiling

The Soaking system is designed for batch-wise soaking in pressure tanks. This is special to Schule where the soaking time schedule with water circulation at a constant water temperature with minimized water consumption can be determined. This offers the highest flexibility by choosing different parboiling parameters.

Schule also has a steaming system that does continuous steaming with the Schule steam cooker. Paddy flow is controlled by a special feeding rotary lock that feeds and discharges the material on a first in-first out basis.

The weighing cells in the system control the minimum speed and the maximum speed of feed and discharge as well as the interval time as also the control tolerance in kilogram (kg).

The electronics oversees the overflow set point, cook time, flow rate in kg as well as provides all production related data that are required in order to monitor production.

Thereafter, what makes the Schule system unique is the use of the Schule Pre-Drying system using hot air to pre dry the paddy with the Schule Fluid Bed Dryer . The Fluid bed drier ensures a constant temperature in the whole dryer and offers a temperature control system. Therefore, the drying and tempering is done in a gentle column drying system in three passes with temperature control for each pass and sufficient tempering zones for equalization between drying passes.

Thereafter, the parboiled paddy is ready for milling and will be uniform in colour and processed properties. It will be completely gelatinized, without white bellies.

Therefore, the Schule system provides a very high quality of product as it results in

- Increased head rice yield during milling as the product is treated and dried evenly.
- Simplified hulling process on account of the above factors as the product will be a uniform and clean one that reduces dependency n subsequent cleaning machines.
- Improved nutritional value and extended shelf life that will enhance the marketability.
- Uniform and stable cooking and processing properties (easy cook rice) Reduced stickiness of cooked rice again making it quite popular among consumers.
- It will provide the typical taste and smell of parboiled rice.

Basmati is the pride and heritage of India which the World acknowledges. In the future, more and more basmati processors will find it necessary to upgrade their facilities to World class standards where Schule will be their choice.

Cimbria A/s Paddy And Rice Processing at its efficient best

Cimbria Group with its cumulative experience of 120 years of processing Seed and Grain over the world has all that it takes to modernize or minimize the inherent problems faced by the Indian Paddy and Rice Sector.

Moreover, the Basmati Sector being more quality conscious, as small inefficiencies built into the process could surmount to huge losses in the long run totally oblivious to the millers in the daily run, Cimbria can actually help the cause take a right direction. Gentle handling at higher capacities and slower speeds. Effective Dust collection and Highly uniform grading built in to the system helps the millers to avoid losses in their process caused by anomalies due to human error and casual approach.

The various areas where Cimbria A/s thru its Indian Office - Cimbria Unigrain India, could cater to in the Indian Basmati Sector are described below:

A) Intake Systems with Complete Dust Control and Collection.

B) Paddy Precleaning and Fine Cleaning

C) Paddy Grading (for Parboiled Paddy Processors more specifically)

D) Paddy Drying Systems (Most Gentle and Dust Free system available in the world today)

E) Complete Paddy and Rice Handling system solutions

F) Rice Cleaning

G) Thickness Grading of Rice

H) Length Grading of Rice

I) Aspiration systems for the complete plant with patented Dust Extraction systems.

J) Control Panels for the complete plant.

A) Intake Systems with Complete Dust Control and Collection.

Cimbria Unigrain India could provide Indian Rice Mills with highly efficient Paddy Intake systems, which could limit the use of labour, gunny bags and inefficient handling to the point of the receiving hopers itself. This action itself converts into he savings for the miller complimented by the huge dust controls adopted by the Intake Systems. The conveying could be done at high capacities and can be stored into storage systems after drying to safe storage moisture limits. The Intake System uses huge filters to scavenge the dust particles and eliminates the dusty and cloudy environment, which causes irritation and negligence from the personnel point of view. It also increases the aesthetic appearance of the plant right at the first point of the process itself.

B) Paddy Pre-Cleaning and Fine Cleaning.

Cimbria Group has a huge program including a vast variety of Pre, Fine and Super Fine Cleaners for the various operations that can be performed on the Raw material, which is being fed into the system. As any process demands, the first machine should be the most sturdy equipment taking away as much impurities and problems away from the material being processed so that the equipment ahead of the same functions in a very efficient manner. Cimbria has cleaners ranging from 2 Tons/Hour to 100 Tons/Hour for Pre-cleaning Paddy, where just the impurities are removed and Paddy is clean enough to be dried to the required moisture levels. Further Fine Cleaning could be performed on Paddy to remove the immature grains. The cleaners are supplied with huge cyclofans or dust filters to avoid the dust spreading problems caused by the conventional cleaning systems.

C) Paddy Grading

When Paddy is being sent to the drying or the parboiling tanks, care should be taken that the paddy grains are uniform in thickness (as far as possible). Cimbria can provide turnkey solutions so that the same can be incorporated in the process avoiding black grains caused by inefficient handling of the grain prior to the drying or parboiling process.

D) Paddy Drying Systems

Cimbria Paddy Dryers are of the LSU type made in galvanized Steel and are fitted with efficient dust collecting cycofans which help in very uniform and gentle drying of the paddy. The dryers could be of a batch or continuous process, depending upon the clients' requirement and are optimally designed to suit the different requirements of the Industry. The unique design of the ducts and the drying principle per se, is what that sets the Cimbria Dryers apart from the conventional ones. The dryers are very energy efficient also compared to the conventional dryers, and can use a variety of mediums to dry Paddy, whether it is parboiled or plain raw (as coming from the fields/mandis).

E) Complete Paddy and Rice Handling Equipment

Cimbria has the complete range of conveying and elevating equipment required to handle the paddy and rice grains within the plant between various equipment and the storage bins. These equipment eliminate the erroneous handling of the grain by labour. It reduces manual error to a great extent and so does it save the grain from getting damaged on the ground. The power consumption also is very less and the compact design of the material handling equipment makes it a very simple and natural choice to be opted for a modernized rice mill. The various equipment in this category are chain conveyors, belt conveyors, jog conveyors, screw conveyors and bucket elevators and pendulum elevators and the various chutes and pipes with the extra safe UHMWPE lining for longer life of the chutes and pipes.

F) Rice Cleaning

The Delta Cleaners in the Cimbria range of Cleaners are the ones that are used again for the fine cleaning of Rice and eliminating all the impurities that are added to it during the milling process. The large, mall, dust particles and also the very fine rice broken grains are removed at this stage to enable efficient grading of rice in the further stages. The huge screen areas and high air volumes allow a very standard cleaning of the grains thereby reducing he loads on the machines further to the same.

G) Thickness and Length Grading of Rice

Here the round cylindrical graders come into operation and allow the oversize and immature grains to be removed from the rice so that a uniform sized grain is obtained.

Further the Rice grains are graded according to their lengths so that final uniformity is obtained in the whole process. Cimbria HEID manufactures the largest Cylinders in the world giving a capacity of 6 T/Hr of Basmati Rice with an average broken kernel percentage of 25. The capacities vary as the rice varieties and their broken kernel percentages vary. The HEID cylinders are offered with a unique air clean out kit that helps clean the indent covers from time to time reducing the load on the operator to keep the indent covers clean.

H) Aspiration Systems for the complete plant

Cimbria has a wide range of equipment for efficient dust collection in different parts of the rice plant with technically superior air locks to capture the most obstinate of the dust particles. The complete dust collection and ducting program of Cimbria can provide any rice mill a great relief from the most common problem in our Indian Rice Mills, and that is of Dust Control.

I) Control Panels for the whole Mill

Cimbria has a separate division to cater to designing of control panels (Mimic panels or PLC based) as per the clients' requirements. The complete plan could be interlocked for an automatic process with provision for manual interferences, when required. The design could be done by Cimbria and the hardware could be locally procured for a techno-economic solution

With the above range of activities Cimbria Unigrain India, is totally equipped to provide turnkey solutions to any Basmati/Non-Basmati Rice Miller in the country for their cleaning, Drying, Storage, Grading and Dust Control requirements.

The satisfied client list of the company includes most of the stalwarts of the Indian Basmati Industry viz:

a) M/s United Riceland Ltd

b) M/s KRBL Limited

c) M/s Amar Singh Chawal Wala

d) M/s Sunstar Overseas Ltd.

e) M/s Amira Foods (I) Ltd.

f) M/s Satnam Overseas Ltd.

g) M/s Navbharat Exports

h) M/s Parmanand Satyarain

i) M/s M R Overseas

j) M/s Adani Exports

k) M/s R.T. Exports Ltd.

For any details about specific machinery/equipment please contact the following address:

Rajiv Iyer Cimbria Unigrain India
B-1/1369,Vasant Kunj, New Delhi - 110070
Tele : 0091-11-2689 4389,
Fax : 0091-11-2689 4574,
Cell : 0091- 98110 66710,
Email : rajiyer@del2.vsnl.net.in

12

Directory of Basmati Rice Exporters/Importers

BASMATI RICE EXPORTERS FROM INDIA REGISTERED WITH APEDA

Mr. Rajesh Agarwal,
Director
Rice India Exports ltd.,
5587, Lahori Gate,
Delhi 110006
Phone: 23984243, 23984343
Fax: 23921212
Email:
ricindia@del2.vsnl.net.in,
ricindia@vsnl.ocm

Mr. Shanti Swarup Aggarwal,
Managing Director
Induss Food Products & Equip.Ltd
238/B, A J S Bose Road
Kolkata 700 019
Phone: 033-22471962, 22478503
Fax: 033-22471874
Email: induss@vsnl.com

Mr. Kameshewar Sharma,
Partner
Shree Hanuman Rice & Gen. Mills,
Hatt Road, Safioon,
Jind, Haryana
Phone: 01686-62101, 62786
Fax: 01686-63501

Mr. Anil Chanana
Chairman-cum-Managing Director
Amira Foods (I) Ltd.,
Chanana Farms ,
Sultanpur,
Bandh Road, Mehrauli
New Delhi 110030
Phone: 26806352, 26806354, 26806346
Fax: 26804282
Email:
amirafoods@vsnl.com
Website:
www.amirafoods.com

Mr. Madan Jindal,
Director
Jindal Niryat Lte.,
B-36, Sanjay Nagar,
Pocket-III Sector 2,
Rohini Delhi 110085
Phone: 27172541
Fax: 27173541, 27267842

Mr. R.D. Agarwal,
Partner
B.R.International
4156, 1st floor, Naya Bazar
Delhi 110006
Phone: 26517962(R)
Fax: 397881

Mr. K.K. Dawar,
Proprietor
Jaishree Exports
70, Kailash Hills
New Delhi 110065
Phone: 27040800
Fax: 26833037, 25417357
Email: gnrice@bol.net.in

Mr. Gurnam Arora,
Jt.M.D
Satnam Overseas Group
201, VIPPS Centre,
Commercial Complex,
Masjid Moth,
Greater Kailash
New Delhi 110017
Phone: 26465757
Fax: 26465959
Email: satnam@
giasdlol.vsnl.net.in

Mr.Vinod Goel,
CMD
Goel International (P) Ltd
Sankara Road, Taraori
Haryana 132 116
Phone: 01745-42244, 42744
Fax: 01745-42544
Email: goelintl@palcom.net
Website: www.goelrice.com

Mr. B M Kapoor,
CEO
Aries Cooper (P) Ltd,
3E/1, East Patel Nagar
Delhi 110008
Phone: 25744342/25724342
Fax: 25744342
Email: aries@vsnl.com

Mr. S C Garg,
General Manager
Rama Association Ltd
Essel House,
B-10, Lawrence Road,
Industrial Area,
New Delhi - 110035
Phone: 27101113, 27101145, 27101154
Fax: 27184709
Email: rama@nde.vsnl.net.in

Mr. K.S.Dimpy,
Managing Director
Karam Singh Raghbir Singh
O/s.Chatiwind Gate,
Tarn Taran Road
Amritsar (Punjab)
Phone: 0183-482111, 482888, 482999
Fax: 0183-482000

Mr. Deepak Bansal,
Partner
Manoj Kumar Sandeep Kumar
2601, 2nd Floor,
Nai Basti, Naya Bazar
Delhi 110006
Phone: 23845547
Email: puoi@bol.net.in

Mr. Jeetpal Singh
Sadhu Singh Gurdip Singh
Outside Chattiwind Gate,
Amritsar 143 001
Phone: 0183-482285, 482286,
Fax: 0183-482287

Mr. Sandeep Singh Kochar,
Partner
Misha Export
318, Ansal Chambers,
6, Bhikaiji Cama Place
New Delhi 110 066
Phone: 26165970, 26182252
Fax: 26188249
Email: misha@del2.vsnl.net.in

Mr. Surender Kumar,
Partner
Rainbow Overseas
Kaithal Road, Pehowa,
Dist. Kurushetra
Haryana 136 128
Phone: 01741-21865, 20765
Fax: 01741-22765

Ganapati International
Gohana Road, Panipat
Haryana
Phone: 01742-52620
Fax: 01742-51667
Email: ganapatilrice@yahoo.com

Mr. Jaideep Khosla,
Managing Director
New Bharat Rice Mills Export Div.
G.C.22, Shivaji Enclave
New Delhi 110027
Phone: 25461399, 25461401
Fax: 25455349
Email: newbharat@yahoo.com

Mr. Ramesh Gupta,
Managing Director
Bharat Industrial Enterprises Ltd
BP-109, Pitam Pura
New Delhi 110034
Phone: 27240549, 27412778-79
Fax: 27240979

Mr. Kawaljeet Singh
K S Overseas
11, Brahm Nagar,
Lawrence Road
Amritsar 143 001
Phone: 0183-210177, 220246
Fax: 0183-213152
Email: kawaljit@jla.vsnl.net.in

Mr. Rajinder Chopra
Proprietor
Remika Overseas
B-46, 2nd Floor, Kalkaji
New Delhi 110019
Phone: 26227479, 26227480, 26816271
Fax: 26201128
Email: remika@ndf.vsnl.net.in

Mr. Prem Garg Shivnath Rai
Harnarain (I) Ltd
B-16, Bhagwab Dass Nagar
New Delhi 110026
Phone: 2454092, 25100251, 25102832
Fax: 25430354, 25446496
Email: Shivnath@del2.vsnl.net.in, lalmahal@ndf.vsnl.net.in
Website: www.shrilalmahal-rice.com

Mr. Jagdish Suri,
Managing Director
Amir Chand Jagdish Kumar
12/1114, Libaspur Road
Sameypur
Delhi 110042
Phone: 27297051/7052
Email: ricebiz@del3.vsnl.net.in

Mr. R P Punjani,
Company Secretary
Doon Vallet Rice Ltd
Outside Jundla Gate
Karnal
Haryana 132001

Mr. Anil Monga,
Managing Director
Emmsons International Ltd
101, South Delhi House,
12, Zamrudpur
Cummunity Centre,
Kailash Colony
New Delhi 110048
Phone: 26216314-15-16, 2648534-35
Fax: 26431926
Email: esssons@inda.vsnl.net.in

Mr. Surendra,
Manager
Puran Chand Rice Mills
Railway Road, Taraori
Haryana 132 116
Phone: 01745-42103, 42923,
42086
Fax: 01745-72323
Email: permnill@nde. vsnl.net.in

Mr. Sunil Goyal,
Export Manager
Veer Overseas Ltd
2637, 2nd Floor,
Naya Bazar,
Delhi 110006
Phone: 23845369, 23915890, 23984263
Email: vopvrm@nda. vsn.net.in

Mr. M L Aggarwal,
Proprietor
Ganesh Rice Mills
Gonder Road nissang
Karnal 132024
Phone: 01745-71062, 71162, 01745-71163(R)
Mobile: 09812040162

Mr. Rajendra Kumar Arora,
Proprietor
P.D.R. International
639, Sector-15, Hissar
Haryana 125 001
Phone: 01662-43235, 22762

Mr. Ashok Sharma,
Commercial Manager
Sumer International Ltd.
SCO 58-61, Sector -8C,
Chandigarh,
Punjab,
Phone: 91-172-2779843
Fax: 91-172-2543732
Website : www.sumeri nternational.com

Mr. M. Ramachandran
Best Food International
PO Box No.05,
Indri, Dist. Karnal,
Haryana.
Phone: 0184-382225, 382467, 382015
Fax: 0184-382201, 250028
Email: bestbasmati@ yahoo.com

Mr. K R S Sobti
Deva Singh Sham Singh
Outside Chatiwind Gate
Amritsar 143 001
Phone: 0183-482230, 482524, 482807
Fax: 0183-490451
Email: dsss@del2. vsnl.net.in
Website: www.817elephant -rice.com

Sahni Rice mills
Village & Post Dhanpur,
Kashipur Road,
Rudrapur, U.S.Nagar
Uttaranchal 263 153

Col.R.K.Sawhney
Vice President
Sudarshan Overseas Ltd
Shivam House,
Karampura Commercial Complex
New Delhi 110015
Phone: 25190462, 25193855, 25432905, 25110838, 25410150
Fax: 25455759, 25113752
Email: group@ sudarshan.wipro.net.in

Mr. Shailendra Sharma
Asst Manager-Business Operations
Amrit International Ltd
G-97, Himalaya House,
23, Kasturba Gandhi Marg,
New Delhi 110001
Phone: 23719677 to 79
Fax: 23711963
Email: amrit@sapta.com

Mr. Devender
Emdiach Exports
9/44, Industrial Area,
Kirti Nagar
Delhi 110015
Phone: 22048309

Mr. S. Gulzar Singh Swani
Swami Enterprises
Katra Hari Singh,
Amritsar. (Punjab)
Phone: 0183-542205, 542202, 225676
Fax: 0183-225670, 221700, 228546
Email: swaniasr@ vsnl.com,
swaniasr@jla.vsnl.net.in

Mr. Jitender Mathur
Worldwide Exports Inc.
J 12/75, Rajouri Garden,
New Delhi 110027
Phone: 25174895/ 9811278075

Mr. Umesh
Navabhat Exports
5192, Naya Bazar, Delhi
Delhi 110006
Phone: 23950675, 23918793, 23911252
Fax: 23916676
Email: deepakg@ del2.vsnl.net.in

Mr. Surinder Pal Singh
Partner
Uttam Exports
3948, 2nd Floor,
Naya Bazar, Delhi
Delhi 110006
Phone: 23926263, 23957948

Mr. Pramod Kumar Garg
Shakti Rice Mills
Railway Road, Taroori,
Haryana 132 116
Phone: 01745-42267, 42967

Mr. Davinder Singal
Janki Dass Rice Mills
Nadana Road, Taroori,
Karnal, Haryana
Phone: 01745-42281

Mr. H L Kaul,
President
SSA International Ltd
M-71, M- Block 1st Floor,
Greater Kailash Part II
New Delhi 1100468
Phone: 26475561, 26476650

Mr. Tejinder Singh
Siri Guru Ram Dass Rice Co
Opp. Jattan Gate
Haryana
Phone: 0184 22668, 22024, 24332
Fax: 0184252138

Mr. Naveen Kumar
Namya Overseas Pvt Ltd
91, Adchini, Adarshini Plaza Sri Aurobinda Marg
New Delhi 110017
Phone: 25123901

Mr. S K Gupta,
Partner
Gopal Rice Mills
Jind Road, Harayana
Phone: 01686-62204
Fax: 63604

Mr. Ravinder Kumar
Sri Ram Rice Unit
Village Chopri Taraori
Phone: 0184-42337, 42373

Mr. Karan Singh Raghbir Singh
O/s Chatiwind Gate,
Tarn Taran Road,
Amritsar
Phone: 0183-482111, 482888, 482999
Fax: 0183-482000

Oasis Exports
16, 1st Floor,
Devangapuram
New Street, Shevapet,
Salem
Tamilnadu 636002
Phone: 0471-501056, 500056,
Fax: 0471-501865

Mr. H L Arora
Partner
Shiv Shakti Industries
Bhurarani Road,
Rudrapur,
Udham Singh Nagar
(Distt.) U.P 263 153,
Phone: 05944-4156, 42444, 41511(R),
Fax: 05944-43694, 43194

Mr. Munish Bansal
Partner
Bansal Overseas
Namestay Chowk, G.T. Road,
Karnal, Haryana 132 001
Phone: 0184-251013, 255762, 255015(R)
Fax: 0542-354334

Mr. Ritu Raman Vohra
Sr. General Manager
Shri Vishnu Eatables (I) Ltd
487, Kohat Enclave,
Pitam Pura,
New Delhi 110 034
Phone: 27105240-41, 27180589,
Fax: 27185858

Sudarshan Overseas Ltd
Regd Office 10/81,
Punjabi Bagh
New Delhi 110026
Phone: 25194062, 25193855
Fax: 25455759, 25113752
Email: group@sudarshan.wipro.net.in

N R M Overseas
D-14, Anand Niketan
New Delhi 110 021

Mr. Gain Chand Garg
G.M. Overseas
5588, Lahori Gate,
Naya Bazar,
Delhi 110006
Phone: 23970063, 23922060, 23983060-070
Fax: 23991064,
Email: gmoverseas@vsnl.com

Mahabir Trading Agency
Jaw Musiang
(Jaintia hills),
Jowai,
Meghalaya 763 150

Mr .Suresh Kumar Singla
Partner
Ramdev Rice Mills
Near Village Daha
Madanpur, G.T.Road
Karnal
Phone: 0184-250674
Fax: 0184-262474
Email: rdrmills@hotmail.com

Mr. Rajpal Singhal,
Partner
R P Exports
Near Village Mandanpur
G T Road
Namestey Chowk,
Karnal, Haryana 132 001
Phone; 0184-252661, 274742,
Fax: 0184-256361,
Email: rpexport@vsnl.com

Mr. K V Rao,
Managing Director
Dolphin International Ltd.
21, Commercial Complex,
Gulmohar Park Extn.,
New Delhi 110049
Phone: 26868224, 26850479
Fax: 26866901

Mr. Deepu Marwah,
CEO
Sachdeva & Sons Ind. Pvt.
78, Rithala Road,
Shahbad Daulatpur,
Phone: 7899456, 7899457, 7899458

Mr. Harish Narag
Managing Partner
Unite Exports
Flat No 21, Ground Floor,
12, Central Lane,
Bengali Market,
New Delhi 110001
Phone: 23319576, 23713390

Mr. Ajay Katyal
Manager Business Division
Indian Organic Food
Himalaya House, I-142,
Kirti Nagar,
New Delhi 110015
Phone: 25123901
Fax: 25122989
Email: himalaya@inda.vsnl.net.in

Mr. Irfan Allana
Director
Allanasoans Ltd
Allana House, 4,
Allana Road
Mumbai 400001
Phone: 022-22874455
Fax: 022-22044821
Email: allana@vsnl.com

Mr. Daljeet S Gill
Director
Himalaya International
Himalaya House, 1-142,
Kirti Nagar,
New Delhi 110015
Phone: 25194853
Fax: 25437247, 25122989
Email: himalaya@nda.vsnl.net.in

Mr. S.K. Dhawan
CEO
Mokul Overseas Ltd
B-71, Paschimi Marg,
Vasant Vihar
New Delhi 110057
Phone: 26141310
Fax: 26141310
Email: mopld@del2.vsnl.net.in

Mr. Subhash Goel
Partner
ARM International
Nadana Road,
Taraori, Dist
Karnal
Haryana 132 116
Phone: 01745-42167, 43367
Fax: 01745-42880, 011-7135371
Email: armint@id.eth.net

Mr. A Bhandari
General Manager
Mr Nareender Sharma,
Hindustan Lever Ltd,
P-6, Ocean Complex,
7th Floor, Sector-18,
Noida 201301
Phone: 6384284, 916384452, 4616274, 3312671
Email: avinashbhandari@unilever.com

Mr. Saptal Arora
Partner
K S International
Near Stateware House,
Tarari, Distt. Karnal,
Haryana 132 116
Phone: 01745-42141, 42025, 43451,
Fax: 01745-42521, 43521
Email: 521rice@hansl.palcom.net

Mr. Abhiram Seth
Director-Exports
Pepsi India Holdings Ltd.,
3-B, DLF Corporate Park,
Phase-111, Gurgaon
Haryana
Phone: 91-6355871 to 80: Extn.659
Fax: 91-6355861
Email: sanyukta.adige@intl.pepsi.com

Mr. Veerkaran Awasthi
Managing Director
Bush Foods
12, Birbal Road, 1st Floor,
Jangpura Extn.,
New Delhi 110014
Phone: 24310106, 24311070, 24320107
Fax: 2316704
Email: bushfood@ndf.net.in

Mr. Arvinder Pal Singh
Partner
Amar Singh Chawalwala
Outside Chattiwind Gate,
Amritsar 143 001 (Punjab)
Phone: 0183-482121
Fax: 0183-482125
Email: arvinder@del2.vsnl.net.in

Mr. Vijay Narang
Narang Impex Pvt Ltd
3-B, New Jawahar Nagar Market,
Jalandhar (Punjab)
Phone: 0181-225978, 224392
Fax: 0181-225111

Mr. Pravesh Manchanda
Partner
Parwaz Overseas (P) Ltd
2258, Gali Raghunathan,
Naya Bazar
Delhi 110006
Phone: 23914514
Fax: 23847369, 23932403
Email: parwaz@del2.vsnl.net.in

Mr. Savinder Gugnani
Partner
S.G.Global
V&PO Giwali,
Tarn Taran Road
Amritsar 143 022 (Punjab)
Phone: 0183-500006, 503776, 501336(R)
Fax: 0183-482904
Email: sgglobal@jla.vsnl.net.in

Mr. Jacob Cherian
Managing Director
Commodities Intertrade
2346, Sector C, Pocket-II,
Vasant Kunj
New Delhi 110070
Phone: 26124211, 26123644
Fax: 26134510
Email: comintde@del3.vsnl.net.in

Mr. Chaman Lal
Managing Director
Chaman Lal Exports Ltd
344-A, Green Avenue
Amristar 143 001
Phone: 0183-503462, 503514
Fax: 0183-503453, 291067
Email: setia@jla.vsnl.net.in

Mr. M Mutha
Partner
M M Exports
30, Ritherdon Road,
Vepery
Chennai 600 007
Phone: 044-25325067,
5344, 3885, 26413935
Fax: 25325057, 26428719
Website: www.mmexports.
com

Mr. Anil Mitta
Chairman
K R B L Ltd
5190, Lahori Gate
Delhi 110006,
Phone: 23951963,
23915813-17-26-27,
Fax: 23915629,
Email: krblrile@del2.
vsnl.net.in
Website: www.kb-group.com

Mr. V K Arora
Chairman
LT Overseas Ltd
A-21, Green Park,
Aurobindo Marg
New Delhi 110016
Phone: 26859244 (6 lines)
Fax: 26859344, 26513450
Email: itoltd@bol.net.in,
Itoltd@del2.vsnl.net.in
Website:
www.itoverseas.com

Mr. Athar Zia
Director
Basic India Ltd.
F-1, U-40 Pitam Pura
Delhi 110034
Phone: 27072590, 27084484
Fax: 27084483
Email: basicJndial@
freedialin.com

Mr. Ajay Jain
Sambhav Agro Foods
Gohana Road
Panipat 132 103
Phone: 01742-55243,
53499, 53243
Fax: 01742-531109

Mr. Ritu Raman Vohra
Sr. General Manager
Shri Vishnu Eatables (I) Ltd
487, Kohat Enclave,
Pitam Pura
New Delhi 110034
Phone: 27105240-41,
237180589,
Fax: 27185858

Mr. MansoorJafri
Sams Grains (India) Pvt.
Ltd
8774, Mittal Chambers,
Opp. Fire station,
Rani Jhansi Road
New Delhi 110005
Phone: 23622919,
23629786, 27538393

Mr . Sujata
Gaaman Global Exports
A-21, Vikas Tower
G-Block,
Commercial Complex,
Vikas Puri
New Delhi 110018
Phone: 25500277, 25606447,
25606447, 25606448
Fax: 25550754, 25511248
Email: gaaman@del2.
vsnl.net.in

Mr. Nitin Aggarwal
Managing Director
SNT Agro Industries (P)
Ltd
4091, Naya Bazaar
Delhi 110006
Phone: 23971415, 23913637
Mobile: 9811229756
Fax: 23935756

Mr. R.S. Seshadri
President
United Riceland Ltd
Unit-II, 42 KM. Stone,
N.H.8,
Delhi-Jaipur Highway,
Gurgaon
Haryana 122 001
Phone: 916-372208-11
Fax: 916-372114
Email: seshadri@
unitedriceland.com

Mr. T.S. Ahluwalia
Dharamvir Exports
A-112, Defence Colony
New Delhi 110024
Phone: 24610455
Email: dvexpo@del3.
vsnl.net.in

Mr. Jatin Nanda
Jay Kay Overseas Inc.
16/941, Faiz Road,
Karol Bagh,
New Delhi 110 055,
Tel: 25726316

Mr. K R S Sobti
Wani Exports
17-A, Amritsar Cantt.
Amritsar,
Phone: 0183-226099,
226199

Mr. Subash Chand
Ambica Rice Mills
Nadana Road, Taraori,
Karnal
Haryana

Mr. Rakesh Agarwal
M.D
Sunstar Oversea Ltd
4119/7, 1st Floor, Naya
Bazar,
Delhi 110006
Phone: 27202591, 27203737
Fax: 27201738
Email: sunstar@del2.
vsnl.net.in
Website: www.
sunstaroverseas.com

Pee Dee Exports
79-C, New Grain Market,
Ladwa, Haryana 136 132
Phone: 01744-60033,
63633,
Fax: 01744-61033
Email: lakshmirice@
yahoo.com
Website: www.lakshmirice.
8m.com

Mr. Krishna Kumar
Balaji Overseas
Kurukshetra Road,
Sandoli (Pehowa),
Kurukshetra (Distt.),
Haryana
Phone: 01741-20336

Mr. L R Garg
Manager Shiv Shakti Rice Mills
BP -109, Pitam Pura,
New Delhi - 110034
Phone: 27240549, 27412778-79,
Fax: 27240979

Mr. V K Jain
Director Jainson Wool Combers Ltd.
266, Industrial Area-A,
Ludhiana 141 003
Phone: 0161-606794, 609277, 609858
Fax: 0161-664276

Mr. Kewal Singh
Director Naranjan Rice Exports (p) Ltd
Katehra Mohalla
Basti Bawa Khel,
Jallandhar 144001
Phone: 0181-891696
Fax: 0181-470729

Mr. A K Khanna
A K Exports A-841,
Asian Game Village Complex,
New Delhi- 110049
Phone: 26492014
Email: akexp@nda.vsnl.net.in

Mr. Sanjiv Khosla
New Bharat Rice Mills
2612/13, 3rd Floor,
Naya Bazar,
Delhi 110006
Phone: 23844438, 23844476
Fax: 23844263,
Email: info@tajmahalrice.com

Mr. Col Narang
Aulakh Overseas
360, Green Avenue
Punjab 143001
Phone: 0183-533896, 503948

Mr. Saurabh Gupta
Bhagwati Rice & General Mills,
Kalsiya Road
UP 247 001,
Phone: 0132-723927, 720674
Email: saurabh_aashi@yahoo.com

Mr. Sanjay Vashista
Kasnal Overseas 38 -39,
Pocket - D11 Sector 7,
Rohini
New Delhi 110085
Phone: 27932159, 2459, 27203243,
Fax: 27931959
Email: kasnal@ndf.vsnl.net.in

Mr. Sajveev Kumar
GRM Overseas Ltd
Near Sugar Mill
Panipat 132 103
Phone: 01742-652476, 652524,
Fax: 653673
Email: grmovers@palcom.net

Mr. Vineet Sood
S D Enterprises Lg -14,
R-23 Nehru Enclave,
New Delhi 110 019,
Phone: 26280027, 26280028

REGISTERED NON BASMATI RICE EXPORTERS WITH APEDA

Mr. Ajay Jain Sanbhav
Agro Foods
Gohana Road, Panipat,
Haryana 132 103
Phone: 01742-55243, 53499, 53243
Fax: 01742-53110-9

Mr. Vishnu Bhagawan Mittal
Managing Director
Shri Vishnu Eatables (I) Ltd
Opp. Bus Stand,
Kaithal 136027,
Phone: 0471-501056, 500056,
Fax: 0471-501865

Mr. Ashish Agarwal
Partner
Shri Deenanath Shrinath Mills
Plot No. 251 to 254,
Village Javadhipur,
P.O. Basantnagar,
Near Ramnagar Industrial Estate,
Chandauli (Distt.)
Old Varanasi
Phone: 0542-331913(R)
Fax: 0542-354334

Mr. Abdul Hamid Munshi
Moosa Exports
HAMD No.3/13,
Berlie St. Cross, Langford Town, Bangalore
Karnataka 560 025

Mr. Harish Narang
Managing Partner
United Exports
Flot No.21, Ground Floor,
12, Central Lane, Bengali Market, New Delhi
Delhi 110001
Phone: 23319576, 23713390

Mr. Summet Saluja
Director White Fields International Pvt Ltd
3/6, Asaf Ali Road
New Delhi 110002
Phone: 23272891, 23276807
Fax: 23266906
E-mail: whitefld@nde.vsnl.net.in

D.S.Exports
Assam Road, Pilibhit
(U.P)

Mr. Satyen Bhatia
Director
D.D.International (P) Ltd
26, The Mall
Amritsar 143 001
Phone: 0183-211966, 563866
Fax: 0183-211866
Email: ddinc@vsnl.com

Mr. G.D.Mittal
Manager
Sri Annapurna Rice mills
Kashipur Road,
Rudrapur, (U.S.Nagar)
Uttar Pradesh

Mr.Vishnu Kumar
Partner
Saraswati Rice Mills
Kashipur Road,
Rudrapur, (U.S.Nagar),
Uttar Pradesh
Phone: 01742-53243, 53243,
Fax: 01742-53119

BASMATI RICE IMPORTERS

Kuwait

Ahmad Hassan Boland Sons & Partners Co., P.O.Box. 20651, 13067-Safat, Kuwait
Tel: 2423985, 2432628
Fax: 2433345, 2449913

Al Honda Kuwaiti Co., P.O.Box. 3167, 13032-Safat, Kuwait
Tel: 2429016, 2408672
Fax: 2408673

W.I. Towell & Co., P.O.Box.75, 130301-Safat, Kuwait
Tel: 4749904
Fax: 4730608

Al Zahem & Malhotra General Trading., P .O.Box.251, 13003-Safat, Kuwait
Tel: 2433432
Fax: 2443420

Kuwait Supply Co., P.O.Box.5932, 130060-Safat, Kuwait Tel: 4832411 Fax: 4812679

Hamza A. Mukamis Est., P.O.Box.94, 13001- Safat, Kuwait
Tel: 4845594
Fax: 4845181

Malik Brodler Co. Ltd., P.O.Box.23169, 13092-Safat, Kuwait Tel: 4348761 Fax: 4348785

The Sultan Centre P.O. Box 26567 13126-Safat, Kuwait Tel: 4343155 Fax: 4849572

Sulaiman Al Abdul Karim & Sons Co. P.O. Box 675 13007-Safat, Kuwait Tel: 2432344 Fax: 2408787

Khalil Bahman Trading Est. P.O. Box 5236 13025-Safat, Kuwait Tel: 2428906 Fax: 2454326

White Stores Co. P.O. Box 3502 13049-Safat, Kuwait Tel: 4819075 Fax: 4848355

Kuwait Indo Trading Co. P.O. Box 2135 13022-Safat, Kuwait Tel: 2422218 Fax: 2416508

Gulf Supply Co., P.O.Box.24410, 13105-Safat, Kuwait
Tel: 4810322, 4849455
Fax: 4840540

Musaed A.Al Sayer Corp., P.O.Box.889, 13009-Safat, Kuwait
Tel: 2424324
Fax: 2431857

Cresent Commercial Est., P.O.Box. 1904, 13020-Safat, Kuwait
Tel: 2429370
Fax: 4842643

Gulf Star Trading Est., P.O.Box.291, 13003-Safat, Kuwait
Tel: 2417327
Fax: 2424055

Jassim Al Wazzan Sons General Trading Co., P .O.Box 124, 13002-Safat, Kuwait
Tel: 4846433
Fax: 4836162

Bahman trading Corporation P.O.Box.24243, 13103-Safat, Kuwait
Tel: 2419272
Fax: 2432833

Boland & Gharabally Co., P.O.Box.649, 13007-Safat, Kuwait
Tel: 2429610
Fax: 2414336

Kuwait Proteins Co. P.O. Box 26332 13124-Safat, Kuwait Tel: 4841733 Fax: 4849572

Abdul Latif Abdul Karim Al Munayes P.O. Box 2446 13025-Safat, Kuwait Tel: 2461396 Fax: 2462868

Abdul Aziz S. Al Babtain P.O. Box 599 13006-Safat, Kuwait Tel: 2405407 Fax: 2424103

Gazwan Agricultural Co. P.O. Box 4878 13049-Safat, Kuwait Tel: 2430274 Fax: 2430276

Al Bait Al Mamur Trading Co.
P.O. Box 21876
13070, Safat, Kuwait
Tel: 4744352
Fax: 4763840

Bahrain

National Imports & Exports Co.
P.O.Box 1080,
Bahrain
Tel: 535005
Fax: 533436

Mohamed Ali Haji Abbas Abdul Aziz Gerashi,
P.O.Box 911, Manama,
Bahrain Tel: 223624/ 212569 Fax: 735115

Saleh Haji Mohamed Al–Durazi Co.,
P.O.Box 309, Bahrain
Tel: 241219
Fax: 252559

Lalchand Laxmi Das,
P.O.Box 163, Bahrain Tel: 211029 Fax: 212387

Hassan Haider Darwish,
P.O.Box 272, Bahrain Tel: 223378/223133
Fax: 240088/224488

Damodhar Devidas & Bros., P.O.Box 97,
Bahrain Tel: 229687 Fax: 228277

Y.K. & P. Maghanmal & Sons
W.L.L,
P.O.Box 173, Bahrain
Tel: 254340
Fax: 274513

General Trading and Food Processing Company, P.O.Box 20202,
Manama, Bahrain Tel: 729731 Fax: 727380

Mohamed Ali Zainal Abdulla,
P.O.Box 593,
Bahrain
Tel: 226616
Fax: 226636

Kazerooni Bros. Est.,
P.O.Box 5844, Bahrain
Tel: 246369 Fax: 276758

Red Leaf Trading Est.,
P.O.Box 2300, Bahrain
Tel: 263298 Fax: 250514

Chunilal Purushottam & Co., P.O.Box 4, Bahrain
Tel: 210738 Fax: 210750

Al-Quraish Inc.,
P.O.20555, Bahrain Tel: 242304 Fax: 253706

Qatar

Ali Bin Ali Establishment,
P.O. Box 75, Doha (Qatar) Tel: 441494, 5,
Fax: 445771

Food Centre
P.O. Box 5164 Doha (Qatar) Tel: 427432, 483, 420703, Fax: 327682

Gulf Foodstuffs, Refrigeration & Trading Co. (Al-Khalaf Bros)
P.O. Box 5774, Doha (Qatar) Tel: 60041, Fax: 601823

Gulf Markets Food Centre, (Al Maha Group Holding) P.O. Box 405
Doha (Qatar) Tel. 333333
Fax. 333399

Ahmed Shaikh Hassan Ansari P.O. Box 277,
Doha (Qatar) Tel: 424137,
Fax: 442169

Central Supply Market,
P.O. Box 2666, Doha (Qatar) Tel: 864625, Fax: 437041

Family Food Centre 5483, Doha
Tel: 424040/438707,
Fax: 448868

Gray Mackenzie & Partners P.O. Box 4792,
Doha (Qatar) Tel: 328921/ 328923 Fax: 326452

Al Mono & Partners WLL
P.O. Box 49 Doha (Qatar) Tel: 422221, Fax: 422690, 1, 2, 3, 439610

A L Mountazah Co-operative Society,
P.O.Box 3371
Dhoha(Qatar)
Tel: 320222, Fax: 419520

Johari Trading Est.,
P.O.Box 155,
Doha(Quatar) Tel: 320910, 428122 Fax: 413722

Kerala Food Centre,
P.O. Box 2867, Doha (Qatar)
Tel: 872932,
Fax: 872947

Sultanate of Oman

Mr. Bernard Vaz,
Manager, Khimji Ramdas (Food stuff Div), P.O Box 19, Muscat, PC 113,
Sultanate of Oman
Tel: 702804,
Fax: 795988

Mr. U. Som, Sales Manager
(Food Div)
Towell Lever LLC.,
P.O Box 1711, Ruwi, PC 112,
Sultanate of Oman
Tel: 786727 Fax: 786722

Mr. H.F. Billimoria
General Manager,
Naranjee Hirjee & Co P.O Box 9, Muscat, PC
113, 1 Sultanate of Oman
Tel: 714842, Fax: 714727

Mr. Haresh Virji
Partner
Virji Purshottam & Co.,

P.O Box 480, Muttrah, PC
114. Sultanate of Oman
Tel: 712805, Fax: 714053

Ali Redha Trading Co LLC., P.O Box 613, Hamriya, PC 131, Sultanate of Oman, Tel: 705792, Fax: 705615

Mr. Ramesh Gulabanii
General Manager
Al Fair Superstores,
P.O Box 418, Madinat Qaboos, PC 115,
Sultanate of Oman.
Tel: 560823
Fax: 561416

Mr. V Krishnan
General Manager,
Khalijana P.O Box 711, Ruwi, PC 112,
Sultanate of Oman
Tel: 592492,
Fax: 592496

Mr. R.J. Williamson
Business Development & Marketing Manager
Assarain Foods,
P.O.Box: 971, CPO
PC 111,
Sultanate of Oman,
Tel: 603166,
Fax: 698162

Mr. Francis D'souza
General Manager
Prisunic,
P.O Box 3985, Ruwi,
PC 112.
Sultanate of Oman
Tel: 563672,
Fax: 564938

Mr. Sridhar, Sales Manager, Bhacker Suleiman Jaffer, P.O Box 39, Muscat,
PC 113.
Sultanate of Oman
Tel: 714922,
Fax: 711335

Mr. Khabbaz
General Manager,
Muscat Cold Stores,
P.O. Box 2365, Ruwi,
PC 112,
Sultanate of Oman
Tel: 707021,
Fax. 704536

Mr. H Vijaysinh
Managing Partner,
Purshottam Damodar & Co., P.O Box 88, Muscat,
PC 113,
Sultanate of Oman
Tel: 712517,
Fax: 713242

Mr. Jitendra Pandya
General Manager
Mugatlal Pandya & Co
P.O Box 1051, Ruwi, PC 112, Sultanate of Oman
Tel: 795404, Fax: 704512

Mr. K Mitra Manager
Sultan Shopping, P.O Box 838, Jibroo, PC 114,
Sultanate of Oman. Tel: 797276, Fax: 789146

Mr. Judd Williams Food Manager,
Matrah Cold Stores,
P.O Box 1158, Ruwi, PC 112, Sultanate of Oman
Tel: 704333, Fax: 785519

Mr. H. Amarnani
General Manager
At Jadeed Stores
P.O Box 330, Hamriya,
PC 131
Sultanate of Oman
Tel: 701389,
Fax: 701391

Mr. PB Thakur
General Marketing Manager Ramniklal Kothary P.O Box 66,
Muscat, PC 113,
Sultanate of Oman
Tel: 709333,
Fax: 703110

Mr. MH Toprani
General Manager
Haridas Nensey
P.O Box 152, Muscat,
PC 113,
Sultanate of Oman
Tel: 750784,
Fax: 703642.

Mauritius

Nak Enterprises Ltd
21, Desforges Street,
Port Louis, Mauritius,
Tel: 2420350,
Fax: (230) 2084819

P. Dabydoy Al 8, Corderie Street, Port Louis,
Mauritius

M Kassamall Y Esmael
32, Bis, Dr. Eugene Laurent Street,
Port Louis, Mauritius

Chan Tai Kong & Sons Ltd
34, Jummah Mosque Street, Port Louis,
Mauritius Tel: 2425207,

Li Hoi Foo,
Li Shun, 11, Corderie Street, Port Louis,
Mauritius,
Tel: 2120923

Sewraz Freres Ltd
27, Queen Street,
Port Louis, Mauritius
Tel: 2411344

Beenesreesing R. Cr 14, Queen & Corderie Streets, Port Louis Tel: (230)2122977,

Soondron D.
Moorvaya, Corderie Street Port Louis
Tel (230)208 1023

Abdullah Ebrahim & Co., 37, Corderie Street, Port Louis, Mauritius,
Ramjuttun Freres 13,
Corderie Street,

Port Louis, Mauritius,
Tel: 2124041

K Mooneesawmy
4, Corderie Street, Port Louis, Mauritius,
Tel: 2121692

Rashid Moosa (Sons) Ltd
30, Louis Pasteur Street, Port Louis, Mauritius, Tel: 2081622, 2407090, Fax: (230)2080423

State Trading Corporation
Fon Sing Building, 3rd Floor, 12,
Edith Cavell Street,
Port Louis, Mauritius
Tel: 2085977, 2080181, 2085440, 2124870,
Fax: (230)2088359

Abdullason co Ltd 23, Louis Pasteur Street, Port Louis, Mauritius
Tel: 2121477

Currimjee Jeew Anjee & Co Ltd
38, Royal Street port Louis, Mauritius
Tel: 2426011,
Fax: (230)2408133

Ramdenee Bros Co Ltd
19, Queen Street, Port Louis, Mauritius, Li Shing Tit 53, Royal Street, Port Louis, Mauritius
Tel: 2420960

A.H.Jackaria & Co. 15, Farquhar Street, Port Louis, Mauritius,
Tei: 2420900

Rammttun Freres
13, Corderie Street, Port Louis, Mauritius
Tel: (230)2124041

Proag & Co Ltd
Cr Farquhar & Louis Pasteur Streets,
Port Louis
Tel: (230)2420147

Ayoob Cassim & Co Ltd
9, Jummah Mosque Street, Port Louis, Mauritius Tel: 2422240

A.A.R.Oosman & Co Ltd
12, Louis Pasteur Street, Port Louis, Mauritius Tei: 2422236, 2400949, 2401026, Fax: 2414468

H.A.M. Ramtoola & Co
24, Queen Street, Port Louis, Mauritius, Tel: 2422926

M H Owadally & Co Ltd
7, Farquhar Street, Port Louis, Mauritius, Tel: 2121619

Fon Sing Brothers 23, Queen Stret, Port Louis, Mauritius, Tel: 2420508, 2408052, Fax: 2128779

Abidjan

Ivoire Cereal 01 BP 393 Abidjan 01
Tel: 214860, Fax: 214862
Jean Abrigail
01 BP 1798 Abidjan 01
Tel: 271417, 275338 Fax: 272279

Ets Roma
01 BP 5672 Abidjan 01
Tel: 241299, Fax: 241014

Secome
13 BP 2119 Abidjan 13
Tel: 394196, Fax: 317233

Sifca
01 BP 1289 Abidjan 01
Tel: 242652, Fax: 240790

Sococe
01 BP 1355 Abidjan 01
Tel: 243664, Fax: 243661

Intercose
01 BP 6556 Abidjan 01
Tel: 255929, Fax: 255134

Nigeria (Lagos)

AlhajiAliko Dangote (president)
Dangote Group of Companies
3 Osborne Road Ikoyi 'Lagos
Tel: 2695010, 688532, 688400, Fax: 2695316

Mr. S.S. Vaswani (Chairman/Chief executive) The Honda Place 270A Ajose Adeogun Street, Victoria Island Lagos, P.O. Box 54767 Falomo Ikoyi Lagos Tel: 2611974, 2618605 Fax: 261773

Dr. Bukola Saraki (Vice President)
Societe Generale Bank,
13 Martins Street, Marina Lagoss.Tel: 2660149, 2664183, Fax: 2663731

Alhaii Isiyaku Rabiu (Group Chairman)
Isiyaku Rabiu Group Of Companies No. 10 Wharf Road Apapa Lagos, Tel: 874231, 5452379
Fax: 874231

Mr. Bhagwan Mahtani (Group Chairman)
Churchgate Group,
No.P .C .30 Afribank Street
Victoria Island Lagos
Tel: 2620419, 2620478
Fax: 2620558

Korea (Seoul)

Mr. D.S.Kim,
Haitai International,
Agricultural Department,
Dabo Bldg, #140,
Mapo-Dong, Mapa-Kuo.
Tel: 32701623,
Fax: 7150150

Mr. Chol Min Kim Myung Bo
#303, Daechi Bldg, Kangnam-Ku, Seoul

Mr. Lee Soo-Young, President,
M/s United Industries International,
Hanjong Bldg,
1460-10, Soch'o-gu, Seoul
Tel: 585-1881 to 1888
Fax: 581-1881

Mr. K.Illee
Rice Team
M/s. Daewoo Corporation, Seoul,
Tel: 882-2-759 2908
Fax: 82-2-7593677

Sri Lanka

Araliya Impex Pvt. Ltd. 69, Old Moor Street, Colombo - 12 Tel: 327901, 445322 Fax: 448957

Careem & Company 549/1, 1st Floor, Galle Road, Mount Lavinia Tel: 714266, 714267 Fax: 733504

The Co-operative Wholesale Establishment (Govt.Organization)
27, C.W.E Secretariat Building, Vauxhall Street, Colombo-2
Tel: 432272, 435577
Fax: 435562, 435546

Golden Pearl Agency Pvt Ltd 25/8, Old Nuge Road Nawloka Garden, Peliyagoda Tel: 910814 Fax: 910814
C. W. Mackie & Co. Ltd.
36, D. R. Wijewardena Mawatha, Colombo - 10
Tel: 436983, Fax: 440228

Nihal Brothers Pvt. Ltd, 340, K. Cyril. C .Perera Mawatha, Colombo - 13
Tel: 338145-7 Fax: 332173

R. A. Associates 1st Floor, 375, R A De Mel Mawatha, Colombo - 12
Tel: 574562, 574956 Fax: 574562, 574956

Suranjee Trading Company 179, Prince Street, Colombo - 11 Tel: 323032, 326317 Fax: 445069

Ceylon & Foreign Trades Ltd.
414 / 18, K.Cyril. C. Perera Mawatha Colombo - 13,
Tel: 449321, 449324,
Fax: 448957,

Chandra Stores
60, New Moor Street, Colombo - 12
Tel: 448420, 343959 Fax: 436108

Cot Lanka Agro Pvt Ltd. 54, 4th Cross Street, Colombo - 11, Tel: 434143, 332830, Fax: 436050

Grandmet (Ceylon) Ltd, 4, Mile Post Avenue, Colombo - 13,
Tel: 423554
Fax: 320199

Mezan Trading Company 201, 4th Cross Street, Colombo - 11,
Tel: 36983,
Fax: 447105

Northwest Holdings Ltd, 99, Cotte Road, Colombo - 8,
Tel: 697321, 699211,
Fax: 687188, 863670

Seneviratne Trading Co. Pvt. Ltd.,
32 A, Old Street, Colombo 12, Tel: 445520, 856212, Fax: 810460, 854674

USA

Sahib overseas inc
P.O. Box # 185
Fairfax Virginia 22030
Outside USA : 1-703-912-3666,
Fax No.: 1-703-923-0·19,
E-Mail: info@sahiboverseas.com

Salwan Trading Inc 1125 Westover Lane
Schaumburg, IL 60193, U.S.A.
Tel: (847) 985-7000
Fax: (847) 985-7005,
Toll Free: 1-888-Mr. Manish
Email: info@salwantrading.com
Bahaar- Premium basmati rice

Asian Brands, Inc. 2251 Orion Street, Building 118, Alameda.CA 94501, USA
Phone: 510-523-7474
Fax: 510-523-4817
Email: info@asianbrands.com

S & W ® Rice
C/o Riviana Foods Inc.
P.O. Box 2636
Houston, Texas 77252

13

Important Details

I. Criteria for Grant of Certification Mark to Exporter of Basmati Rice from India.

1. Units exporting Basmati Rice complying with the requirements laid down under notification issued by the Ministry of Commerce under the Export (Quality Control and Inspection) Act 1963.
2. Compliance with AGMARK, PFA or any other requirements as applicable to Rice.
3. Basmati Rice mills complying with the inspection procedure laid down under Basmati Rice Mills Certification and Pre-shipment Inspection Scheme issued by APEDA.
4. Availability of in-house testing laboratories equipped to carry out relevant tests to ensure compliance with the quality requirements of importing countries.
5. Record of any other requirements of Food Regulatory Authority of respective country(ies).
6. Nature of technical expertise available with exporter.
7. Status with respect .to the detentions/ rejections of consignments exported during the last three years.
8. Nature of complaints, if any, received from importing country with respect to quality and safety of the product exported by the party during the last three years.

Certification of Basmati Rice

The scheme for compulsory quality control and pre shipment inspection of Basmati Rice was introduced with effect from 19 April 1980 in pursuance of the Ministry of Commerce and Civil Supplies Notification Nos. S.O. 1025 & 1026 dated 19 April 1980. Based on the experience gained and keeping in mind the objective of the development of export trade of India, the above notifications were superseded by Ministry of Commerce, GOI Notification No. S.O. 2538 and 2539 dated 14. 9. 1990.

Based on the notifications two systems of certifications are being followed for basmati rice namely:

A. Consignment wise Inspection (CWI) system

B. In-Process Quality Control (IPQC) system

A. Consignment wise Inspection for Basmati Rice

1. General

1.1 Under the consignment wise inspection (CWI), each consignment is inspected and tested by Export Inspection Agency (EIA). Under the system the samples are drawn, inspected and tested for verifying the conformity of the consignment to the notified standards. Tests are carried out in the EIAs laboratory. Only on passing the field inspection and tests in laboratory, the certification of inspection is issued by Export Inspection Agencies.

1.2 An exporter intending to export shall process the consignment of Basmati rice so as to conform to any of the three grades, namely, Special, A or B based on the characteristics prescribed in respect of these grades specified in the Notification.

1.3 The graded basmati rice shall be packed in standard new gunny bags/ Polypropylene bags with following informations:

(1) Name and address of the exporter

(2) Variety (raw or parboiled)

(3) Grade (Special, A or B)

(4) Lot No.

(5) Gross weight & net weight

(6) Produce of India

(7) Shipping Mark

1.4 The premises used for preparation and storage of basmati rice for export requires to be maintained free from insanitary conditions and infestation by rodents and insects.

2. Notice of Inspection

2.1 An exporter intending to export Basmati Rice is required to give intimation for inspection in duplicate as per Proforma given at Annexure-Ia, to the nearest office of the Export Inspection Agency.

2.2 The intimation for inspection needs to be given

(a) Not less than two days before the inspection is to be carried out at the premises situated at the same station as the office of the Export Inspection Agency; and

(b) Not less than ten days before the inspection is to be carried out at the premises, which are not situated at the same station as the office of the Export Inspection Agency.

3 Place for inspection

3.1 The inspection will be carried out by Export Inspection Agency either at the port of shipment or at the premises of the packer or any other premises where the goods are offered by the exporter provided adequate facilities for the inspection exist therein. It will be the responsibility of the exporter to provide the facilities for inspection.

3.2 In addition to the inspection at the premises mentioned in 3.1 above, the agency will have the right to exercise such supervision of the inspected consignments at any place of storage, in transit or at wharf before the actual shipment as it may consider necessary for satisfying the purpose of compulsory pre shipment inspection scheme.

4. Basis of Inspection

4.1 Inspection of the Basmati Rice meant for export will be carried out with a view to seeing that the same conforms to the standard specifications recognized under Section 6 of the Export (Quality Control and Inspection) Act, 1963

5. Procedure of Inspection

5.1 On receipt of the intimation for inspection, the Export Inspection Agency will get the consignment examined. For the purpose of examination, representative samples will be drawn from each lot offered for inspection. A lot in this context will mean the total number of bags of the same variety and grade offered for inspection under one intimation

5.2 For the purpose of drawing samples the Sampling for Basmati Rice in Bags

No of bags in the lot	*Scale of sampling for Basmati Rice in Bags*
Up to 30	All
31 - 300	30
301 - 1000	50
1001 - 2000	100
2001 - above	5%

Scale of sampling for Basmati Rice in Bulk

Quantity of Rice (Tons)	*Number of the spots to be sampled*
Up to 300 tonnes	30
301 to 1000 tonnes	50
1001 and above	100

5.3 The selection of bags/spots for inspection will be done at random and should cover bags/ spots from various positions and depths in the stack.

5.4 For drawal of primary sample from each selected bag an appropriate sampler such as tube sampler or bag-trier etc. will be used. The sampler shall be inserted diagonally in such a way that it reaches the centre of the bag. All the primary samples so drawn from the lots will be thoroughly mixed to form a homogeneous composite sample weighing 2.5 kg. The composite sample will be divided into 3 final samples weighing each 500 gms. Each final sample will be packed in a cloth bag with identification tag and will be closed and securely sealed. The identification tag will contain Intimation No., Date of Sampling, Lot No., Variety and Grade declared, Name, Designation & Signature of Inspecting Officer. Out of 3 final samples, one will be sent to the Laboratory under code for analysis, the second handed over to the exporter under proper acknowledgement and third retained in the Export Inspection Agency office for future reference.

5.5 Selected bags for sampling will be sealed using lead seal and sealing pliers bearing EIC monogram as a mark of identification of sampled bags.

5.6 The following sampling procedure will be adopted when the consignments of basmati rice are shipped in containers:

(a) There should be no necessity of sealing each bags by EIA officers. The basmati rice should be stuffed into containers in the presence of Inspecting Officers;

(b) Once the containers is fully stuffed it is to be sealed by the Inspecting Officers with EIC seals;

(c) The fact that the containers has been sealed with EIC seal, should be recorded in the inspection certificate.

5.7 On completion of sealing and drawal of samples, the inspecting officer will prepare a Field Inspection Report in respect of each consignment.

5.8 If the lot, after analysis of sample, does not conform to the declared variety and grade, the lot will be rejected and a rejection letter issued and the exporter/processor will be required to return the seals affixed on the sampled bags. The exporter/processor will be further permitted to re-grade the lot.

5.9 If the exporter desires, the exporter's sample may be tested in the presence of senior officers of EIA and EIC and a representative from the trade.

5.10 Each final sample drawn during spot checks will be packed in a cloth bag with identification tag and shall be securely sealed. The identification tag will contain intimation; No. date of sampling, lot No, variety and grade declared, and Name, Designation and Signature of the Inspecting Officer. Out of the three final samples, one will be sent to the laboratory under code for analysis, the second handed over to the exporter under proper acknowledgement and third retained in the Export Inspection Agency office for future reference.

6. Testing of samples in the Laboratory

6.1 The samples of basmati rice received in the laboratory will be analysed for different characteristics mentioned in the specification.

7. Certificate of Inspection

7.1 Export Inspection Agency will issue the certificates of inspection as per Annexure -I b after the consignment/lot(s) has/have duly passed. The first three copies of the certificates will be given to the exporter, fourth copy sent to Export Inspection Council, New Delhi and the fifth copy retained by the Agency for its official records. For rejected lots, a rejection letter as at Annexure -I c will be issued with reasons of rejection.

7.2 The Exporter will be required to get the cleared lot(s) duly fumigated within forty-five days of the date.

7.3 Certificate of inspection will be valid for the period of fifteen days from the date of fumigation.

7.4 In case the certificate of inspection has expired before the expiry of the period of sixty days from the data of inspection, the certificate of inspection may be revalidated, after subjecting the lot(s) covered by the certificate to fresh fumigation, as per clause 7.5 above. Validity of certificate will, in any case, not exceed sixty days from the date of inspection of the lot(s) by Export Inspection Agency.

7.5 In case of material covered by the certificate is not shipped within sixty days from the date of inspection, the consignment shall have to be re-inspected after charging necessary inspection fee, before fresh certificate of inspection is issued.

8. Fumigation

8.1 Fumigation as at 7.2 and 7.3 will be required to be carried out by any of the approved fumigation agencies in a manner specified at Annexure-I d.

8.2 All charges towards the fumigation of basmati rice will be borne by the exporter and paid directly to the fumigation agency and a certificate to this effect will be obtained as per Annexure-I e.

9. Inspection Fee

9.1 A fee at the rate 0.4% of FOB will be paid by the exporter to the Export Inspection Agency as inspection fee. The inspection fee will be paid in advance along with intimation for the inspection by Cheque or Bank Draft or Indian Postal Order drawn in favour of Export Inspection Agency concerned.

The exporter also has to open a Deposit Account with the Export Inspection Agency for this purpose.

10. Appeal

Any exporter aggrieved by the refusal of the Export Inspection Agency to issue the certificate of inspection, may, within 10 days of the receipt of the communication of such refusal prefer an appeal which will be referred by the Agency to a Panel of Experts consisting of not less than three, but not more than seven persons appointed for the purposes by the Central Government. The appeal will be disposed of within fifteen days from its receipt. The decision of the panel in such appeal will be final.

B. In-Process Quality Control Scheme for Basmati Rice

General

Under the In-process Quality Control (IPQC) Scheme, only those units having all the prescribed facilities to produce sound product shall be approved for processing and packing Basmati Rice for export under their own supervision and control. Accordingly, exercising total surveillance of the entire processing operation to ensure quality of the product shall be the responsibility of the processor themselves and the main duties of Export Inspection Agencies (EIAs) shall be to ensure that the norms of approval are being followed by the approved units. This shall be done through a system of surveillance to include monitoring and supervisory visits by EIAs and corporate audits by EIC. In this system, any unit of Basmati Rice approved as per norms given hereunder shall be permitted to issue certificates of export worthiness for individual consignments itself without any inspection and analysis by the EIA prior to certification.

1. Definitions

For the purpose of this Scheme, the following definitions shall apply:

1.1 Processor - A processor shall mean any unit which processes basmati rice from paddy or from any other intermediate stage using brown basmati rice (raw or parboiled) or milled basmati rice (raw or parboiled).

1.2 Processing Unit - In the processing unit the basic raw material may be paddy, brown basmati rice (raw or parboiled) or milled basmati rice (raw or parboiled).

2. Norms for Approval

2.1 Surroundings and construction

a) The surroundings of units, which are under the physical control of the processor, shall be such as not to pose any sanitary problems.

b) The building shed shall be maintained satisfactorily.

c) The working rooms shall be maintained in good repair.

2.2 Raw Material Control

- The raw material may be paddy, brown basmati rice (raw or parboiled) and milled basmati rice (raw or parboiled).
- Specifications shall be laid down in detail for the raw material by the processing units.

- Inspection and analysis shall be conducted on the material to ensure quality by comparing them with the laid down specification. At the time of actual feeding of raw material, samples should be drawn at regular intervals and analyzed.
- The results shall be tabulated indicating the date, variety and quantity represented by the sample.
- Such inspection and analysis shall be conducted on the basis of laid down sampling plan and procedures.
- Systematic method shall be adopted in segregating accepted/ rejected lots so as to effectively avoid mix up.

2.3 Process Control

Detailed process specification shall be laid down for different stages of processing namely:

(i) Hot soaking, steaming and drying in case of par-boiled rice etc

(ii) Removal of husk

(iii) Removal of bran

(iv) Polishing

(v) Sieving

(vi) Cleaning

(vii) Grading

(viii) Sortex/finishing operation

Adequate in-process inspection shall be carried out during different stages of processing.

2.4 Product Control

- Product i.e. basmati rice so obtained shall confirm to laid down specifications. Final inspection and analysis shall be conducted on the processed product to ensure quality of the product and its conformity to the notified specifications.
- Such inspection and analysis is to be carried out on the basis of laid down sampling plan.

2.5 Metrology Control

- The laboratory equipment like moisture meter, balance etc. should be calibrated.

- Sieves, grinding stones/rubber rollers etc. should be checked periodically.
- The frequency of such calibration and checks should be laid down.

2.6 Minimum Sanitary and Hygiene Requirements Basmati Rice shall be processed and packed for export only by a unit approved by the Agency. For this purpose the unit shall satisfy the minimum facilities as specified below.

2.6.1 General Sanitation

- The entire premises used for processing, storage and packing Basmati Rice shall be maintained in good hygienic and sanitary conditions. Accumulations of dust, cobwebs, objectionable foreign matters like
- Mammalian excreta, stone, etc., shall not be present in the premises. Such materials shall be removed on a daily cleaning schedule.
- Open gutters shall be flushed and always kept clean. Toilets in the premises shall be maintained with a high degree of cleanliness and adequate facilities provided for workers to wash their hands and feet with running water using soap.
- All machines, equipments, utensils, etc. coming in contact with Basmati Rice shall be maintained clean without permitting dust accumulation and harborage of insects, weevils and other pests.
- Processing premises should be provided with exhaust fans to control air circulation in processing hall.
- The entrance door to the processing hall shall be fitted with wire mesh door/air curtains.

2.6.2 Drying yard.

- The open yard used for sun drying of Basmati Rice shall be cemented and properly covered with suitable netting, adequate to prevent entry of birds.
- Open sides of the drying yard shall be skirted by cemented single brick wall of sufficient heigaht and all openings to the yard suitably closed in order to prevent entry of rodents into the yard.

2.6.3 Storage

- Basmati Rice shall be stored separately. In the particular area where Basmati Rice is stored, no other products shall be stored.
- Basmati Rice shall be filled only in new gunny bags and such gunny bags stored in an area where other products are not stored.
- Basmati Rice packed in new gunny bags ready for export shall be stacked 30 centimeter away from walls and on wooden pallets at the bottom.
- Final products meant for export shall not be handled or stored in the room used for machines that generate dust.
- Outlet of machines that bring out light particles, extraneous matters and dust shall be properly secured to avoid such materials being wind-blown or otherwise carried into other areas and thus being admixed with final products.

2.6.4 Control of Animals, Rodents, Birds and Pests

- All openings leading to outside of the premises such as, gates, drain outlets, etc. shall be fitted with suitable grills/wire meshes to prevent entry of animals and rodents, etc.
- All windows, ventilators, gaps between the roof and wall and other openings that permit entry of birds into the godown shall be suitably secured to ensure that birds do not enter the godowns.
- If built-in foot-steps have been provided for godowns, doors of such godowns shall be fitted with trap-planks that prevent entry of rodents.
- Suitable number of rodent and pest repeller devices of required rating shall be fitted in all godowns.
- Periodic pest control of the premises by spraying or fumigation shall be done using one of the fumigants depending upon type of infestation.
- The godown floors shall be at a height of at least 18" from the ground level in order to avoid entry of rainwater in the godown.

2.7 Equipment and Metrological Control

- The unit shall have its own laboratory facilities with all necessary equipments and chemicals to carry out analysis and testing of basmati rice for the purpose of export.
- Unit shall have competent and qualified trained personnel to carry out testing of basmati rice.
- The unit shall check few instruments in relation to their history cards for its accuracy and proper calibration as per laid down frequency.

2.8 Personnel Hygiene

- Responsibility is required to be fixed of the Supervisor to check personnel hygiene of the employees.
- Workers are apparently free from communicable disease, open sores and worms or any other source of contamination.
- Workers to be medically examined after each illness from contagious diseases.
- Worker to be provided with sufficient sets of clean work dress.

2.9 Packing

Detailed specification shall be laid down for packing material and tests carried out on small pack/master cartons/bags.

2.10 Maintenance of records Necessary records related to all the above aspects shall be maintained systematically in order to ensure effective control on the system and this shall be made available to the agency as an when required.

2.11 Transportation facilities

It shall be ensured that the finished products are transported under hygienic conditions.

3. Procedure for Approval

3.1 The unit shall apply for grant of approval to the concerned EIA (through its nearest office) in the prescribed proforma (Annexure-I f) with requisite application fee of Rs. 5,000/-. Attested/ certified copy of the consent letter issued by the pollution control board concerned. If no consent letter is given, the period of approval shall be for the period of three months.

3.1.1 The application in the prescribed format shall be accompanied by the documents as given in the application form.

3.2 If the application is found to be complete in all respects and it is established prima-facie that the IPQC facilities are to the desired level, the EIA will depute an officer of the rank of not less than AD to conduct a survey of the unit within ten days.

3.3 On the basis of survey report, if the unit is considered as satisfying the norms of IPQC approval, the EIA will arrange a visit by an Inter-Departmental Panel (IDP) of experts constituted for the purpose within 15 days. The panel shall be constituted from among the following comprising not less than 3 members including the convener:

i) A representative of APEDA

ii) A representative of IARI

iii) A representative of FCI

vi) A representative of Haryana/ Punjab Agriculture University

v) Joint Commissioner (S&R) Ministry of Consumer Affairs G.O.I

vi) Deputy Director (F&A) - EIA- Convener.

3.4 Based on satisfactory IDP visit approval will be granted for a period of two years and decision will be communicated to the unit by the Agency. An approval number will be allotted to the unit.

3.4.1 No provisional or conditional approval will be accorded. In case any deficiencies are observed by IDP, these would be verified before according approval.

3.4.2 If the unit does not meet the norms specified, the findings of the IDP visit will be communicated to the processor by the EIA for rectifying the defects and making further request for reassessment which will be carried out by IDP or as recommended by IDP. If the unit is not ready for reassessment within 3 months, or is found deficient by the IDP convener during reassessment, the application will be rejected. The unit will however be free to apply afresh for approval.

3.4.3 In case, an approved unit is shifted to new premises with the same managerial/technical/ labourers etc. and is following the same procedures and practices in its operation, the processing units may be granted approval in the new premises subject to verification by the officers of EIAs.

4. Responsibilities of Processing Units

4.1 Under the IPQC Scheme, the entire processing operations to ensure quality of the product will be the responsibility of the processor himself. The responsibilities of the processor under these rules are as given below:

i) To carry out-processing operations in hygienic conditions under the supervision of experienced personnel of the unit.

ii) To draw samples at various stages of processing and from the finished product for the purpose of tests. For the purpose of examination representative sample shall be drawn from each lot offered under IPQC certification. A lot in this context shall mean total number of bags of same variety and grade offered for inspection under one IPQC certificate.

For the purpose of drawing samples the inspecting officer shall select the bags according to the scale of sampling given below:

Sampling for Basmati Rice in Bags

No of bags in the lot	***Scale of sampling for Basmati Rice in Bags***
Up to 30	All
31 - 300	30
301 - 1000	50
1001 - 2000	100
2001 - above	5%

Scale of sampling for Basmati Rice in Bulk

Quantity of Rice (Tons)	***Number of the spots to be sampled***
Up to 300 tonnes	30
301 to 1000 tonnes	50
1001 and above	100

iii) To evaluate the results of the samples tested and decide on the conformity of these samples to the prescribed specifications and to take remedial action wherever necessary;

iv) To evaluate of inspection and laboratory testing results to decide their conformity with the prescribed specifications.

v) To decide whether the lots of basmati rice processed and packed are export worthy or not on the basis of inspection carried out as per rule;

vi) To carry out the instructions issued by the Council from time to time.

4.2 If, at any time, there is any difficulty in maintaining the conformity of the product to the specification for any reason, production for export shall be suspended under intimation to the agency.

4.3 On completion of corrective actions, the unit may resume production for export under information to the Agency.

4.4 The processing of Basmati Rice for export shall be resumed only after the same is approved by the Agency in writing.

4.5 The Processing operations shall be subject to check by the Agency officers as and when found necessary.

4.6 The processing unit shall cover 'all exports' under IPQC certification.

5. Surveillance of Approved Units

A three-tier surveillance system is being adopted by the EIC/EIAs to supervise the operation of the IPQC Scheme by the approved units:

5.1 Monitoring Visits

5.1.1 The monitoring visits to an approved unit would be carried out at a frequency of minimum once in three months depending upon the performance of the units based on:

- Reports of surveillance visits in the previous year;
- Reports of analysis of samples drawn during monitoring visits;
- Quality complaints received from the foreign buyers;

During the Monitoring Visits, the Inspecting Officers will draw three sets of samples, from any consignment available and meant for exports, one for laboratory, one as referee sample and one for the exporter from the finished product, pack in standards new gunny bags/ poly propylene bags with the following informations.

- Name and address of processor/exporter.

- Variety (raw & parboiled)
- Grade (Special, A & B)
- Lot No.
- Gross weight & Net weight
- Produce of India.
- Shipping mark.

The scale of sampling will be given in Sl. No. 4.1 above will be followed.

The selection of bags/spots for inspection shall be done at random and will cover bags/spots from various positions and depth in stack.

For drawal of primary sample from each selected bag, an appropriate sampler such as tube sampler or bag- drier etc. be used. One third of the sampler shall be inserted diagonally in such a way that it reaches center of the bag. All the primary samples drawn from the lots will be thoroughly mixed to form a homogenous composite sample weighing 2.5 kg. The composite sample shall be divided into three final samples each weighing 500 grams. Each final sample shall be pack in a cloth bag with identification tag and shall be securely sealed and one of these shall be sent to the laboratory, the second handed over to the exporter under proper acknowledgement and third retained in the Export Inspection Agency office as referee sample for the future.

Note: In case of any failure of sample tested/ drawn during monitoring visits, the Agency shall subject all subsequent consignments to spot checks till such time three consecutive consignments are found conforming to the prescribed specifications.

5.2 Supervisory Visits

Supervisory visits to check compliance to the norms as well as quality of monitoring by EIAs would be conducted by EIAs at the frequency of approximately once in six months.

5.2.1 In pursuance of this report, the Agency would communicate to the unit within seven days the observations and recommendations for effecting necessary improvements within a stipulated period.

5.2.2 If any discrepancies are observed in process quality control exercised by the unit till such time as necessary improvements is made by the unit, the frequency of spot checks would be increased by the Agency.

5.2.3 The unit shall take adequate steps to implement the recommendations made by the Agency within the stipulated period and shall immediately thereafter intimate the Agency in writing of having done so, to enable the Agency to verify the adequacy of implementation of the recommendations.

5.3 Corporate Audits

Internal Audits of each Agency under the corporate audit mechanism will be carried out from EIC at the frequency of once every year. These will comprise:

- Examination of records of processor maintained by the agency like reports of visits, lab reports etc.
- Visit by the audit team to some of the units.

6 Guidelines for dealing with unsatisfactory reports of visits and/ or test reports.

6.1 All deficiencies observed during any visit to the processor's establishment including failure of samples tested will be conveyed to the processor through the Corrective Action Report (CAR) duly signed by the EIA officer and representative of the establishment.

6.2 In case of minor deficiencies, the corrective actions will be verified by the officer conducting the next visit.

6.3 In case of major deficiencies, any one of more of the following actions may be taken depending upon seriousness of deficiencies.

i) The explanation of the processor may be called with time frame for rectification.

ii) The processor may be placed under spot check until the rectification is done and verified to EIA's satisfaction by a visit and satisfactory test results of 3 consecutive consignments.

iii) The processor may be advised to suspend production and export until rectification is done and verified by a visit.

6.4 Similar actions may be taken in case laboratory reports show failure in major requirements.

7. Renewal of Approval

7.1 The approved unit shall apply for renewal in the prescribed format with renewal fee of Rs. 5,000/- at least 60 days before the expiry of the earlier approval to the in charge of the concerned EIA.

7.2 The approval may be renewed for a period of 2 years' at a time on the basis of assessment conducted by IDP besides review of performance covering monitoring visits/supervisory visits, lab reports and complaints during then period of validity and a fresh certificate of approval shall be issued.

8. Withdrawal of Approval

8.1 The approval accorded to a unit may be withdrawn with due approval of the head of the Agency, due to any of the following reasons:-

a) If the norms as laid down in clause 2 are not met;

b) If the samples drawn for testing repeatedly fail to meet the notified standards;

c) If the processor has violated/deliberately attempted to violate the provisions of the notification or instructions issued from time to time,

d) If complaints are received from foreign buyers regarding the quality of Basmati Rice or on any other matter related to EIA approval and investigation.

8.2 In case the approval accorded under IPQC Scheme is withdrawn for any reason, the consignments of such units may be allowed for export based on consignment wise inspection system provided that the unit satisfies the requirements of such system.

9. Certification

Certificate of Inspection may be issued either by the processor or the EIA as per details given below.

9.1 Issue of Certificate by Processor.

The IPQC approved units may issue the certificate of inspection themselves as follows:

- The processor exporter shall ensure that the Basmati Rice certified as export worthy conforms to the specifications recognized by the Government/Export Inspection Council for the products.

- Certificate of inspection of Basmati Rice shall be issued in the prescribed Annexure-I b.
- The certificate shall be issued by the official (s) authorised by the processor /exporter and such official (s) shall not be lower than the head of the Quality Control Department of the processing units.
- Name(s), designation (s) and specimen signatures of the official(s) authorised above shall be furnished by the processor exporter to the Custom Authorities at the port of shipments. The same should also be furnished to the nearest office of the EIA head quarter of the EIA.
- Blank certificate book can be obtained from the nearest office of Export Inspection Agency at the cost of Rs.20/- per certificate.
- Every certificate issued shall bear a distinct serial number, which will never be repeated, and the certificate shall be issued chronologically in the order of their serial numbers. In a given time only one book shall be used. All the certificates shall bear the date of issue.
- Certificate shall be neatly typed. There must be no over-typing/erasing. Correction, if any, must be countersigned by the certifying official of the unit.
- Since the system of certification is restricted to exports by the approved unit itself, name of the exporter and processor under Box 1 & 2 of the certificate should be the same. Their address may be different in case the processing unit and its registered office are situated at different places.
- Under box 12 "Description of goods" of the certificate, the approved unit must indicate the title as Basmati Rice as given in the relevant gazette notification.
- One copy of the certificates issued by the unit during the week shall be forwarded to the nearest sub office or Head Office of the EIA from where the processors/exporters were getting the certificate of inspection, on the last working day of the week along with the following:
- A copy of the export invoice duly attested and carrying cross reference of the serial number and date of the certificate to which it relates.

- A copy of the export contract indicating the contractual specifications of the products duly attested.
- A demand draft or cheque drawn in favour of the concerned EIA covering the inspection fee prescribed for the products under IPQC system, for the consignments certified by the processor exporter during the last week.
- For any change in the FOB value in the certificate of inspection already issued the concerned office of the EIA through a letter incorporating therein the certificate number and date and details of changes made in the FOB Value. In case of upward revision of the value, proportionate additional inspection fee shall also be paid to the EIA.
- For the payment of inspection fee, the approved unit may also open a deposit account with the concerned office of EIA by paying initial lump sum and remitting further amount periodically depending on the quantum and value of the exports certified. For this purpose the unit shall operate a pass book system with the concerned EIA.

  If a certificate, after it is issued by the unit, is required to be cancelled, the original copy (Custom's copy) of such certificate with endorsement of cancellation shall be forwarded to the concerned sub-office of the EIA. Another copy with similar endorsement should be sent to the head office of the concerned EIA.

  Whenever a fresh certificate is required to be issued in lieu of a certificate issued earlier and subsequently cancelled, the following entry may must be made in Box 15 Remarks, if any.

- " Issued in lieu of Certificate Book No. ______________ Sr. No. ______________ of ______________ (date)".
- In the event of cancellation of the certificate before its issuance, the unit must preserve all the 5 copies of the certificate.
- The IPQC unit shall submit a quarterly return to the Incharge EIA giving following particulars:

  a) Number and date of certificates issued.

  b) Total FOB Value of the consignments certified.

  c) Quantity and value of exports, country wise.

d) A statement of inspection fees paid to the EIA.

e) Details of complaints received and corrective actions taken.

9.2 Issue of Certificate by Export Inspection Agencies

- An exporter intending to export a consignment of Basmati Rice, processed under the in-process Quality Control Scheme, shall submit 5 copies of self certified inspection certificate to the office of the Export Inspection Agency under whose jurisdiction the unit is situated along with inspection fees at the prescribed rates, requesting for the issuance of necessary certificate for the purpose of export.
- The Export Inspection Agency shall issue IPQC certificate after deduction of inspection fee at the prescribed rate. The first three copies of the certificate shall made available to the exporter, fourth and fifth copy retained by Agency for records. For rejected lots a rejection letter is to be issued with reasons of rejection. In case monitoring of consignment is required all the copies of certificate will be retained by the Deputy Director in charge of the scheme and will be released after clearance of monitoring.
- The IPQC certificates shall be valid for 45 days from the date of issuance by EIAs. The certificate of inspection may be revalidated for further period of 15 days after physical verification of the consignment. Validity of certificate shall in any case not exceed 60 days from the date of issuance by EIAs.
- In case material covered is not shipped within 60 days from the date of issuance of IPQC certificate the certificate will be treated as cancelled and inspection fee paid for such certificate will not be returned/readjusted.
- Subsequent to certification, the Export Inspection Agency shall have the right to reassess the quality of the consignments in the godown, in transit or at the docks. In the event of the consignment being found not conforming to the notified standards specifications at any of these stages, the certificate of export worthiness originally issued by the Agency shall be withdrawn. In such cases, the final decision shall be taken by a senior officer of the Agency. If any defect is observed, the entire bags of the defective lot shall be detained.

- In case an approved unit seeks certificate from other offices of the respective agency or from the offices of other Agencies, the office issuing such certificates shall intimate the details thereof to the concerned office of the Agency under whose jurisdiction the approved unit is operating, for the purpose of effective monitoring of the performance of the unit.

10. Fumigation

The Exporter shall get export material (lots) covered under IPQC certification duly fumigated within 45 days of issuance of certificate. Fumigation may be got done by any of the approved fumigation agency, in a manner specified in Annexure-I g and certificate to this effect will be obtained. All charges towards fumigation of Basmati Rice shall be borne by the exporter and paid directly to fumigation agency.

11. Inspection Fee

Inspection fee at the @ 0.2% of FOB value shall be paid by the exporter to Export Inspection Agency as inspection fee. The inspection fee will be paid in advance along with inspection certificate by a bank draft in favour of concerned Export Inspection Agency.

Advance inspection fee calculated @ 0.1% of the average annual exports based on the last two years figures shall be paid for six months at the time of approval. Fees will be charged for all export and not only for export to ED. The exporter, if he desires may open a deposit account with Export inspection Agency for the purpose.

12. Complaint

If a complaint is received from a forging buyer or consignment of Basmati Rice is detained by importing country on food safety ground etc. the EIA will follow the procedure given below:

- Complaint would be immediately referred to the concerned EIA.
- The exporter would be immediately placed 'on alert' by the concerned EIA which shall mean that frequency of monitoring will be increased to at least once a month and each consignment will need clearance by EIA before export.
- EIA will collect complete information from exporter as given below:

  Full particulars of consignment such as product name, quantity, grade along with attested copies of documents such as purchase order, letter of credit, certificate of export. Bill of lading, labs test report, location of consignment. If the processor has got his consignment where it was detained it is required to be surveyed by an independent surveyor in the country where it was detained. Such survey report shall be made available to EIAs.

- An immediate visit will be made by an EIA officer to check records and compliance to the norms.
- Based on assessment, the EIAs may:
  1. Revoke 'on alert'.
  2. Resort to normal frequency of surveillance but continue with testing of next ten consignments.
  3. Suspend production for export in case major deficiencies are observed.

13. Issue of Certificate of Authenticity for European Union

13.1 EIC/EIAs have been designated by the Government of India for issuing Certificate of Authenticity for the consignments of basmati rice shipped from India to the countries of ED as per EC regulations for allowing the benefit of reduced import duty as per Annexure I g.

13.2 The following parameters have to be certified by EIAs for issuing certificates of authenticity:

i) Region of cultivation

ii) FOB value

iii) Description of goods i.e. grade of Basmati Rice;

iv) Rice meant for export is Basmati Rice;

v) Quantity/packing

13.3 The following procedure is adopted for issue of certificates:

i) Submission of the documents like invoice, affidavit, certificate of inspection issued by the exporter etc in respect of the consignment for which certificate of authenticity is required by the exporter. The EIA will verify that the consignment(s) are inspected/tested to ensure that they are basmati rice as per the provisions of the notification.

ii) The exporters will inform 'Region and place of cultivation' so as to confirm the origin of Basmati Rice through an affidavit.

iii) EIAs will attest the Certificate of Authenticity based on the verification/inspection and testing carried out by them. These certificates are stamped with EIC seal and signed by authorized signatories of EIAs.

iv) The details on the certificates include the certificate no. date of its issue, name of the buyer, consignee, value, quantity, gross weight and net weight etc.

v) After attesting the Certificate, first and second copies are given to the exporters for getting them attested by the Customs at the time of shipment and for sending these copies to their overseas buyer. The third copy is sent to Brussels, the EC HQs, on monthly basis, and the fourth copy is retained with EIAs for records.

vi) As per the EC requirement, the validity of Certificates of Authenticity is 90 days.

vii) In case the exporter so desires, the certificate of authenticity may be issued from EIA head office rather than the concerned sub office for saving time and better service to the exporter subject to fulfilling all other requirements.

viii) In case the date of validity of certificate of authenticity is over and there is request from the processor/ exporter for revalidation, sampling and testing of consignment(s) of basmati rice in the importing country and issue fresh certificate of authenticity, is being considered on merit. The issue of certificate of authenticity will be based on the test results. However, the exporter has to bear the cost of visit of EIA officials for drawal of samples and test.

14. Appeal

Any exporter aggrieved by the refusal of the Export Inspection Agency to issue the certificate of inspection, may, within 10 days of the receipt of the communication of such refusal prefer an appeal which shall be referred by the Agency to a panel of Experts consisting of not less than three, but not more than seven persons appointed for the purposes by the Central Government. The appeal panel will dispose of the appeal within fifteen days from its receipt. The decision of the panel in such appeal shall be final.

Annexure – I a

Application for Inspection

<table>
<tr><td colspan="3">Exporter's Name Address 1</td><td>Invoice No. & Date 10</td><td>Exporter's Ref. 11</td></tr>
<tr><td colspan="3">Manufacturer's Name & Address 2</td><td colspan="2">Buyer's Order No. & Date 12</td></tr>
<tr><td colspan="3">Details of the Manufacturer's Seal, if any 3</td><td colspan="2">To 13
The
(Name & Address of the Inspection Authority)
Please inspect the consignment and issue a Certificate of inspection under the ....Act. A crossed cheque for Rs................................drawn on...is enclosed as inspection fee/Please debit our Account Pass Book No.................... enclosed.

Date Signature of Exporter</td></tr>
<tr><td>Inspection required on 4</td><td colspan="2">Weekly Holiday 5</td><td colspan="2" rowspan="3">Address where consignment is to be inspected 14</td></tr>
<tr><td>Vessel/Flight No. 6</td><td colspan="2">Port of Loading 7</td></tr>
<tr><td>Probable Date of Landing 8</td><td colspan="2">Date of Sealing/ Flight 9</td></tr>
<tr><td>Mark & Nos. 15</td><td>No. & Kind of Pkgs. 16</td><td>Description of Goods (*) 17</td><td>Quantity As declared 18</td><td>FOB Value (in Rs.) 19</td></tr>
<tr><td></td><td></td><td></td><td></td><td></td></tr>
<tr><td colspan="5">Technical requirements including specifications/approved samples with its characteristics as stipulated in the export contract. 20</td></tr>
</table>

<table>
<tr><td colspan="2">Other Relevant Information 21</td></tr>
<tr><td colspan="2">Declarations: Certified that the goods mentioned above have been manufactured/ produced to satisfy the conditions relating to quality 22 control/inspection applicable to them under the ___________Act and that consignment conforms to the specification

Certified that the goods have been offered previously for inspection vide intimation no. _______. Dated _____and the defects as pointed out earlier have been duly rectified.

Certified that no additional technical or quality requirements other than mentioned above have been stipulated by the overseas buyer.

(*) Description should include grade, size and brand, if any. @ As motor car</td></tr>
<tr><td>parts, Components and accessories are covered under statutory preshipment inspection, exporter in this case would need to prefix the description of goods

reproduced from Master Document-1 by typing "Components and Accessories fitted in" and fill in the quantity column accordingly.</td><td>[Signature & Date:</td></tr>
</table>

Annexure – I b

Certificate Of Inspection/In-Process Quality Control

<table>
<tr><td rowspan="2">Exporter's Name Address 1</td><td>Invoice No. &
Date 6</td><td>COPY</td></tr>
<tr><td colspan="2">Buyer's Order No. & Date 7</td></tr>
<tr><td>Manufacturer's Name & Address 2</td><td colspan="2" rowspan="2">Grams: SHIPMENT QUALITY
Telex : 031-66351 8
EXPORT INSPECTION AGENCY
DELHI
(Ministry of Commerce)
Government of India
Municipal Market Building,3,
Saraswati Marg,
Karol Bagh (4th Floor)
New Delhi-110 005-INDIA</td></tr>
<tr><td>Details of the Manufacturer's
Seal, if any 3</td></tr>
<tr><td>Details of Seal of Inspection
authority, if any 4</td><td colspan="2" rowspan="2">Valid upto and including......
Certificate No. 03-</td></tr>
<tr><td>Specification Reference 9</td></tr>
</table>

<table>
<tr><td rowspan="2">Mark & Nos. 10</td><td rowspan="2">No. & Kind of Pkgs. 11</td><td rowspan="2">Description of Goods (*) 12</td><td colspan="2">As declared by Exporters</td></tr>
<tr><td>Quantity As declared 13</td><td>FOB Value (in Rs.) 14</td></tr>
<tr><td></td><td></td><td></td><td></td><td></td></tr>
<tr><td colspan="5">Remarks, if any Stamp for FOB Revision 15</td></tr>
</table>

<table>
<tr><td><u>** CERTIFICATION UNDER INSPECTION SYSTEM</u> 16

It is hereby declared that the consignment as per details given above has been inspected as required under the Honey Export (Quality Control and Inspection) Rules 2002

It satisfies the conditions as applicable to it and is certified export worthy.

Date of inspection ....

OR

**CERTIFICATION UNDER IN PROCESS QUALITY CONTROL SYSTEM

It is hereby certified, on the basis of controls carried out, that the commodities as per details given herein are in specifications prescribed under the Honey Export (Quality Control and Inspection) Rules 2002.</td><td>SEAL OF THE ISSUING AUTHORITY

Signature

Name

Designation Accordance with the standard

Date</td></tr>
</table>

(*) Description should include grade, size and brand, if any. @ Refer to footnote in 'Intimation for Inspection).

(**) Strike out whichever is not applicable

Annexure – I c

Rejection Letter Format

Export Inspection Agency ____________

No. Eia/

To

M/S.____________________

____

____

Sub : **Pre shipment Inspection of** ________________________________

Ref : **Your Intimation No.** ____________________**dated** ____________

Dear Sirs,

With reference to your above mentioned intimation for inspection, this is to inform you that the consignment of ________________________________ was inspected and it was not found confirming to the specification recognized under Export (Quality Control and Inspection) Act, 1963. It is, therefore, regretted that the certificate of export worthiness cannot be issued due to the following reason (s).

Reason (s) for rejection

1)

2)

3)

4)

5)

Yours faithfully,

For **Export Inspection Agency,**

Annexure – I d

Procedure for Fumigation of Basmati Rice

1) Under atmospheric pressure (Tent fumigation)

a) Use 2.0 kg to 2.8-kg methyl bromide for 100 cu. metres at 25 degree centigrade and above and give 16 to 24 hours exposure.

Note: a) At the rate of 2.00 kg. Methyl bromide per 100 cu. metres, the duration of the exposure shall be 24 hours.

b) At the rate of 2.8 kg. methyl bromide per 100 cu. metres, the duration of the exposure shall be 16 hours.

2) In Vacuum Chambers

a) Use 2.8 kg. Methyl bromide per 100 cu. metres at 250 degree centigrade and above at 28 inches vacuum pressure inside the fumigation chambers. Minimum duration of exposure shall be 3 hours.

Annexure – I e

Certificate of Fumigation

Book No. __________ Serial No. __________

This is to certify that the consignment of Basmati Rice as per details given below has been fumigated in Tents / Vaccum Chambers.

1) Name & address of the exporter	:	
2) Basmati Rice	:	Raw / Parboiled
3) Number of bags	:	
4) Quantity packed in each bag	:	
5) Details of sealing done by the Inspection Agency	:	
6) Marks on the Packages	:	
7) Name of the Fumigant used	:	
8) Rate of application	:	_______kg. Per 100 cu. Metre.
9) Duration of exposure in Vacuum/ Tent inches Vacuum Pressure	:	
10) Date of Fumigation	:	

Signature :

____

Name & Designation :

____

Seal of Fumigation Agency:______________

Place : __________

Date : __________

Annexure – I f

Application for Approval Form

From:
M/s. ____________________

____

To:
The Joint Director Incharge, Export Inspection Agency-Kolkata/Mumbai/Cochin
The Deputy Director Incharge, Pilot Test House, Mumbai
Sir,
Please carry out the assessment of our establishment as required under the Rules. We furnish below the information regarding facilities existing in our establishment. We undertake that our establishment meet the stipulated as per the Rule ________________.
Please find enclosed herewith DD/Cheque bearing No. ____________ for Rs. ______________ towards application.

1. General

1.1 Name and address of the processing unit with telephone No/Telex No/ Fax No

1.2 Name & Address of the registered office with telephone No/Telex No/ Fax No

1.3 Production capacity per month

(a) Quantity

(b) Value

1.4 It the unit is hired/leased, full address of owner.

1.5 Weather the surrounding kept clean. Whether the unit is maintained in good hygienic condition to present rodent harborage and infestation?

1.6 Value of export during proceeding three years?

1.7 A list of machinery and equipment available be attached.

1.8.1 Is there any in house testing facility available.

1.8.2 Whether all required chemicals are available.

1.8.3 Whether tests conducted and proper records thereof maintained.

1.8.4 List of testing equipment.

1.9 Is all the sections of units are kept clean.

2.0 Is there adequate veilation and lighting in all sections of the unit.

2.1 Is there adequate space for free movement in all the sections units for workers.

2.2 Is there restriction of entry into processing and packing area of unauthorised persons.

2.3 Whether workers provided with clean working cloth Apron and to prevent contamination of consignment with sweat and dust/dirt.

2.4 Is these arrangement in all the sections for preventing entry of rodents, birds and pegions.

2.5 Are the doors of all sections fitted with fly proofing and self closing device.

2.6 Is there adequate protection in the unit for loading and unloading of consignment during rainy season.

2.7 Facilities of toilets/washing for workers with liquid soap, disinfectant and towel.

2.8 Are the toilets having self closing doors and kept in clean.
2.9 Are the toilet away from processing area.
2.10 Whether the walls and floors of the premises are free from pits, crevices and peeling off.
2.11 Whether there is an adeuate failities of fumigation.
3.0 Personnel
3.1 Number of workers
3.2 Number of supervisors
3.3 Number of technical personnels
(a) Production
(b) Inspection
(c) Testing and analysis
3.1 Qualification
3.4 The Name/qualification/designation and experience of quality control chief.
4.0 Material control
4.1 Is there specification laid down for paddy/basmati rice.
4.2 Is inspection and test on paddy/basmati rice conducted based on laid down sampling plan and procedure?
4.3 Is there effective method systematically adopted in segregated the rejected items.
5.0 Process control
5.1 Are detailed process specifications laid down at different stages of processing /
5.2 Are production samples/guides available ?
5.3 Is there any stage inspection and/or petrol inspection give (details)
6.0 Product Control
6.1 Are instruments serially numbered and calibrated at laid down frequency
6.2 Are final inspection and test conducted on finished rice based on laid down sampling plan (give details).
7.0 Metrological control
7.1 Are instruments serially numbered and calibrated at laid down frequency.
8.0 Preservation and packing control.
8.1 Are Products well preserved during storage and transit.
8.2 Are there specification laid down for packing and packing material and relevant test carried out on packages.
9.0 Documentation
9.1 Are essential records systematically maintained at all the above stage.
10 Other particular/remarks, if any

Place-
Date:
List of enclosures
1. DD/Cheque No.
2. Date ________ of Rs. ________
3. Upto date lay out plan of establishment.
4. Certified copies of legal identity of establishment.

Yours faithfully
Signature
Name
Designation
Company Seal

Annexure – I g

Certificate of Authenticity Basmati Rice

<table>
<tr><td rowspan="5">Exporter (Name & Full Address) 1

Consignee (Name & Full Address) 2</td><td>For ex
No
9566 DUPLICATE
Issued by (Name and full address of issuing body)</td></tr>
<tr><td>3. Region or place of cultivation</td></tr>
<tr><td>4. FOB value in US dollars</td></tr>
<tr><td>5. Number and date of invoice</td></tr>
<tr><td>7. Gross weight (kg.)</td></tr>
<tr><td>6. Marks and numbers- Number and kind of packages–
Description of goods</td><td>8. Net weight (kg)</td></tr>
<tr><td colspan="2">9. DECLARATION BY EXPORTER
The undersigned declares that the information shown is correct/
Place and date: Signature</td></tr>
<tr><td colspan="2">10. CERTIFICATION BY THE ISSUING BODY
It is hereby certified that the rice described above is BASMATI RICE and that the information shown in this certificate is correct.
Place and date: Signature: Stamp:</td></tr>
<tr><td colspan="2">11. CERTIFICATION BY COMPETENT CUSTOMS OFFICE OF COUNTRY OF EXPORT
Customs formalities for export to the European Economic Community of the rice described above have been completed.
Type, number and date of export document: Name and country of Custom office:
Signature : Stamp:</td></tr>
<tr><td colspan="2">12. FOR COMPLETENT AUTHORITIES IN THE COMMUNITY</td></tr>
</table>

(*) Description should include grade, size and brand, if any. @Refer to footnote in 'Intimation for Inspection).

(**) Strike out whichever is not applicable

II. Grade Designation and Quality Specification for various froms of Basmati Rice Exported from India as per New Delhi Order dt. 14th September, 1990

In exercise of the powers conferred by section 6 of the Export (Quality Control and Inspection Act, 1963 (22 of 1963), the Central Government, after consulting the Export inspection council, being of opinion, that it is necessary and expedient so to do for the development of the export trade of India, hereby:-

(1) Notifies that Basmati Rice shall be subject to quality control and inspection prior to export;

(2) Specifies the type of quality control and inspection in accordance with the export of Basmati Rice (Inspection) Rules, 1990 as the type of quality control and inspection which shall be applied to such Basmati Rice prior to export;

(3) Recognises-

(a) The national standards of importing countries and international standards;

(b) The contractual specifications agreed to between the foreign buyer and the exporter; provided that such specifications are not below the minimum specifications stipulated in schedules I to III;

(c) The grade designation formulated under Basmati Rice (Export) Grading and Marketing Rules, 1990; provided that such specifications are in conformity with clause (b);

(d) In the absence of contractual specifications, minimum specifications set out in the Schedules to this Order; provided that the specifications under clauses (a), (b), (c) and (d) shall also conform to the Food Laws; if any, in force in the importing country;

(4) Prohibits the export, in the course of international trade of Basmati Rice unless a mark or seal recognised by Central Government indicating that it conforms to the standard specifications applicable to it has been affixed or applied to packages or containers of such Basmati Rice and is accompanied by a certificate Grade/Inspection issued by the Agricultural Marketing Adviser to the Government of India or by any of the agencies established under section 7 of the Export (Quality Control and Inspection) Act, 1963 (22 of 1963) to the effect that such Basmati Rice conforms to the aforesaid standard specifications and is export worthy.

Nothing in this Order shall apply to export by sea, land or air of samples of Basmati Rice not exceeding in value of rupees fifty, to prospective buyers.

In this Order, "Basmati Rice" (Oryza sativa)" shall mean Basmati Raw Milled Rice, Parboiled Rice and Dehusked and Unpolished (Brown) Basmati Rice produced in India.

Schedule – I

Grade designation and definition of quality of Basmati Rice Raw milled (for export)

Grade designation	Maximum permissible limit (in percent by weight)					General Characteristics
	Foreign Matter	Brokens & Fragments	Other rice including Red Grains	*Damaged, discoloured and chalky grains	Moisture	
1	2	3	4	5	6	7
Special A B	0.5 1.0 2.0	5.0 10.0 10.0	10.0 15.0 20.0	1.0 2.0 3.0	14.0 14.0 14.0	**(1)** The grains shall be long slender of white or greyish or creamy white colour and translucent.
						(2) The rice,:-(a) shall be dried matured kernelsof Oryza/sativa; and shall haveuniform size, shape and colour;(b) shall possess in a marked degree the nature fragrance, characteristic of Basmati Rice both in the raw and cooked state;(c) shall not have been artificially coloured and shall be free from polishing agents;(d) may contain upto 3 percent of grains with an appreciable amount of bran thereon;(e) shall be free from musty of noxious odour and shall carry no sign of mould or containing webs and dead or live weavils;(f) shall have length 6.0 mm and above, and length breadth ratio 3 and above;(g) shall be in sound marchantable condition. Definitions :-(i) "Foreign matter" includes dust, stones, lumps of earth, chaff, stems or straw and any other impurity(ii) "Brokens and fragements" includes pieces of rice kernels which are less than three-fourth of a whole kernel. The pieces of kernels. Smaller than one-fourth of the whole kernels shall be treated as fragments. (iii) "Other rice including red grains" shall consist of contrasting and/or inferior varieties of rice. Red grains shall be the kernels, whole or broken, which have 25 per cent. Or more of their surface coated with red bran.(iv) "Damaged, discoloured and chalky grains" includes rice kernels, broken, fragments of whole that are internally damaged or discoloured materially affecting the quality. Chalky grains shall be the grains atleast half of which are milky white in colour and brittle in nature.

*Red grains shall not exceed 2%.

Schedule – II

Grade designation and definition of quality of Basmati Parboiled Rice (for export only)

Grade designation	Maximum permissible limit (in percent by weight)					General Characteristics
	Foreign Matter	Brokens & Fragments	Other rice including Red Grains	*Damaged, discoloured and chalky grains	Moisture	
1	2	3	4	5	6	7
Special A B	0.5 1.0 2.0	5.0 10.0 10.0	10.0 15.0 20.0	1.0 2.0 3.0	14.0 14.0 14.0	**(1)** The grains shall be long slender of white or greyish or creamy white colour and translucent.
						The rice,:-(a) shall be dried matured kernels of Oryza/sativa; and shall have uniform size, shape and colour;(b) shall possess in a marked degree the nature fragrance, characteristic of Basmati Rice both in the raw and cooked state;(c) shall not have been artificially coloured and shall be free from polishing agents; (d) may contain upto 3 percent of grains with an appreciable amount of bran thereon;(e) shall be free from musty of noxious odour and shall carry no sign of mould or containing webs and dead or live weavils;(f) shall have length 6.0 mm and above, and length breadth ratio 3 and above;(g) shall be in sound marchantable condition.Definitions :-(i) "Foreign matter" includes dust, stones, lumps of earth, chaff, stems or straw and any other impurity(ii) "Broken and fragments" includes pieces of rice cernels which are less than three-fourth of a whole kernel. The pieces of kernels. Smaller than one-fourth of the whole kernels shall be treated as fragments. (iii) "Other rice including red grains" shall consist of contrasting and/or inferior varieties of rice. Red grains shall be the kernels, whole or broken, which have 25 per cent. Or more of their surface coated with red bran.(iv) "Damaged, discoloured and chalky grains" includes rice kernels, broken, fragments of whole that are internally damaged or discoloured materially affecting the quality. Chalky grains shall be the grains atleast half of which are milky white in colour and brittle in nature.

*Red grains shall not exceed 2%.

Schedule – III

Grade designation and definitions of quality of Basmati unpolished/dehusked/brown basmati rice (for Export only)

Grade designation	Maximum permissible limit (in percent by weight)					General Characteristics
	Foreign Matter	Brokens & Fragments	Other rice including Red Grains	*Damaged, discoloured and chalky grains	Moisture	
1	2	3	4	5	6	7
Special A B	0.5 1.0 1.5	5.0 10.0 15.0	14.0 26.0 41.0	1.0 3.0 5.0	14.0 14.0 14.0	(1) The grains shall be long slender of light brown colour and having vitreous lustre (glossy in appearance).
						(2) The rice,:-(a) shall be the dried matured kernels of Oryza sativa from which the hulls have been removed and have not been subjected to further milling and shall have uniform size, shape and colour; (b) shall possess marked degree of the natural fragrance characteristics of basmati rice, both in the raw and cooked state;(c) shall not have been artificially coloured and shall be free from polishing agents;(d) shall be free from musty or obnoxious odour and shall carry no sign of mould or contain of webs and dead of live weavils;(e) shall have length 6.0 mm and above and length breadth ratio 3.0 and above;(f) shall be in sound merchantable condition.Definitions :-1. "Foreign matter" includes dust, stones, lumps of earthy chaff, stem or straw and any other impurity.2. "Brokens and fragments "includes pieces of rice kernels, which are less than three fourth of the whole kernels, shall be treated as fragments; 3."Other rice" shall consist of contrasting and/or inferior varieties of rice; 4."Green grains' shall be the kernels, whole or brokens, which are greenish in colour;5."Red grains" shall be kernels, whole or broken, which have their surface coated with red grain; 6. "Damaged, discoloured and chalky grains" includes rice kernels, broken, fragements of whole, that are internally damaged or dicoloured materially affecting the quality. Chalky grains shall be the grains at least half of which are milky white in colour and brittle in nature.

*Red grains shall not exceed 2%.

14

Plant Economics of Rice Puff

Capacity = 300 Tons/Annum

Land & Building (LandArea 1000sq.ft.) = Rentel

PLANT & MACHINERY

1. Automatic Puffed Rice making machine
2. Bag stiching machine
3. Hot pouch sealing machine
4. Weighing balance and Weight measurement

Rs. 1,26,200.00

FIXED CAPITAL

1. Plant & Machinery	Rs.	1,26,200.00
2. Other Fixed Assets	Rs.	25,000.00
TOTAL	**Rs.**	**1,51,200.00**

RAW MATERIALS

1. Rice
2. Salt
3. Jute bags
4. Polythene bags (Woven sacks)
5. Polypack

TOTAL WORKING CAPITAL/MONTH

1. Raw Material	Rs.	3,72,250.00
2. Salary and Wages	Rs.	25,935.00
3. Utilities & Overheads	Rs.	24,325.00
TOTAL	**Rs.**	**4,22,510.00**

TOTAL CAPITAL INVESTMENT

Total Fixed Capital	Rs.	1,51,200.01
Total Working Capital for 2 Months	Rs.	8,45,020.00
TOTAL	**Rs.**	**9,96,220.01**

TURN OVER/ANNUM

By sale of Puffed Rice 300 tons	Rs.	55,50,000.00

PROFIT SALES RATIO = Profit / Sales x 100 = 6.25 %

RATE OF RETURN = Operating profit / T.C.I x 100 = 34.80 %

BREAK EVEN POINT (B.E.P) = 51.92 %

15

Plant Economics of Rice Bran Oil

Capacity = 6000 MT/Annum

Land & Building (Land & Building 10 Bigha)= Rs. 1,45,50,000.00

PLANT & MACHINERY

1. Extractor
2. Hydrocycloner
3. Preveaporator
4. Post evaporator
5. 2-stage stripping column
6. Gas tight conveyor
7. Desolventizer Toaster/drier
8. Condenser for surplus D-T vapor
9. Condenser for micella vapor
10. Solvent water separator
11. Solvent holding tank
12. Inection condenser
13. Waste water evaporator
14. Solvent recovery plant
15. Distillation column & accessories
16. Boiler
17. Oil storage tank
18. Miscellaneous jigs, fixtures & fittings
19. Valves, pumps, pipes, motors etc.

20. Other equipments
21. Various tanks

FIXED CAPITAL

1. Land&Building	Rs.	1,45,50,000.00
2. Plant & Machinery	Rs.	1,36,57,000.00
3. Other Fixed Assets	Rs.	60,50,000.00
TOTAL	**Rs.**	**3,42,57,000.00**

RAW MATERIALS

1. Rice bran
2. Hexane solvent
3. Miscellaneous

TOTAL WORKING CAPITAL/MONTH

1. Raw Material	Rs.	70,80,000.00
2. Salary and Wages	Rs.	3,35,058.29
3. Utilities & Overheads	Rs.	13,57,500.00
TOTAL	**Rs.**	**87,72,558.29**

TOTAL CAPITAL INVESTMENT

Total Fixed Capital	Rs.	3,42,57,000.00
Total Working Capital For 2 Months	Rs.	1,75,45,116.58
TOTAL	**Rs.**	**5,18,02,116.58**

TURN OVER/ANNUM

By Sale of 6000 MT. Rice Bran oil Rs. 13,20,00,000.00

PROFIT SALES RATIO = Profit / Sales x 100 = 11.97 %

RATE OF RETURN = Operating profit / T.C.I x 100 = 30.51 %

BREAK EVEN POINT (B.E.P) = 54.66 %

16

Plant Economics Rice Polishing and Packing

Capacity	=	1350 Ton/Annum
Land & Building (Land 1000 sq. mts.)	=	Rs. 24,50,000.00

PLANT & MACHINERY

1. Conveyor Belt
2. Magnetic Seperator
3. Destoner
4. Paddy Seperator
5. Cyclone System
6. Silky Polishing Machine
7. PVC Water storage tank
8. Grader
9. Automatic Weighing, Filling, pouch sealing machine with Nitrogen Flush arrangement.

FIXED CAPITAL

1. Land & Building	Rs.	24,50,000.00
2. Plant & Machinery	Rs.	12,95,000.00
3. Other Fixed Assets	Rs.	1,70,000.00
TOTAL	**Rs.**	**39,15,000.00**

RAW MATERIALS

1. Rice
2. Packaging material

TOTAL WORKING CAPITAL/MONTH

1. Raw Material	Rs.	22,75,000.00
2. Salary and Wages	Rs.	62,000.00
3. Utilities & Overheads	Rs.	2,38,500.00
TOTAL	**Rs.**	**25,75,500.00**

TOTAL CAPITAL INVESTMENT

Total Fixed Capital	Rs.	39,15,000.00
Total Working Capital For 2 Months	Rs.	51,51,000.00
TOTAL	**Rs.**	**90,66,000.00**

TURN OVER/ANNUM

1. By Sale of RICE 1350 M.T.
2. Broken Rice 120 M.T.
3. Bran 30 M.T.

TOTAL	**Rs.**	**4,18,80,000.00**

PROFIT SALES RATIO = Profit / Sales x 100 = 22%

RATE OF RETURN = Operating profit / T.C.I x 100 =104%

BREAK EVEN POINT (B.E.P) = 24%

17

Plant Economics of Modern Rice Mill

Rated Plant capacity	=	50 Mt Paddy Per Day for Rice Mill
Land & Building (Land 3 Acres)	=	Rs. 1,99,50,000.00

PLANT & MACHINERY

1. Drum Sieve with 2 H.P. motor
2. Paddy Cleaner
3. Gravity Selector Cum Destoner
4. Horizontal Cyclone with Air Seal.
5. Bucket Elevator with 3 H.P. motor and other accessories
6. Ducting, Gravity, Packing, Chuts, Hopper and other.
7. Magnets.
8. Grain Separator
9. Rubber roll Paddy Dehusker with motor, husk blower.
10. Paddy Separator
11. Cone Polisher
12. Sieve Separtor Aspiration Channels Cyclone, Air Seal etc.
13. Indented Grador
14. Bucket Elevator
15. Magnet.
16. Bran Conveying System with 25 H.P. motor.
17. Ducting Gravity, Packing Spot etc.
18. Erection Changes.

FIXED CAPITAL

1. Land&Building	Rs.	1,99,50,000.00
2. Plant & Machinery	Rs.	39,46,000.00
3. Other Fixed Assets	Rs.	23,50,000.00
TOTAL	**Rs.**	**2,62,46,000.00**

RAW MATERIALS

1. Paddy
2. Gunny Bags
3. Jute Twine.
4. Miscellaneous. Consumables.

TOTAL WORKING CAPITAL/MONTH

1. Raw Material	Rs.	77,44,000.00
2. Salary and Wages	Rs.	2,92,500.00
3. Utilities & Overheads	Rs.	9,24,400.00
TOTAL	**Rs.**	**89,60,900.00**

TOTAL CAPITAL INVESTMENT

Total Fixed Capital	Rs.	2,62,46,000.00
Total Working Capital For 2 Months	Rs.	1,79,21,800.00
TOTAL	**Rs.**	**4,41,67,800.00**

TURN OVER/ANNUM

1. By Sale of Rice 11700 M.T.
2. Broken Rice 900 M.T.
3. Bran 900 M.T.
4. Husks 3960 M.T.

TOTAL **Rs. 14,09,94,000.00**

PROFIT SALES RATIO = Profit / Sales x 100 = 17.95 %

RATE OF RETURN = Operating profit / T.C.I x 100 = 57.31 %

BREAK EVEN POINT (B.E.P) = 35.60 %

18

Plant Economics of Modern Rice Mill

Capacity = 30,000 MT/Annum

Land & Building (Land 4.5 Acres) = Rs. 2,07,87,500.00

PLANT & MACHINERY

1. Drum Sieve
2. Paddy Cleaner
3. Gravity Selector Cum Destoner
4. Horizontal Cyclone
5. Bucket Elevator
6. Ducting, Gravity, Packing, Chuts, Hopper and other.
7. Magnets.
8. Grain Separator with Complete accessories.
9. Rubber roll Paddy Dehusker with motor, husk blower.
10. Paddy Separator 36 Compartment
11. Cone Polisher
12. Sieve Separtor Aspiration Channels Cyclone, Air Seal etc.
13. Indented Grador with 2 H.P. motor.
14. Bucket Elevator.
15. Magnet.
16. Bran Conveying System with 25 H.P. motor.
17. Ducting Gravity, Packing Spot etc.
18. Erection Changes.
19. Technical Consultancy charges.

FIXED CAPITAL

1. Land & Building	Rs.	2,07,87,500.00
2. Plant & Machinery	Rs.	57,59,000.00
3. Other Fixed Assets	Rs.	23,00,000.00
TOTAL	**Rs.**	**2,88,46,500.00**

RAW MATERIALS

1. Paddy
2. Gunny Bags
3. Jute Twine.
4. Miscellaneous. Consumables.

TOTAL WORKING CAPITAL/MONTH

1. Raw Material	Rs.	1,04,05.000.00
2. Salary and Wages	Rs.	4,01.040.00
3. Utilities & Overheads	Rs.	13,97.000.00
TOTAL	**Rs.**	**1,22,03,040.00**

TOTAL CAPITAL INVESTMENT

Total Fixed Capital	Rs.	2,88,46,500.00
Total Working Capital For 3 Months	Rs.	3,66,09,120.00
TOTAL	**Rs.**	**6,54,55,620.00**

TURN OVER/ANNUM

1. By Sale of Rice 19500 M.T.
2. Broken Rice 1500 M.T.
3. Bran 1500 M.T.
4. Husks 6600 M.T.

TOTAL	**Rs. 19,13,70,000.00**

PROFIT SALES RATIO = Profit / Sales x 100 = 17.64 %

RATE OF RETURN = Operating profit / T.C.I x 100 = 51.59 %

BREAK EVEN POINT (B.E.P) = 36.96 %

19

Plant Economics of Modern Rice Mill

Capacity	=	3000 TPD/Annum
Land & Building (Land area 1 acre)	=	Rs. 62,00,000.00

PLANT & MACHINERY

1. Total Cost of Plant & Machinery	Rs.	20,00,000.00

FIXED CAPITAL

1. Land & Building	Rs.	62,00,000.00
2. Plant & Machinery	Rs.	20,00,000.00
3. Other Fixed Assets	Rs.	85,000.00
TOTAL	**Rs.**	**82,85,000.00**

RAW MATERIALS

1. Paddy required
2. Octroi, Taxes
3. Consumable stores eg. Packaging and Other expenses

TOTAL WORKING CAPITAL/MONTH

1. Raw Material	Rs.	10,50,000.00
2. Salary & Wages	Rs.	49,840.00
3. Utilities & Overheads	Rs.	1,85,000.00
TOTAL	**Rs.**	**12,84,840.00**

TOTAL CAPITAL INVESTMENT

Total Fixed Capital	Rs.	82,85,000.00
Total Working Capital For 2 Months	Rs.	25,69,680.00
TOTAL	**Rs.**	**1,08,54,680.00**

TURN OVER/ANNUM

1. By Sale of 3000 M.T. of Rice
2. By Sale of 260 MT of Bran

TOTAL	**Rs.**	**2,32,80,000.00**

PROFIT SALES RATIO = Profit / Sales x 100 = 23.84 %

RATE OF RETURN = Operating profit / T.C.I x 100 = 51.12 %

BREAK EVEN POINT (B.E.P) = 38.27 %

20

Plant Economics of Basmati Rice Trading

Capacity	=	90000 Mt/Annum
Land & Building (Land area 500 sq.mt.)	=	Rs. 15,25,000.00

PLANT & MACHINERY

1. Weighing Machines
2. Packaging & Scaling equipments

FIXED CAPITAL

1. Land & Building	Rs.	15,25,000.00
2. Plant & Machinery	Rs.	1,25,000.00
3. Other Fixed Assets	Rs.	85,000.00
TOTAL	**Rs.**	**17,35,000.00**

RAW MATERIALS

1. Basmati Rice
2. Packaging (Stout) Exp.
3. Transportation exp.
4. Shipment Charges
5. Miscellaneous Exp.

TOTAL WORKING CAPITAL/MONTH

1. Raw Material	Rs.	10,50,000.00

2. Salary and Wages	Rs.	32,500.00
3. Utilities & Overheads	Rs.	49,800.00
TOTAL	**Rs.**	**11,32,300.00**

TOTAL CAPITAL INVESTMENT

Total Fixed Capital	Rs.	17,35,000.00
Total Working Capital For 2 Months	Rs.	22,64,600.00
TOTAL	**Rs.**	**39,99,600.00**

TURN OVER/ANNUM

By Sale of 300 MT. of Basmati Rice	Rs.	1,87,50,000.00

PROFIT SALES RATIO = Profit / Sales x 100 = 24%

RATEOF RETURN = Operating profit / T.C.I x 100 = 113%

BREAK EVEN POINT (B.E.P) = 18.69 %

21

Plant Economics of Rice Sorting / Grading Plant

Capacity	=	3600 Tons/Annum
Land & Building (Land Area 750 sq.mtrs.)	=	Rs. 24,00,000.00

PLANT & MACHINERY

1. Roto Sifter separator
2. De Stoner cum Classifier
3. Versatile Plansifter
4. Length Grader
5. Precision Sizer
6. Sortex Cabin
7. Grain Color Sorter Color Master
8. Materials for Fabrication at site
9. Gear Boxes
10. Motors
11. Electrical Engineering Items
12. Other Items for Colour Sorting Machine
13. Platform Structure
14. Materials for civil works
15. Tools & Tackles
16. Sales Tax, P & F, Insurance, Cartage, Excise

FIXED CAPITAL

1. Land&Building	Rs.	24,00,000.00
2. Plant & Machinery	Rs.	83,26,000.00
3. Other Fixed Assets	Rs.	19,50,000.00
TOTAL	**Rs.**	**1,26,76,000.00**

RAW MATERIALS

1. Basmati Rice
2. Sheila Rice
3. Rice Packaging Bags

TOTAL WORKING CAPITAL/MONTH

1. Raw Material	Rs.	56,40,000.00
2. Salary and Wages	Rs.	1,98,702.00
3. Utilities & Overheads	Rs.	2,50,000.00
TOTAL	**Rs.**	**60,88,702.00**

TOTAL CAPITAL INVESTMENT

Total Fixed Capital	Rs.	1,26,76,000.00
Total Working Capital for 2 Months	Rs.	1,21,77,404.00
TOTAL	**Rs.**	**2,48,53,404.00**

TURN OVER/ANNUM

1. By Sale of Transparent Head rice (Basmati Rice)	1620 MT
2. By sale of Basmati Broken Rice (Middle Broken)	126 MT
3. By sale of Basmati Rice by Product	54 MT
4. By sale transparent Sheila (head - rice)	1620 MT
5. By sale of Sheila Rice (Middle - Broken)	126 MT
6. By sale of Sheila RIce 54 MT	
TOTAL	**Rs. 9,09,54,000.00**

PROFIT SALES RATIO = Profit / Sales x 100 = 14%

RATE OF RETURN = Operating profit / T.C.I x 100 = 51%

BREAK EVEN POINT (B.E.P) = 37%

15

Suppliers of Plant and Machineries

BOILERS: ELECTRIC

Shri Indtex Boiler Pvt. Ltd.
Plot No. 1601
GIDC Est., Phase-I
Naroda
Ahmedabad,
Gujarat-382330
India
TEL : +91(0)79 22823057
FAX : +91(0)79 22820047
E-mail: shiyug@wilnetonline.net

Alfa Entech (Guj.) Pvt. Ltd.
504, Suyojan
Hotel President Lane
Off C G Rd.
Navrangpura
Ahmedabad,
Gujarat-380009
India
TEL : +91(0)79 26426444
FAX : +91(0)79 26566106
E-mail: parikh@icenet.net

Energy Process Equipments
29 GIDC Indl. Est.
National Highway No. 8
Por Ramangamdi
Vadodara,
Gujarat-391243
India
TEL : +91(0)265 2830375
FAX : +91(0)265 2830975
E-mail: energyboiler@satyam.net

Fuelpac Boilers & Engg. Company (I) Pvt. Ltd.
H-94 Gujrati Soc.
Nehru Rd.
Vile Parle (E)
Mumbai,
Maharashtra-400057
India
TEL : +91(0)22 26112782
FAX : +91(0)22 26110475

Ross Thermal Systems Pvt. Ltd.
#5, Amir Terrace
Al-Ameen Soc.
Gultekdi Pune,
Maharashtra-411037
India
TEL : +91(0)20 24272293
FAX : +91(0)20 24269562

Enmax Systemz
Block C - 60B
Kalkaji
New Delhi,
NCT of Delhi-110019
India
TEL : +91(0)11 26447880
FAX : +91(0)11 26473243
E-mail: enmax@satyam.net.in

Heatex Boilers (India) Pvt. Ltd.
2nd Flr., 1
Motia Khan
Rani Jhansi Rd.
New Delhi,
NCT of Delhi-110055
India
TEL : +91(0)11 23530642
FAX : +91(0)11 23530645
E-mail: heatexboilers@rediffmail.com

Indcon Boilers Ltd.
D-170 Phase-I
Okhla Indl. Area
New Delhi,
NCT of Delhi-110020
India
TEL : +91(0)11 26811440
FAX : +91(0)11 26812425
E-mail: indcon@vsnl.com

BOILERS: GAS FIRED

Heatex Boilers (India) Pvt. Ltd.
2nd Flr., 1
Motia Khan
Rani Jhansi Rd.
New Delhi,
NCT of Delhi-110055
India
TEL : +91(0)11 23530642
FAX : +91(0)11 23530645
E-mail: heatexboilers@rediffmail.com

Kemtech International Ltd.
A-125 Shivalik
Malviya Ngr. P.O.
New Delhi,
NCT of Delhi-110017
India
TEL : +91(0)11 26688343
FAX : +91(0)11 26680899
E-mail: info@kemtech international.com

LG Thermoflo Systems Pvt. Ltd.
Ground Flr., Paigah Plaza
Basheer Bagh
Hyderabad,
Andhra Pradesh-500029
India
TEL : +91(0)40 23242468
E-mail: rk_lgindia@yahoo.com

Balkrishna Boilers Inds.
Plot No. 14
Jay Khodiyar Indl. Est.
Nr. Subhash Est.
Ramol Rd.
Ahmedabad,
Gujarat-380026
India
TEL : +91(0)79 25855883
E-mail: info@balkrishn.com

Alfa Entech (Guj.) Pvt. Ltd.
504, Suyojan
Hotel President Lane
Off C G Rd.
Navrangpura
Ahmedabad,
Gujarat-380009
India
TEL : +91(0)79 26426444
FAX : +91(0)79 26566106
E-mail: parikh@icenet.net

The Indian Sugar & General Engg. Corp. Industrial Machinery Divn.
Yamuna Nagar,
Haryana-135001
India
TEL : +91(0)1732 251700
FAX : +91(0)1732 251495
E-mail: exports@isgec.com

IMA Boilers Pvt. Ltd.
8/1 Meghal Indl.Est.
Devidayal Rd.
Mulund (W)
Mumbai,
Maharashtra-400080
India
TEL : +91(0)22 25602369
FAX : +91(0)22 25683220
E-mail: imaboilerspltd@yahoo.com

Cheema Boilers Ltd.
SCO 66
Phase-3B-2
Mohali,
Punjab-160059
India
TEL : +91(0)172 2220067
FAX : +91(0)172 2271691
E-mail: cheema@cha.i91.net

IBIL Tech Ltd.
47 Gandhi Ngr.
1st Main Rd. Adyar
Chennai,
Tamil Nadu-600020
India
TEL : +91(0)44 24910638
FAX : +91(0)44 24911283
E-mail: gnifluid@giasmd01.vsnl.net.in

ISGEC John Thompson
A-4 Sec. 24
Noida,
Uttar Pradesh-201301
India
TEL : +91(0)120 24524072
FAX : +91(0)120 24551686
E-mail: ijtsales@isgec.com

BOILERS: STEAM

Vacunair Engineering Company Pvt. Ltd.
Nr. Gujarat Bottling
Rakhial
Ahmedabad,
Gujarat-380023
India
TEL : +91(0)79 22747771
FAX : +91(0)79 22747770
E-mail: vadherad1@sancharnet.in

Indcon Boilers Ltd.
D-170 Phase-I
Okhla Indl. Area
New Delhi,
NCT of Delhi-110020
India
TEL : +91(0)11 26811440
FAX : +91(0)11 26812425
E-mail: indcon@vsnl.com

Vivek Chem-Fabs
Plot No. 71
Sect. 27A, 15/1 Mile Stone
Mathura Rd.
Faridabad,
Haryana-121003
India
TEL : +91(0)129 25274848
FAX : +91(0)129 28843308

Ambica Engg. Works
16/A, 1st Main,
Modi Hospital Rd.,
W.O.C Road, 2nd Stage.
Bangalore,
Karnataka-560086
India
TEL : +91(0)80 3495370
FAX : +91(0)80 3496120
E-mail: ambica_e_w@vsnl.com

Swaraj Engg. Industries
Camp Bazar
Kannur,
Kerala-670001
India
TEL : +91(0)4297 267245

Unicon Boilers (I) Pvt. Ltd.
581 M G Rd.
Indore,
Madhya Pradesh-452006
India
TEL : +91(0)731 2536442
FAX : +91(0)731 2536444

Asian Boiler Engineers Pvt. Ltd.
130-A Golanji Hill Rd.
Sewree
Mumbai,
Maharashtra-400015
India
TEL : +91(0)22 24131630
FAX : +91(0)22 24139624
E-mail: abengg@bom3.vsnl.net.in

Cheema Boilers Ltd.
SCO 66
Phase-3B-2
Mohali,
Punjab-160059
India
TEL : +91(0)172 2220067
FAX : +91(0)172 2271691
E-mail: cheema@cha.i91.net

ISGEC John Thompson
A-4 Sec. 24
Noida,
Uttar Pradesh-201301
India
TEL : +91(0)120 24524072
FAX : +91(0)120 24551686
E-mail: ijtsales@isgec.com

Esco Engg. Pvt. Ltd.
53/1 Garcha Rd.
Kolkata,
West Bengal-700019
India
TEL : +91(0)33 24745656
FAX : +91(0)33 24745656
E-mail: escoengineering@rediffmail.com

DRYERS: FOOD

Pragati Engineering Works
Plot No. 114 New Chikhloli
MIDC Ambernath,
Maharashtra-421505
India
TEL : +91(0)251 2687407
FAX : +91(0)251 2685054
E-mail: shantaflaker@vsnl.com

NSW India Ltd.
Plot No. 43, Sect. 34
EHTP Gurgaon,
Haryana-122001
India
TEL : +91(0)124 26371106
FAX : +91(0)124 26372859
E-mail: corporate@nswindia.com

Ultrafilter International, AG Branch Office
334, 14th Main Rd.
Rajmahal Vilas Extn.
Bangalore,
Karnataka-560080
India
TEL : +91(0)80 23612304
FAX : +91(0)80 23614128
E-mail: ufiag@vsnl.net

Enfab Industries Pvt. Ltd.
C-2, Shanthi Niwas
Mettuguda
Secunderabad,
Andhra Pradesh-500017
India
TEL : +91(0)40 27824343
FAX : +91(0)40 27830010
E-mail: enfabs@hd1.vsnl.net.in

Cool Connections
Shop No. F-39 & 40
LSC Mansarovar Garden
New Delhi,
NCT of Delhi-110015
India
TEL : +91(0)11 25109004
FAX : +91(0)11 25934156
E-mail: ajeetsuri@hotmail.com

SMID Engineering Co.
25-A Rama Park Bus Stop,
Nr. Medicine Factory
Uttam Ngr.
New Delhi,
NCT of Delhi-110059
India
TEL : +91(0)11 22351450
FAX : +91(0)11 25649879

Premium Engineers Pvt. Ltd.
603 Chinubhai Centre
Nehru Bridge Corner
Ashram Rd.
Ahmedabad,
Gujarat-380009
India
TEL : +91(0)79 26579293
FAX : +91(0)79 26577197
E-mail: premiumgroup@hotmail.com

Stadler Corporation
A-3/3 Surjit Singh
Compound, Shivaji Ngr.
Off Vakola Bridge
Santacruz (E)
Mumbai,
Maharashtra-400055
India
TEL : +91(0)22 26105212
FAX : +91(0)22 26105093
E-mail: stadler44@hotmail.com

Doris (India) Engineers Pvt. Ltd.
No. 389, 390
Arcot Rd.
Kodambakkam
Chennai,
Tamil Nadu-600024
India
TEL : +91(0)44 24801098
FAX : +91(0)44 24815652
E-mail: machines@dorisindia.com

Jay Kay Enterprises India (Regd.)
H-23-25 Sect. 9
Noida,
Uttar Pradesh-201301
India
TEL : +91(0)120 24557023
FAX : +91(0)120 24535045
E-mail: jaykayenterprises@hotmail.com

FORM, FILL & SEAL MACHINERY

EC Packaging Pvt. Ltd.
14/7 Milestone
Mathura Rd.
Faridabad,
Haryana-121003
India
TEL : +91(0)129 25277796
FAX : +91(0)129 25255602
E-mail: ecppl@del3.vsnl.net.in

Chaudhary Precision Mouldings
D-44/5 East Of Kailash
New Delhi,
NCT of Delhi-110065
India
TEL : +91(0)11 26435578
FAX : +91(0)11 26225293
E-mail: chaudhrypet@hotmail.com

New Indo International
135-A Begumpur
Malviya Ngr.
New Delhi,
NCT of Delhi-110017
India
TEL : +91(0)11 26683289
FAX : +91(0)11 26688290
E-mail: nii@ndf.vsnl.net.in

Bharati Trade & Engg. Enterprise
16, Gayatri Chmbrs.
Nr. GD High School
Krishnanagar Rd.
Saijpur Bogha
Ahmedabad,
Gujarat-382345
India
TEL : +91(0)79 22812291
FAX : +91(0)79 22823201

Abhilash Industries
Plot No. VI/80A
Devp. Plot
S. Kalamassery
Kochi,
Kerala-683109
India
TEL : +91(0)484 2544142
FAX : +91(0)484 2556628
E-mail: gempac@spectrum.co.in

Shivalaya Machinery Manufacturing Co.
1 Shivaji Ngr.,
B/h Hukumchand Mill
Vishranti Chouraha
Indore,
Madhya Pradesh-452003
India
TEL : +91(0)731 2530669
FAX : +91(0)731 2533274
E-mail: shivalaymcm@satyam.net.in

Frigmaires Engineers
Janta Indl. Est. Gala No. 8,
Opp. Phoenix Mill
Senapati Bapat Marg
Lower Parel
Mumbai,
Maharashtra-400013
India
TEL : +91(0)22 24945624
FAX : +91(0)22 22187750
E-mail: fe@vsnl.com

Global Packaging Systems
D-347 Sect. 10
Noida,
Uttar Pradesh-201301
India
TEL : +91(0)120 24518015
FAX : +91(0)120 24532229
E-mail: globalpack@mantraonline.com

Asian Power Cyclopes
Rochipura Majra
Dehradun,
Uttaranchal-248171
India
TEL : +91(0)135 2620488
FAX : +91(0)135 2620961
E-mail: asian@nde.vsnl.net.in

Sikri Packaging Corp.
44 Palace Court, 1
Kyd St.
Kolkata,
West Bengal-700016
India
TEL : +91(0)33 22298166
FAX : +91(0)33 23280475
E-mail: sikri@vsnl.com

New Indo International
135-A Begumpur
Malviya Ngr.
New Delhi,
NCT of Delhi-110017
India
TEL : +91(0)11 26683289
FAX : +91(0)11 26688290
E-mail: nii@ndf.vsnl.net.in

Nimco Engg. Corp.
M-14, Gali No. 2
Anand Parbat Indl. Area
New Delhi,
NCT of Delhi-110005
India
TEL : +91(0)11 25742228

Shreyas International
A-68 Brotherhood Soc.
Vikaspuri
New Delhi,
NCT of Delhi-110018
India
TEL : +91(0)11 25615706
FAX : +91(0)11 25615706
E-mail: shreyas.intl@sm5.sprintrpg.ems.vsnl.net.in

Unitek Packaging Systems
RZ-64/10
Tughlakabad Extn.
New Delhi,
NCT of Delhi-110019
India
TEL : +91(0)11 26412851
FAX : +91(0)11 26982628
E-mail: unitek@vsnl.com

Global Packaging Systems
D-347 Sect. 10
Noida,
Uttar Pradesh-201301
India
TEL : +91(0)120 24518015

FAX : +91(0)120 24532229
E-mail: globalpack@
mantraonline.com

L&M Automatics
60/7 Old Dal Mandi
Kanpur,
Uttar Pradesh-208001
India
TEL : +91(0)512 2208001
E-mail: lm_automatics@
rediffmail.com

Modern Engg. Works
B-47 Sect. 10
Noida,
Uttar Pradesh-201301
India
TEL : +91(0)118 24555778
FAX : +91(0)118 24520399

NS Packaging Pvt. Ltd.
C-69 Sect. 2
Noida,
Uttar Pradesh-201301
India
TEL : +91(0)120 24535119
FAX : +91(0)120 24514973
E-mail: nsindia@
mantraonline.com

Rado Packaging Machines Pvt. Ltd.
A-41 Sect. 10
Noida,
Uttar Pradesh-201301
India
TEL : +91(0)118 24555190
FAX : +91(0)118 24525699

Select Packaging Systems
F-43 Sect. 9
Noida,
Uttar Pradesh-201301
India
TEL : +91(0)120 24444512

Baba Packaging
9C/5
Nityanand Bagh
Chembur Camp
Mumbai,
Maharashtra-400074
India
TEL : +91(0)22 25572568
E-mail: sumitvidya@
yahoo.com

Gujrat Polypet
Plot No. A-261
Rd. No. 16-A
Wagle Indl. Est.
Thane,
Maharashtra-400604
India
TEL : +91(0)22 25831164
FAX : +91(0)22 25805899
E-mail: gujratpolypet@
vsnl.net

Gurdeep Packaging Machines
Harichand Mills
Compound
LBS Marg
Vikhroli (W)
Mumbai,
Maharashtra-400079
India
TEL : +91(0)22 25783521

Hassia Redatron Packaging Machinery Pvt. Ltd. An IWKA Group Company
Gat No. 768/3
Sanaswadi
Shirur,
Maharashtra-412207
India
TEL : +91(0)8254 253211
FAX : +91(0)8254 253206
E-mail: redatron_india@
vsnl.com

HB Engg.
118, Gobind Udyog
Bhawan
Bal Rajeshwar Rd.
Mulund (W)
Mumbai,
Maharashtra-400080
India
TEL : +91(0)22 25603491
FAX : +91(0)22 25688916
E-mail: pacwel@bom7.
vsnl.net.in

Interpack Machines Pvt. Ltd.
44/5 Nav Sahyadri Soc.
Pune,
Maharashtra-411052
India
TEL : +91(0)20 25439475
FAX : +91(0)20 25411633
E-mail: interpack@vsnl.net

GRAIN CLEANING MILLS

Indopol Food Processing Machinery Pvt. Ltd.
Indl. Plot No.28
Sect. 27-C
Faridabad,
Haryana-121003
India
TEL : +91(0)129 25276161
FAX : +91(0)129 25720549
E-mail: info@indopol.com

Khalsa Metallic Fabrics
D-10 Focal Point
Rajpura,
Punjab-140401
India
TEL : +91(0)1762 224290

Kovai Engg. Works
88 Iyer Hospital Rd.
Souripalayam P.O.
Coimbatore,
Tamil Nadu-641028
India
TEL : +91(0)422 2316456

Airex Engineering
129 Babaji Est.
B/h Bhiksuk Gruh
Odhav
Ahmedabad,
Gujarat-382415
India
TEL : +91(0)79 22970055
FAX : +91(0)79 22876872
E-mail: airexengg@
indiatimes.com

Premium Engineers Pvt. Ltd.
603 Chinubhai Centre
Nehru Bridge Corner
Ashram Rd.
Ahmedabad,
Gujarat-380009
India
TEL : +91(0)79 26579293
FAX : +91(0)79 26577197
E-mail: premiumgroup@hotmail.com

GRAINING DRYER

Bry-Air (Asia) Pvt. Ltd.
21C Sect. 18
Gurgaon,
Haryana-122015
India
TEL : +91(0)124 28991111
FAX : +91(0)124 28991100
E-mail: enquire@pahwa.com

Mathesis Engineers Pvt. Ltd.
Plot No. B-35, Bhel AIE
R C Puram
Hyderabad,
Andhra Pradesh-500032
India
TEL : +91(0)40 23022298
FAX : +91(0)40 23020628

Cool Connections
Shop No. F-39 & 40
LSC Mansarovar Garden
New Delhi,
NCT of Delhi-110015
India
TEL : +91(0)11 25109004
FAX : +91(0)11 25934156
E-mail: ajeetsuri@hotmail.com

Mojj Engineering Systems Ltd.
81-B/15 MIDC
Bhosari
Pune,
Maharashtra-411026
India
TEL : +91(0)20 27120360
FAX : +91(0)20 27122836
E-mail: mojjpune@vsnl.net

Sharpenn Technologies Pvt. Ltd.
P.O. Box No. 19
Shanmugananda, D-56,
MIDC B/h London Pilsner
Nerul Navi Mumbai,
Maharashtra-400706
India
TEL : +91(0)22 27907201
FAX : +91(0)22 27907205
E-mail: subra@bom3.vsnl.net.in

Commerce Corporation
A-22, Anurag
Shivram Soc.
Devidayal Rd.
Mulund (W)
Mumbai,
Maharashtra-400080
India
TEL : +91(0)22 25676956
FAX : +91(0)22 25676956
E-mail: kumar812@hotmail.com

RICE MILLS

Kiran Engineering Works
111 Ajay Bizli Mkt.,
2865/66 Shah Ganj
G B Rd.
Delhi,
NCT of Delhi-110009
India
TEL : +91(0)11 23219310
FAX : +91(0)11 23210002
E-mail: kewbbb@vsnl.net.in

Vashisht Food Pvt. Ltd.
315, Ambika Vihar
Paschim Vihar
New Delhi,
NCT of Delhi-110087
India
TEL : +91(0)11 25271636
FAX : +91(0)11 25672639

Central Engineering Corporation
Bhaktinagar Stn. Rd.
P.O. Box 540 & 104
Bhaktinagar
Rajkot,
Gujarat-360002
India
TEL : +91(0)281 2462003
FAX : +91(0)281 2461590
E-mail: centralengg01@hotmail.com

Forsberg Agritech (I) Pvt. Ltd.
123 GIDC Est.
Makarpura
Vadodara,
Gujarat-390010
India
TEL : +91(0)265 2645752
FAX : +91(0)265 2641583
E-mail: forsagri@satyam.net.in

Gujarat Castings
233, Adovaiya Est
Gheekantha Rd.
Ahmedabad,
Gujarat-380015
India
TEL : +91(0)79 25620263
FAX : +91(0)79 25625570
E-mail: gujratcastings@im.eth.net

Amira India
P.O. Box No. 8
12/7 Urban Est.
Gurgaon,
Haryana-122001
India
TEL : +91(0)124 26373010
FAX : +91(0)124 26322997
E-mail: septu@del3.vsnl.net.in

Flow Tech Engineering Pvt. Ltd.
16/5 Mathura Rd.
Faridabad,
Haryana-121001
India
TEL : +91(0)129 25263017
FAX : +91(0)129 25291556

Indopol Food Processing Machinery Pvt. Ltd.
Indl. Plot No.28
Sect. 27-C
Faridabad,
Haryana-121003
India
TEL : +91(0)129 25276161
FAX : +91(0)129 25720549
E-mail: info@indopol.com

Ramani Automation Systems Pvt. Ltd.
140 Phase-II
Indl. Area Panchkula,
Haryana-134113
India
TEL : +91(0)172 2592105
FAX : +91(0)172 2591971
E-mail: ramani_engg@hotmail.com

Septu (India) Pvt. Ltd.
"Septu House", 12/7
P.O. Box 4 Urban Est.
Gurgaon,
Haryana-122001
India
TEL : +91(0)124 26373010
FAX : +91(0)124 26322997
E-mail: septu@del3.vsnl.net.in

Saboo Stone Flour Mills Pvt. Ltd.
10/5 New Palasia
Indore,
Madhya Pradesh-452001
India
TEL : +91(0)731 2432562
FAX : +91(0)731 2433239
E-mail: sabstone@bom4.vsnl.net.in

Western India Mfg Co.
Opp. Narayan Kothi
Dr. R S Bhandari Marg
Indore,
Madhya Pradesh-452003
India
TEL : +91(0)731 2431541

Garima Global Enterprises
215 Ruby Indl. Est.
Off New Link Rd.
Malad (W)
Mumbai,
Maharashtra-400064
India
TEL : +91(0)22 28771656
FAX : +91(0)22 28765693
E-mail: garima@bom3.vsnl.net.in

Majestic Auto Components
D-8/9 Focal Point
Rajpura,
Punjab-140401
India
TEL : +91(0)1762 2424276

Nayyar Belting House (Regd.)
Gurudwara Dukh
Niwaran Rd.
Ludhiana,
Punjab-141008
India
TEL : +91(0)161 2663954
FAX : +91(0)161 2607591

Navdeep Products
123-124 Nr. Pital Factory
Pink City Tower
Jaipur,
Rajasthan-302016
India
TEL : +91(0)141 2304006
FAX : +91(0)141 2304006

Sabko Industries
Sanatorium Rd. Madar
Ajmer,
Rajasthan-305024
India
TEL : +91(0)145 2429750
FAX : +91(0)145 2426684
E-mail: sabko@sabko.com

Synthetic Stones
E-24 Marudhar Indl. Area,
Phase-II Basni
Jodhpur,
Rajasthan-342005
India
TEL : +91(0)291 2740904
FAX : +91(0)291 2742329

Sri Rudran Instruments Co.
56 Vaikundapuram
2nd St.
Nungambakkam
Chennai,
Tamil Nadu-600034
India
TEL : +91(0)44 28172803
FAX : +91(0)44 28175843
E-mail: srico@satyam.net.in

AVR Engg.
83 Rajalakshmi Ngr. St.,
TVS Ngr.
Edayarpalayam P.O.
Coimbatore,
Tamil Nadu-641025
India
TEL : +91(0)422 2401129

Binny Engg. Ltd.
P. O. Box 8677
Meenambakkam
Chennai,
Tamil Nadu-600114
India
TEL : +91(0)44 22341151
FAX : +91(0)44 22345251
E-mail: bew@vsnl.com

Navinchandra & Co.
179, Navin House
Thambu St.
Chennai,
Tamil Nadu-600001
India
TEL : +91(0)44 25228675
FAX : +91(0)44 25229450
E-mail: navin@mds.vsnl.net.in

Newtec Milling Pvt. Ltd.
450/1
G K Indl. Est.
Porur
Chennai,
Tamil Nadu-600116
India
TEL : +91(0)44 24767320
FAX : +91(0)44 24769697

Sree Balaji Industries
283 Dr. Ambedkar Rd.
Velandipalayam
Coimbatore,
Tamil Nadu-641025
India
TEL : +91(0)422 2430510
FAX : +91(0)422 2301598

SS Engg. Products
SF No. 461
Maruthamalai Gounder Layout
Sakthi Main Rd.
Ganapathy
Coimbatore,
Tamil Nadu-641006
India
TEL : +91(0)422 2531564

St. Johns Engg. Works
Thaneerpandal
V K Rd.
Peelamedu
Coimbatore,
Tamil Nadu-641004
India
TEL : +91(0)422 2573792
FAX : +91(0)422 2570310
E-mail: kuruvila@md3.vsnl.net.in

Gurucharan Engg. Works
142 Indl. Est.
Nunhai
Agra,
Uttar Pradesh-282006
India
TEL : +91(0)562 2345452

Mukul Enterprises
Mala Roller Flour Mills Compound
Delhi Rd.
Partapur
Meerut,
Uttar Pradesh-250103
India
TEL : +91(0)121 2512284
FAX : +91(0)121 2514714
E-mail: mukuletp@vsnl.com

Somnath Industries
B-21 Foundry Ngr.
Agra,
Uttar Pradesh-282006
India
TEL : +91(0)562 2344110
FAX : +91(0)562 2345050
E-mail: sommark@sancharnet.in

AT Mohsin & Co.
P.O. Box 2736, 71/B
N S Rd.
Kolkata,
West Bengal-700001
India
TEL : +91(0)33 22433777
FAX : +91(0)33 22252319
E-mail: firozukani@sify.com

GG Agro Products Pvt. Ltd.
25, Marshall House,
Room No. 653
Strand Rd.
Kolkata,
West Bengal-700001
India
TEL : +91(0)33 22200876
FAX : +91(0)33 22200769

Grain Processing Industries (I) Pvt. Ltd.
Mohta House, 1st Flr.
29 Strand Rd.
Kolkata,
West Bengal-700001
India
TEL : +91(0)33 22431639
FAX : +91(0)33 22204508
E-mail: grainpro@cal3.vsnl.net.in

Baba Auto Mechanical Works
1-1-186/A/4
Charminar Cross Rd.
Hyderabad,
Andhra Pradesh-500020
India
TEL : +91(0)40 27636297

Circars Lakshmi Mill Stores
Machinery Merchants
Convent St.
Vijayawada,
Andhra Pradesh-520001
India
TEL : +91(0)866 2424642
FAX : +91(0)866 2420034
E-mail: circars1@rediffmail.com

Farm Steel Products
Indl. Est. Vijayawada,
Andhra Pradesh-520007
India
TEL : +91(0)866 2553958
FAX : +91(0)866 2555358

Hardcase Engineering Works Pvt. Ltd.
Plot No. P/10/1 IDA
Nacharam
Hyderabad,
Andhra Pradesh-500007
India
TEL : +91(0)40 27534446
FAX : +91(0)40 27535567
E-mail: hardcase@hd2.dot.net.in

Intel Systems
5-234/2 H P Rd.
Moosapet
Hyderabad,
Andhra Pradesh-500018
India
TEL : +91(0)40 23711379
FAX : +91(0)40 23713567
E-mail: intelarch@mantraonline.com

Raghavendra Innovative Industries
3-55 Gopal Puram
Hanmakonda,
Andhra Pradesh-506015
India
TEL : +91(0)8712 2565669

ROASTERS BEANS & CEREAL GRAIN & NUT

Ace Pack Machines
55 Sri Lakshmi Ngr.
Nava India Rd., Opp.
Hindustan College
Sowripalayam
Coimbatore,
Tamil Nadu-641028
India
TEL : +91(0)422 2562386
FAX : +91(0)422 2568212
E-mail: acepack@
satyam.net.in

Acufil Machines
S.F. 120/2
Kalpatty P.O.
Coimbatore,
Tamil Nadu-641035
India
TEL : +91(0)422 2866108
FAX : +91(0)422 2866255
E-mail: acufil@
md4.vsnl.net.in

Apnaa Industries
M-2 Indl. Est.
Guindy
Chennai,
Tamil Nadu-600032
India
TEL : +91(0)44 22340963
FAX : +91(0)44 22331107
E-mail: apna@
md3.vsnl.net.in

Durai Industrial Works
1143 Mettupalayam Rd.
Coimbatore,
Tamil Nadu-641043
India
TEL : +91(0)422 2442380
FAX : +91(0)422 2444453
E-mail: duro@eth.net

KLRF Sheet Metal Industries
SRKV Post
Perianaickenpalayam
Coimbatore,
Tamil Nadu-641020
India
TEL : +91(0)422 2692102
FAX : +91(0)422 2693741
E-mail: klrfsmi@vsnl.com

Sree Valsa Engg. Works
36 Nandanagar Rd.
Singanallur
Coimbatore,
Tamil Nadu-641005
India
TEL : +91(0)422 2574268
E-mail: sreevals@
epatna.com

SP Engg.
E-53 Sect. 7
Noida,
Uttar Pradesh-201301
India
TEL : +91(0)120 24529703
E-mail: sp_engg@
hotmail.com

Mechem Engineering Works
Plot No.J-80 MIDC
Bhosari
Pune,
Maharashtra-411026
India
TEL : +91(0)20 27120903
FAX : +91(0)20 2780239

SEPARATORS DUST

Thermax Ltd. Enviro Divn.
D-13 MIDC Indl. Area
Chinchwad
Pune,
Maharashtra-411019
India
TEL : +91(0)20 27475941
FAX : +91(0)20 27440845
E-mail: dbhanja@
thermaxindia.com

Vascon Engineering Equipments
C-31/1 Indl. Est.
(Nr. SBH, Opp. RMSC
Stockyard)
Sanathnagar
Hyderabad,
Andhra Pradesh-500018
India
TEL : +91(0)40 23708586
FAX : +91(0)40 23708586
E-mail: vasconengg@
yahoo.com

Airfilt Technologies Pvt. Ltd.
C-51 B/h Rajdhani College
Bali Ngr.
New Delhi,
NCT of Delhi-110015
India
TEL : +91(0)11 25162303
FAX : +91(0)11 25432191
E-mail: airfilt@sify.com

Airex Engineering
129 Babaji Est.
B/h Bhiksuk Gruh
Odhav
Ahmedabad,
Gujarat-382415
India
TEL : +91(0)79 22970055
FAX : +91(0)79 22876872
E-mail: airexengg@
indiatimes.com

Abbott Air Systems
Plot No. 28 Sect. 27A
Mathura Rd.
Faridabad,
Haryana-121002
India
TEL : +91(0)129 25778572
FAX : +91(0)129 25271574
E-mail: abbott@id.eth.net

Metallizing Wires & Conductors
C-433 Phase-II
MIA Basni
Jodhpur,
Rajasthan-342005
India
TEL : +91(0)291 2741011
FAX : +91(0)291 2741014
E-mail: metallizing@
vsnl.com

ARF Engg. Ltd.
4-C/2, Devp. Plot
Indl. Est.
3rd Main Rd.
Ambattur
Chennai,
Tamil Nadu-600058
India
TEL : +91(0)44 26250312
FAX : +91(0)44 26258099
E-mail: art2000in@yahoo.com

Manmachine (India) Pvt. Ltd.
E-98 Sect. 6
Noida,
Uttar Pradesh-201301
India
TEL : +91(0)120 24422725
FAX : +91(0)120 24422303
E-mail: info@manmachineindia.com

WEIGHING AND PACKAGING MACHINERY

Kalsi Micro Measurements & Instrumentation Pvt. Ltd.
K-35 Site-III
Panki Indl. Area
Kanpur,
Uttar Pradesh-208022
India
TEL : +91(0)512 2691971
FAX : +91(0)512 2691628
E-mail: kalsi_micro@sify.com

Optima Novel Packaging Technologies
5-9-22/19-315
Adarshnagar
Hyderabad,
Andhra Pradesh-500063
India
TEL : +91(0)40 23298020
FAX : +91(0)40 23298020
E-mail: optima@pol.net.in

Aprotech Engineers Pvt. Ltd.
1573 Sect. 7E
Faridabad,
Haryana-121006
India
TEL : +91(0)129 25242140
FAX : +91(0)129 25243452
E-mail: aprotech@vsnl.com

Jasubhai Richard Simon Ltd.
101-103, Thacker Towers,
Plot No. 86 Sect.-17
Vashi
Navi Mumbai,
Maharashtra-400703
India
TEL : +91(0)22 27893822
FAX : +91(0)22 27898824
E-mail: dave@vsgrp.com

Vikaash Packaging
120 Mugappair Rd.
Padi
Chennai,
Tamil Nadu-600050
India
TEL : +91(0)44 26521703
FAX : +91(0)44 26521703
E-mail: rvs@eth.net

Unique Machine Company Pvt. Ltd.
2, 4th Flr., Commerce House
G C Avenue
Kolkata,
West Bengal-700013
India
TEL : +91(0)33 22155441
FAX : +91(0)33 22155441
E-mail: unimac@cal2.vsnl.net.in

23

Suppliers of Packaging Materials

JUTE BAGS

Capital Laminators Pvt. Ltd.
190, Ram Darbar
Phase-II Indl. Area
Chandigarh,
Chandigarh (UT)-160055
India
TEL : +91(0)172 2653093

Arts N Crafts
C-157 Indl. Area, Phase-I
Naraina
New Delhi,
NCT of Delhi-110028
India
TEL : +91(0)11 25794977
FAX : +91(0)11 25797239
E-mail: ancdel@hotmail.com

Bansal Auto Spares
8815 Raja Lane
Nr. Krishna Battery,
Sidhpura
New Rohtak Rd.
New Delhi,
NCT of Delhi-110005
India
TEL : +91(0)11 23512149
E-mail: bansauto@vsnl.com

Deep Enterprises
School Rd.
Village Badli
Delhi,
NCT of Delhi-110042
India
TEL : +91(0)11 27293760

Jutex
Joshi Building, 2nd Flr.
Vasco-Da-Gama
Goa,
Goa-403802
India
TEL : +91(0)832 2512421

Atlas Laminate Industries
525/526
Nr. Grid Stn.
Indl. Area
Odhav
Ahmedabad,
Gujarat-382415
India
TEL : +91(0)79 22872032
FAX : +91(0)79 22872981

Norquest Brands Pvt. Ltd.
Norquest House
Nr. Lions Hall
Udhyan Marg
Mithakhali
Ahmedabad,
Gujarat-380006
India
TEL : +91(0)79 26463331
FAX : +91(0)79 26569140
E-mail: rajiv@badlani.com

South Bihar Plastic Pvt. Ltd.
Chowk Bazar
Jugsalal
Jamshedpur,
Jharkhand-831006
India
TEL : +91(0)657 2434512
FAX : +91(0)657 2433413
E-mail: sbpp1@rediffmail.com

Kollanoor Industries
37/1817
Azad Rd. (S) End
Kaloor
Kochi,
Kerala-682017
India
TEL : +91(0)484 2345314
FAX : +91(0)484 2349784

PKAL Jute Industries
Salman Manzil
Chembumuke
BMC P.O.
Kakkanad
Kochi,
Kerala-682021
India
TEL : +91(0)484 2424114

Allinace Marketing
2 Brijeshwari Area
Kanadia Rd.
Indore,
Madhya Pradesh-452001

India
TEL : +91(0)731 2592987
FAX : +91(0)731 2592987

Dalal Industries
"Dhairyavir", 41
Presidency Soc.
8th Rd., JVPD Scheme
Juhu
Mumbai,
Maharashtra-400049
India
TEL : +91(0)22 26206270
FAX : +91(0)22 26253169
E-mail: vffi@hotmail.com

Gunny Gujarat
5, Shriji Apt.
Opp. Hotel Pooja
Ghatkopar (E)
Mumbai,
Maharashtra-400077
India
TEL : +91(0)22 25157965

Jamnadas Lakhmidas & Co.
Ground Flr.,
13, Krishna Niwas, 305
Yusuf Meherali Rd.
Mumbai,
Maharashtra-400003
India
TEL : +91(0)22 23427027
FAX : +91(0)22 23430278
E-mail: nthakker@
vsnl.com

Jaybharat Gunny Co.
61-A Dr. Atmaram
Merchant Rd.
Bhuleshwar
Mumbai,
Maharashtra-400002
India
TEL : +91(0)22 22013601
FAX : +91(0)22 22401875
E-mail: jbgunny@
bom3.vsnl.net.in

Jodhpur Bags (Regd.)
Near Akhalia Crossing
K N Ngr. Rd.
Jodhpur,
Rajasthan-342001
India
TEL : +91(0)291 2756555
FAX : +91(0)291 2612307
E-mail: kishorlaxman@
yahoo.com

Shekhawati Export
A-252 Vidyut Ngr.
Ajmer Rd.
Jaipur,
Rajasthan-302013
India
TEL : +91(0)141 2351196
FAX : +91(0)141 2302364

Carrtel Exports
10 Raja St.
T Ngr.
Chennai,
Tamil Nadu-600017
India
TEL : +91(0)44 24344953
FAX : +91(0)44 24313398
E-mail: ksmanic@
md3.vsnl.net.in

Maris Associates Pvt. Ltd.
6T/1 North Cotton Rd.
Tuticorin,
Tamil Nadu-628001
India
TEL : +91(0)461 2326709
FAX : +91(0)461 2326446

Raj Kamal Lamination
Krishna Ngr.
Meerut Rd.
Ghaziabad,
Uttar Pradesh-201001
India
TEL : +91(0)120 24721592

Khadi Sadan
BA/18B Phase-I
Ashok Vihar
New Delhi,
NCT of Delhi-110052
India
TEL : +91(0)11 27247837
FAX : +91(0)11 27242427
E-mail: saritatrehan@
hotmail.com

Manu International
C-44B Shivaji Park
Punjabi Bagh
New Delhi,
NCT of Delhi-110026
India
TEL : +91(0)11 25429845
FAX : +91(0)11 25110887
E-mail: manu@
nde.vsnl.net.in

Shyam Jute Industries
1720, Pilikothi
S P Mukherjee Marg
Naya Bazar
Delhi,
NCT of Delhi-110006
India
TEL : +91(0)11 23944305
FAX : +91(0)11 23946960

Swastik Poly-Coat Industries
402, Express Tower
Comml. Cmplx.
Azadpur
Delhi,
NCT of Delhi-110033
India
TEL : +91(0)11 27113461
FAX : +91(0)11 27431743

The Hans
98-A Pocket-C,
Nr. Ashram Chowk
Sidharth Extn.
New Delhi,
NCT of Delhi-110014
India
TEL : +91(0)11 26903527
FAX : +91(0)11 26903529
E-mail: hansjute@usa.net

SK Industries
E-120 Indl. Area
B S Rd.
Ghaziabad,
Uttar Pradesh-201001
India
TEL : +91(0)120 24700305
FAX : +91(0)120 24701112

Agmo International
4th Flr., 22
Brabourne Rd.
Kolkata,

West Bengal-700001
India
TEL : +91(0)33 22250655
FAX : +91(0)33 22259013

TEL : +91(0)33 22436401
FAX : +91(0)33 22202260
E-mail: alliance@cal2.vsnl.net.in

Secunderabad,
Andhra Pradesh-500003
India
TEL : +91(0)40 26216251

Alliance Mills (Lessees) Ltd.
18 N S Rd.
Kolkata,
West Bengal-700001
India

Hyderabad Enterprises
2-4-495, Door No. 513
Nr. New Maharashtra Tower
Ramgopalpet

Vijaya Industries
P9/19 Indl. Est.
Nacharam
Hyderabad,
Andhra Pradesh-500076
India
TEL : +91(0)40 27153044

117. MANUFACTURE OF TIN CONTAINERS
118. MANUFACTURE OF STORAGE TANKS, PRESSURE VESSELS, HEAT EXCHANGERS
119. MARK II HAND PUMPS
120. MARUTI WORKSHOP CUM - SERVICE STATION
121. MECHANICAL JACKS
122. METAL CUTTING DIE DESIGN
123. METAL CUTTING OF AND GRINDING WHEELS (ABBRASIVE CUTTING WHEELS)
124. METAL HOOKS & CLIPS
125. METAL SEPARATION (COPPER, TIN, LEAD) FROM SPENT WASH ACID
126. METALLIC RING JOINTS
127. METALLIC GASKET (SPIRAL WOUND)
128. MICROVEE & ABSOLUTE FILTER
129. MICROWAVE OVEN
130. MILD STEEL INGOTS
131. MINI STEEL PLANT
132. MODERN VEHICLE WORKSHOP
133. MOPED
134. M.S.HINGES
135. M.S.INGOT AND HR. STEEL STRUCTURALS
136. M.S.INGOT BY INDUCTION FURNACES
137. M.S.PIPES
138. M.S. WELDING ELECTRODE
139. MUFFLERS & SILENCERS FOR THREE WHEELERS
140. NAIL CUTTER WITH FILER & MANICURE
141. NICHROME WIRE
142. NICKEL LINED SCREENS
143. NON-FERROUS ALLOY ROLLING
144. NON-FERROUS FORGING
145. NON-FERROUS FOUNDRY
146. NON PRESSURE
147. INCANDESCENT LAMP
148. NUMBER COMBINATION LOCKS FOR LUGGAGES
149. NUTS & BOLTS
150. PAPER COATED ALUMINIUM AND COPPER WIRE
151. PETROMAX CONTAINER
152. PHOTO ETCHING OF STAINLESS STEEL PLATES
153. PIPE GALVANIZING PLANT
154. PISTON RING-AUTOMOBILE
155. PLANT PROTECTION EQUIPMENTS
156. PLATINUM LABORATORY APPARATUS
157. PRESSURE COOKER & ALUMINIUM UTENSILS
158. PRESSURE COOKER (ALUMINIUM)
159. PRESSURE DIE CASTING
160. PRINTED ALUMINIUM COLLAPSIBLE TUBES
161. PRINTED TIN CONTAINERS
162. PRINTING PRESS (CYLINDER MACHINE)
163. PUMPS FOR CHEMICAL INDUSTRY (SPECIAL)
164. RAILWAY SLEEPERS (M.S.)
165. RAZOR TWIN BLADE
166. R.C.C SPUN PIPES
167. RECONDITIONING OF M.S. DRUMS/BARRELS
168. RE-ROLLING COPPER AND BRASS SHEET AND RODS
169. RE-ROLLING MILLS
170. RESIN COATED SAND
171. RESIN CORED SOFT SOLDER WIRES
172. ROLLING MILL (BY INDUCTION FURNACE) & MANUFACTURE OF BARS, ANGLES, SQUARES, TUBES AND OTHERS
173. ROLLER BEARING & FORGING
174. ROLLING OF STAINLESS STEEL PATTA
175. RUBBER INSULATED PLIERS (HAND TOOLS)
176. RUBBING COMPOUND FOR AUTOMOBILES
177. SCIENTIFIC LABORATORY EQUIPMENTS
178. SCOOTER ASSEMBLING
179. SECONDARY LEAD EXTRAC-TION BY SCRAP BATTERY PLATES,PIPES & SHEET
180. SEAMLESS M.S. TUBES & PIPES
181. SELF TAPPING STEEL SCREW
182. SEWING NEEDLES
183. S.G. IRON & ALLOY STEEL
184. SHEET METAL PRODUCTS, (FERROUS/NON-FERROUS)
185. SHIP/MARINE CONTAINER
186. SHOCK ABSORBERS
187. SHOE EYELETS
188. SHOT AND GRITS BY AUTOMIZATION PROCESS
189. SHOVELS
190. SILICO MANGANESE ALLOYS
191. SILENCERS (MUFFLERS) EXHAUST & TAIL PIPE FOR ALL TYPES OF VEHICLES
192. SINTERED BEARING
193. SINTERED BUSHES
194. SINTERED METAL PRODUCTS
195. SOFT AND HARD FERRITES
196. SPANNERS
197. SPARK PLUGS
198. STEEL PLANT (ELECTRIC ARC FURNACE BASED- EAF)
199. SPHERIODAL GRAPHITE CAST IRON
200. SPRAY DRYER
201. STAINLESS STEEL HINGES
202. STAINLESS STEEL SHEET ROLLING TO PRODUCE STAINLESS STEEL UTENSILS
203. STAINLESS STEEL UTENSILS
204. STAPLE PINS,PAPER PIN, GEM CLIPS ETC.
205. STEEL CASTINGS
206. STEEL CHAIN
207. STEEL FOUNDRY
208. STEEL FURNITURES AND ELECTRICAL APPLIANCES
209. STEEL PLANT (MINI)
210. STEEL RODS AND COILS FROM SCRAPS
211. STEEL ROLLING MILL
212. STEEL STRIPS (COLD ROLLED) SILICON WITH GRAIN RIENTED FOR ELECTRIC USE
213. STEEL TRANSMISSION LINE TOWERS & ROLLING MILL TO PRODUCE STEEL SECTION
214. STEEL FURNITURES AND ELECTRICAL APPLIANCES
215. STEEL WIRE DRAWING AND GALVANIZING
216. STEEL WOOL
217. SUBMERGED ARC WELDED PIPES
218. SUBMERSIBLE PUMP MANUFACTURING
219. SUPER ENAMELLED COPPER WIRE
220. THREE WHEELERS
221. TIE-ROD ENDS
222. TIN CONTAINERS
223. TOOLROOM AND SHEET METAL PRODUCTS
224. TRACTOR TRAILERS
225. TRANSMISSION POWER FITTING
226. TUBULAR POLES
227. SUPER ENAMELLED COPPER WIRES
228. TUBULAR POLES FOR ELECTRICAL TRANSMISSION (BY FABRICATION PROCESS)
229. TUBULAR POLES OF M.S. & HIGH TENSILE STEEL
230. VACUUM CLEANERS
231. VACUUM FLASK (STAINLESS STEEL)
232. VALVES FOR REFRIGERATION AND AIR-CONDITION
233. VEHICLE WELDING & PAINTING
234. VENETION BLIND
235. WASHING MACHINES (AUTOMATIC & COMPUTERISED)
236. WATER CONTROLLER (AUTOMATIC)
237. WATCH STRAPS/CHAINS/ BRACELETS/BELT BRASS & STAINLESS STEEL
238. WATER COOLERS
239. WELDED WIRE MESH
240. WELDING ELECTRODES
241. WICK STOVES
242. WIND MILL WINDOW FRAME (FERROUS & NON-FERROUS)
243. WRIST WATCH

359. DI ETHYL OXALATE
360. DI METHYL ORTHOPHTHALATE
361. DI-METHYL PHTHALATE
362. DICLOFENAC GEL
363. DIOCTYL PHTHALATE (DOP)
364. DI PHENYL GLYCERINE
365. DI PHENYL OXIDE
366. DINITRO-CHLORO BENZENE
367. DISTILLED WATER
368. DODECYL BENZENE SULPHONATE
369. DUSTLESS CHALK
370. EDTA & ITS SALTS
371. ELECTROLESS NICKEL PLATING ON PLASTICS
372. ENDOSULFAN
373. EPOXY RESIN BASED COMPOUND
374. ETHYL ACETATE
375. EHTYL ETHER
376. ETHYL ALCOHOL (POTABLE LIQUOR)
377. ETHYL HEXANOL
378. EXTRACTION OF ESSENTIAL OILS BY SUGAR CRITICAL FLUID (CARBON DIOXIDE) METHOD FROM FLOWERS, HERBAL & SPICES
379. FERRIC ALUM
380. FERRO CHROME LIGNO SULPHONATE
381. FERRO MANGANESE
382. FERRO SILICONE
383. FERRO VANADIUM FROM VANADIUM SLUDGE
384. FERROUS SILICATE
385. FERROUS SULPHATE
386. FERTILIZER FROM ANIMAL BLOOD & LEATHER WASTE
387. FLUORESCENT TUBE LIGHT POWDER
388. FOAMED PVC COMPOUNDING & ITS PRODUCTS
389. FORMALDEHYDE
390. FRACTIONAL DISTILLATION OF D.M.O (DEMENTHOLIZED OIL)
391. FRACTIONAL DISTILLATION OF ESSENTIAL OIL & MEDICINAL PLANT EXTRACT
392. FRICTION DUST (LIQUID & POWDER) FROM CNSL
393. FRUIT FLAVOURS
394. FURFURAL FROM RICE HUSK
395. GARLIC ACID
396. GASKET SHELLAC COMPOUND
397. GEAR OIL
398. GIBBERELLIC ACID
399. GLASS PUTTY
400. GLYCERINE
401. GOSSYPOL (POLY PHENOL) FROM COTTON SEED OIL
402. GUAR GUM POWDER
403. HAIR FIXER (HAIR GEL TYPE)
404. H - ACID
405. HENNA PASTE MAKING
406. HEPTAL DEHYDE
407. HIGH CARBON FERRO CHROME
408. HYDRATED CALCIUM SILICATE BRICK
409. HYDRATED LIME FROM SEA SHELL
410. HYDROCHLORIC ACID
411. HYDRO FLUORIC ACID
412. HYDROGEN PEROXIDE (BY AUTO-OXIDATION PROCESS)
413. ICE PACKS (SOLUTIONS TYPE, WHITE GEL TYPE, VIOLET SEMI SOLID POLYMER TYPE)
414. IMPROVING DROP POINT PARAFFIN WAX FROM 45-50°C TO 75-80°C
415. INDUSTRIAL ALCOHOL
416. INTEGERATED COMPLEX OF EASTER & ALLIED PRODUCTS (D.O.P, D.B.P, ETHYL ACETATE WIRE ENAMEL & CABLE JELLY)
417. IMFL (WHISKY) & COUNTRY LIQUOR
418. IRON OXIDE FOR MAKING FERITTE
419. IRON SULPHIDE
420. JUTE BATCHING OIL
421. KESH KALA TEL (HAIR DYE LOTION) (VASMOL 33, BLACK NITE TYPE)
422. L-LYSINE MONOHYDROCHLORIDE
423. LACTIC ACID FROM WHITE SUGAR BY FERMENTATION PROCESS
424. LDPE GRANULES FROM VIRGIN (LDPE RESIN)
425. LEAD EXTRACTION FROM BATTERY SCRAP
426. LEAD OXIDE (A) LEAD MONOXIDE
(B) LEAD TETRA OXIDE
(C) GREYLEAD OXIDE
427. LIQUID GLUCOSE & ITS BY PRODUCTS
428. LIQUID OXYGEN BOTTLING PLANT
429. LIQUID SHOE POLISH
430. LIQUID FLOOR POLISH
431. LUBE OIL VISCOSITY IMPROVED FOR P.P.G/P.E.G.
432. LUBRICANTS ASHLESS 100% COMBUSTION
433. MAGNESIUM CARBONATE AND MAGNESIUM BICARMONATE
434. MAGNESIUM HYDROXIDE POWDER
435. MAGNESIUM SILICATE
436. MAGNESIUM SULPHATE
437. MALACHITE GREEN
438. MALEIC ANHYDRIDE
439. MANGANESE SULPHATE
440. MANUFACTURING OF CARBON MONO-OXIDE WATER GAS
441. MENTHOL BOLD CRYSTALS FROM FLAKES
442. MENTHOL CRYSTAL & MENTHA OIL
443. MERCURIC OXIDE
444. METAL PRE-TREATMENT CHEMICALS
445. METHANE GAS BY SODIUM ACETATE & SODA LIME
446. METHYL ACETYL RICINOLATE
447. METOL
448. METOL FROM HYDROQUINONE & METHYLAMINE
449. MICANITE
450. MICRO NUTRIENT MIXTURE
451. MINERAL WATER
452. MINERAL WATER AND PET BOTTILNG PLANT
453. MINERAL WATER IN BOTTLES, GLASS AND POUCHES
454. MINI CEMENT PLANT (BY ROTARY KILN PROCESS)
455. MIXED FERTILIZER
456. MOSQUITO & FLIES REPELLENT AGARBATTI (INCENSE STICKS)
457. MONO CHLORO ACETIC ACID
458. MONOCROTOPHOS (TECHNICAL)
459. MOSQUITO COIL
460. MOSQUITO COIL & MAT
461. MOSQUITO MAT
462. MOTHER TINCTURE & BIO CHEMIC MEDICINES
463. NAPHTHALENE & PHENYL (INTEGRATED UNIT)
464. NATURAL MINERAL WATER BY REVERSE OSMOSIS PROCESS
465. NICKEL PLATING BRIGHTNER (PRIMARY OR CARRIER BRIGHTNER & SECONDARY BRIGHTNER)
466. NICKEL SULPHATE
467. NICOTINE FROM TOBACCO WASTE
468. NICOTINE SULPHATE FROM TOBACCO WASTE
469. NITRO BENZENE
470. NITRO CELLULOSE SANDING SEALER/LACQUER
471. NITRO MUSK
472. NITROGEN & OXYGEN GAS PLANT
473. NON-IONIC SURFACTANT (WETTING AGENT)
474. NO-CARB PASTE
475. OCTANOL
476. ORTHO NITRO PHENOL
477. OXALIC ACID FROM MOLASSES
478. OXALIC ACID FROMRICE HUSK
479. OXALIC ACID FROM TREE BARK
470. OXALIC ACID FROM WASTE VEGETABLES
471. OXYGEN GAS PLANT
472. OXYGEN GAS PLANT (AIR SEPERATION METHOD)
473. PARA-AMINO BENZOIC ACID
474. PARA-AMINO PHENOL
475. PARA TOLUENE SULPHONIC ACID
476. PECTIN FROM RAW PAPAYA
477. PERFUME (LEMON & OTHERS)

CRUDE NAPHTHA
570. TRIMETHYL AMMONIUM CHLORIDE
571. TRIPHENYL PHOSPHITE (T.P.P)
572. ULTRAMARINE BLUE (LIQUID)
573. UREA FORMALDEHYDE & MELAMINE FORMALDEHYDE POWDER
574. UNDECYLINIC ACID
575. VINYL ACETATE MONOMER
576. VITAMIN C
577. VITAMIN E
578. WASTE WATER TREATMENT PLANT FOR INDUSTRIAL SECTOR IN INDIA (ONLY MARKER SURVEY)
579. WIRE DRAWING LUBRICANT
580. WIRE ENAMEL
581. XANTHATES
582. YELLOW DEXTRIN
583. ZINC CHLORIDE
584. ZINC OXIDE
585. ZINC PHOSPHATING BY COLD PROCESS
586. ZINC SILICATE
587. ZINC STEARATE
588. ZINC SULPHATE
589. ZINC SULPHATE MONOHYDRATE
590. ACID BLACK
591. AURAMINE'O'
592. AZO DYES STUFF
593. DYE & DYE INTERMEDIATE
594. DYE INTERMEDIATES
595. MALACHITE GREEN
596. METHYLENE BLUE
597. PHTHALOCYANINE BLUE
598. PHTHALOCYANINE BLUE & GREEN
599. REACTIVE DYES
600. SULPHUR BLACK DYE
601. VAT DYES
602. WATER CHILLING PLANT
603. WADDING OIL (100%) FOR WADDING OF COTTON HOSIERY CLOTH IN THE DYEING PROCESS
604. WHITE OIL
605. WAX FLOOR POLISH

ELECTRICAL, ELECTONICS, COMPUTERS AND INFOTECH/IT PROJECTS

606. AIR CONDITIONING
607. ALUMINIUM ALLOY CONDUCTOR
608. ALUMINIUM CABLE
609. ALUMINIUM ELECTROYTIC CAPACITORS
610. AUDIO CASSETTE ASSEMBLING & RECORDING
611. AUDIO CASSETTES DUPLICATING RECORDING
612. AUDIO CASSETTES & AUDIO STUDIO
613. AUDIO CASSETTES PLANE & RECORDED
614. AUDIO MAGNETIC HEADS
615. AUDIO MAGNETIC TAPE
616. AUDIO/VIDEO CASSETTES
617. AUTO BULB/LAMPS
618. AUTOMATIC VOLTAGE STABILIZER
619. BATTERY PLATES
620. BACK OFFICE (Rs. 5000/-)
621. B/W TV & COMPUTER MONITOR PICTURE TUBE
622. BREAD BOARDS
623. CALL CENTRE
624. CAMERA (35 MM)
625. CAPACITORS
626. CARBON ELECTRODE USED FOR BATTERY CELL
627. CARBON POTETIOMETERS
628. CEILING FAN
629. CERAMIC INSULATOR
630. CHILDREN INFOTECH TRAINING INSTITUTE (Rs. 5000/-)
631. CHOKE AND PATTI
632. CHOKE AND STARTER
633. CHOKE USED FOR FLUORESCENT LAMPS
634. COLOUR TELEVISION
635. COLOUR AND BLACK & WHITE TELEVISION
636. COMPACT DISC
637. COMPACT DISC PLAYER (AUDIO/VIDEO)
638. COMPUTER EDUCATION INSTITUTE
639. COMPUTER ASSEMBLY
640. COMPUTER HARDWARE
641. COMPUTER KEYBOARD
642. COMPUTER PERIPHERALS
643. COMPUTER PRINTERS
644. COMPUTER RIBBON
645. COMPUTER RIBBON REINKING OR REFILLING
646. COMPUTER STATIONERY
647. COMPUTER STATIONERY &

IMPORTED HARDWARE PARTS
648. COMPUTER TERMINALS
649. COMPUTERISED WASHING MACHINE (AUTOMATIC)
650. COMPUTER SOFTWARE
651. CONDENSER FOR MOTOR USING MPP FILM
652. CONTENT DEVELOPMENT CENTRE (EOU) (Rs. 5000/-)
653. CONTROL PANEL BOARD
654. COOLING COIL FOR AIR CONDITIONERS
655. COPPER STRIP COIL FROM SCRAP
656. CORDLESS TELEPHONES
657. CYBER CAFE
658. CYBERKIOSK (Rs. 5000/-)
659. DATA PROCESSING CENTRE (Rs. 5000/-)
660. D.C. MICRO MOTORS
661. D.G.SETS
662. DISH ANTENNA AND CABLE T.V. NETWORK EQUIPMENT
663. DISTRIBUTION TRANSFORMERS & REPAIRS
664. DOMESTIC ELECTRICAL APPLIANCES- ROOM COOLER, WASHING MACHINE, WATER HEATER, ELECTRIC ROOM HEATER
665. E-SCHOOL
666. E-COMMERCE/BUSINESS
667. ELECTRIC ENERGY METER
668. ELECTRIC FANS
669. ELECTRIC HORN FOR AUTOMOBILE
670. ELECTRIC LAMP/GLS (INCANDESCENT LAMP)
671. ELECTRIC MIXER
672. ELECTRIC MOTORS UP TO 10 HP. REWINDING OF ALL TYPES OF MOTORS WATER PUMPS
673. ELECTRIC MOTOR WINDING (FOR FAN, MIXIES, ETC.)
674. ELECTRIC STEAM IRON
675. ELECTRICAL APPLIANCES
676. ELECTRICAL FIXTURES
677. ELECTRICAL STAMPING
678. ELECTROLYTIC CAPACITORS
679. ELECTROMAGNETIC RELAY
680. ELECTRONIC BALAST/CHOK
681. ELECTRICAL CHOKE
682. ELECTRONIC DIGITAL WATCHES
683. ELECTRONIC DIGITAL WEIGHING MACHINE
684. ELECTRONIC FIRE ALARM
685. ELECTRONIC GAS STOVE LIGHTERS
686. ELECTRONIC PRESSURE INDICATORS, ELECTRICALS, ELECTRONIC LIQUID LEVEL INDICATORS, ELECTRONIC TEMPERATURE INDICATOR, DIGITAL TACHOMETER
687. ELECTRONIC TELEPHONE INSTRUMENTS
688. ELECTRONIC TOYS
689. ELECTRONIC WATCHES & CLOCKS
690. FAX MACHINES
691. F.H.P MOTORS
692. FLOPPY DISKETTES
693. FLUORESCENT LAMP STARTER
694. FLUORESCENT TUBULAR

LAMPS WITH INTRODUCTION TO MERCURY VAPOUR LAMP
695. FRANCHISEE COMPUTER EDUCATION CENTRE (Rs. 5000)
696. GAS DETECTOR (L.P.G)
697. GENERATOR SET & PUMP SETS
698. GENERATOR (BATTERY OPERATED)
699. GIS SERVICE CENTRE (GEOGRAPHICAL INFORMATION SYSTEMS)
700. HARDWARE FITTING FOR TRANSMISSION LINE OVERHEAD LINE MATERIAL
701. HEADERS FOR TRANSISTOR ICS SEMI CONDUCTOR
702. H.T & L.T INSULATORS
703. H.T & M.V INDUSTRIAL CUBICAL SWITCH BOARD
704. INFORMATION MOVING DISPLAY (L.E.D TYPE)
705. INSURANCE CLAIM PROCESSING CENTRE (EOU) (Rs. 5000/-)
706. INTEGRATED CIRCUITS
707. INTERNET BASED STOCK TRADING (Rs. 5000/-)
708. INTERNET SERVICE PROVIDER (I.S.P.)
709. JELLY FILLED TELEPHONE CABLES
710. LAP TOP COMPUTERS
711. LEAD ACID BATTERIES
712. LEAD ACID BATTERY PLATES AND ASSEMBLING OF BATTERY
713. LEGAL TRANSCRIPTION & SECRETARIAL SERVICES CENTER (EOU)(Rs. 5000/-)
714. LIGHT EMITTING DIODES (L.E.D)
715. LINEAR ICS TRAINER KIT
716. LOUD SPEAKER
717. L.T TRANSFORMER REPAIRING
718. MEDICAL TRANSCRIPTION CENTRE
719. METAL FILM RESISTORS
720. METALLISED POLYPROPYLENE, POLYESTER FILM CAPACITOR
721. MICA BASE ELECTRONIC COMPONENTS
722. MICA PAPER WASTE PAPER FROM MICA WASTE
723. MICRO PROCESSORS TRAINER KITS BASED ON MICRO PROCESSORS
724. MINI COMPUTER (PERSONAL COMPUTER)
725. MINIATURE CIRCUIT BREAKER (M.C.B)
726. MINIATURE WATCH BATTERIES (BUTTON CELL)
727. MIXER/GRINDER (MIXI)
728. MONO CHROME COMPUTER MONITOR
729. MOTOR START ELECTROLYTIC CAPACITOR
730. MULTI LAYER P.C.B
731. MULTIPLE RELAY FOR LOW VOLTAGE
732. NEON INDICATOR
733. NEON SIGN MANUFACTURE
734. OPTICAL FIBRE CABLES
735. ON LINE SHOPPING MALL (Rs. 5000/-)
736. OPTO MECHANICAL & ELECTRICAL EQUIPMENTS
737. PHOTO COLOUR LAB
738. PICTURE TUBE (B/W)
739. PLAIN PAPER COPIER
740. PLASTIC FILM CAPACITORS
741. POLYESTER CAPACITORS
742. PORTABLE GENERATOR SET
743. PORTAL
744. PORTABLE TELEVISION(TV)
745. POWER CAPACITORS
746. POWER INVERTERS
747. POWER PLANT
748. POWER TRANSFORMERS UP TO 600 KVA
749. PRINTED CIRCUIT BOARD
750. PVC WIRES & CABLES
751. RE-CONDITIONING OF PICTURE TUBE
752. RESIN CAST CT & PT (1 KV)
753. SEMI CONDUCTOR DEVICE
754. SEMI CONDUCTORS FOR TRANSISTORS & DIODES
755. SETTING UP OF A VIDEO STUDIO
756. SMOKE DETECTORS
757. SOLAR CELLS
758. SOLAR MODULES
759. SOLAR PHOTO VOLTAIC SYSTEM
760. SOLDER FLUXES
761. SOLAR WATER HEATING PANELS
762. STEEL FURNITURE & ELECTRICAL APPLIANCES
763. STEREO AMPLIFIERS
764. STEREO CASSETTE RECORDERS/PLAYERS
765. STREET LIGHT FITTINGS SURGE SUPPRESSOR
766. TANTALUM CAPACITORS
767. TEFLON COATED ELECTRIC CABLE
768. TELEMEDICINE (DISTANCE HEALTH CARE) (Rs. 5000/-)
769. TELEPHONE CORD/CABLE
770. TELEPHONE (PUSH BUTTON TYPE)
771. TELEPHONE (PUSH BUTTON & CORDLESS)
772. TELEVISION (CTV & B/W)
773. TELEVISION (3-D)
774. TELEVISION DEFLECTION COMPONENTS
775. TELEVISION SIGNAL BOOSTERS
776. TELEVISION TUNERS
777. TRACTION BATTERIES
778. TRAINING INSTITUTE OF MEDICAL TRANSCRIPTION
779. TRANSFORMER FOR B/W TV
780. TRANSFORMER FOR VOLTAGE STABILIZER & E.H.T
781. TRANSMISSION POWER LINE FITTING
782. TRANSMISSION TOWER FITTING
783. TV AUDIO EQUIPMENT CABINETS & THEIR ASSEMBLING UNIT
784. UN-INTERRUPTED POWER SUPPLY (U.P.S)
785. VARIABLE FREQUENCY
786. VARIABLE VOLTAGE A.C. DRIVE
787. VIDEO CASSETTES (COMPLETE MANUFACTURING & ASSEMBLING)
788. VIDEO CASSETTES RECORDER (V.C.R)
789. VIDEO FILM STUDIO
790. VOLTAGE REGULATOR FOR AUTOMOBILES
791. VOLTAGE STABILIZERS
792. VOLTAGE STABLIZER & T.V. GAIN BOOSTER
793. WAX AND CHEMICAL COATED, BRAIDED TINSEL WIRE
794. WEBSITE DESIGN & E-MAIL REGISTERING
795. WELDING ELECTRODES
796. WIND ENERGY POWER PROJECT (10 MW)
796A WIRES (METAL)

FOOD, AGRO FOOD, PROCESSED FOOD, AGRO PLANTATION, CULTIVATION, FARMING, DAIRY/MILK, TOBACCO/PAN MASALA, BREWERY & DISTILLERY, EDIBLE OILS, EOU FOOD PRODUCTS AND ALLIED PRODUCTS

797. ALCOHOLIC BEVERAGES & VENEGAR FROM COCONUT WATER
798. ALCOHOL DRINKS FROM ETHYL ALCOHOL BY MIXING OF VARIOUS FLAVOURS
799. ANTI SCALE COMPOUND FOR ADDING INTO SUGAR JUICE BOILING
800. APPLE JUICE CONCENTRATED & DEHYDRATED FRUIT & VEGETABLES
801. ARTIFICIAL FISH MEAL FOR POULTRY FEED
802. AUTOMATIC BISCUIT PLANT
803. BABY CEREAL FOOD AND MILK POWDER
804. BACTERIA FOR CANE JUICE
805. BAKER'S YEAST
806. BAKERY INDUSTRY
807. BANANA PUREE
808. BEER & WINE
809. BEER PLANT (BREWERY)
810. BIDI
811. BIDI & CIGARETTE
812. BISCUIT PLANT

813. BREAD (AUTOMATIC PLANT)
814. BLACK PEPPER (SPICES)
815. BREAD AND BISCUITS
816. BREEDING FARM
817. BROILER CHICKEN
819. BUTTON MUSHROOM CULTIVATION & PROCESSING
820. CANNING OF RASAGULLAS IN METAL CANS
821. CAFFEIN FROM TEA WASTE
822. CANNING OF FRUITS & VEGETABLES
823. CASEIN AND BY-PRODUCTS
824. CASHEW FRUIT JUICE FROM CASHEW FRUIT APPLE
825. CASHEWNUT KERNEL EXTRACTION FROM CASHEWNUT FRUIT
826. CASHEWNUT SHELL LIQUID & KERNEL PROCESSING
827. CASHEW FENI
828. CATECHEU (BY CHEMICAL PROCESS)
829. CATTLE FEED FROM TAPIOCA
830. CHEWING & BUBBLE GUM
831. CHICKEN/SHEEP MEAT PROCESSING
832. CHOCOLATE (MILK)
833. CIGARETTE AND BEEDIES
834. COCOA BUTTER FROM COCOA MASS
835. COCONUT PRODUCTS & BY PRODUCTS PROCESS COMPLEX
836. COLD/SOFT DRINKS
837. COLLECTION OF MILK AND MILK MAKING POWDER
838. COLLECTION OF MILK AND PACKING IN POLYTHENE POUCH (1/2 KG.1 KG. & 2 KG.)
839. CONDENSED MILK (SWEETNED)
840. CONFECTIONERY INDUSTRY (TOFFEE & CANDY, SEMI-AUTOMATIC PLANT)
841. COUNTRY LIQUOR FROM MOLASSES
842. CIGARETTE
843. DAIRY FARM AND DAIRY (MILK) PRODUCTS (PASTEURISED MILK, BUTTER, GHEE, PANEER)
844. DAIRY FARM TO PRODUCE MILK & PACKING IN POUCHES (50%) & CAN(50%)
845. DAIRY FOR MILK PROCESSING
846. DAIRY FARM (BUFALO)
847. DAL (PULSE) MILL UNIT
848. DEHYDRATION OF CARROT & GARLIC
849. DEHYDRATION & CANNING OF FRUITS & VEGETABLES
850. DEHYDRATION OF FIGS
851. DEHYDRATION OF FRUITS AND VEGETABLES
852. DEHYDRATED ONIONS AND ONION POWDER
853. DRY ICE BY BREAKING OF AIR
854. DRYING OF RED CHILLIES, HALDI, DHANIA, AND GREEN PEAS
855. EGG POWDER (40,000 EGGS PROCESSING PER DAY)
856. EXPORT OF PROCESSED FOODS AND MARINE PRODUCTS
857. FISH CANNING & POUCHING
859. FISH FARMING (PRAWN & OTHER MARINE PRODUCTS)
860. FISH MEAL
861. FLOUR MILL AND MUSTARD OIL
862. FOOD COLOUR & ORASTED GROUNDNUT GRAM PEAS, ETC IN POUCHES
863. FROG LEGS PROCESSING
864. FROZEN MEATS PROCESSING
865. FOOD FLAVOURS (WHISKY) VODKA, GRAPE, BUTTER SCOTCH)
866. FOOD PRODUCTS COMPLEX (DEHYDRATED ONIONS, GARLIC POWDER & FLAKES, CATTLE FEED, TOMATO POWDER, TOMATO PRODUCTS, CANNED FRUITS & VEGETABLES, TOMATO PURE, GROUN NUT OIL, REFIND OIL, DEHYDRATED GRAPES, BANANA POWDER & WAFFERS)
867. FRUIT JUICE, JAM, JELLIES & ALLIED PRODUCTS
868. FRUIT JUICE, PICKLES PROCESSING AND CANNING
869. FRUIT JUICE MAKING & PACKING IN PLASTIC CONTAINER/POUCHES
870. FRUIT PROCESSING (JAM & JELLIES)
871. FRUIT PULP & JUICE CONCENTRATES
872. FRUIT & VEGETABLE DRYING (FREEZE DRYING METHOD)
873. GOAT & SHEEP FARMING
874. GRAM DALL/PULSE MILL
875. GRAPE DEHYDRATION
876. HARD BOILED CANDY (TOFFEE & CANDY)
877. HERBAL CIGARETTES
878. HONEY PROCESSING & PACKAGING
879. ICE CREAM OF DIFFERENT FLAVOURS
880. ICE CREAM STABILIZER
881. ICE MAKING PLANT
882. INDIAN MADE FOREIGN LIQUOR (I.M.F.L)
883. INSTANT FOOD (IDLI MIX, DOSA MIX, GULAB JAMUN MIX)
884. INSTANT FOOD (INSTANT FOOD & FAST FOOD PARLOUR)
885. INSTANT NOODLES
886. INSTANT TEA
887. INSTANT TEA FROM BLACK TEA
888. INTEGERATED STARCH BAKING POWDER/YEAST INDUSTRY
889. IODIZED SALT
890. IODIZED SALT (ORDINARY MOISTURE-LESS FREE FLOWING IN PLASTIC BAGS AND CONTAINERS
891. JAM, JELLIES, FRUIT JUICE & ALLIED PRODUCTS
892. KATHA AND CUTCH
893. KHANDSARI SUGAR
894. KHANDSARI SUGAR & IMFL
895. LACTIC ACID FROM WHITE SUGAR BY FERMENTATION PROCESS
896. LACTOSE & BY PRODUCTS PROCESSING FROM MILK
897. LIQUID GLUCOSE AND ITS BYE PRODUCTS
898. MACRONI AND VERMICILLI
899. MALT EXTRACTION FROM BARLEY
900. MANGO PROCESSING (MANGO PULP, JUICE & SLICES)
901. MAYUR BRAND TYPE CHEWING TOBACCO
902. MINERAL WATER
903. MILK PRESERVATION & MARKETING TO WHOLE SELLERS (INPOUCH PACKING BY UHT TECHNOLOGY)
904. MILK PROCESSING AND PACKAGING OF MILK PRODUCTS
905. MILK PRODUCTS (CASEIN, LACTOSE, GHEE & WHEY POWDER)
906. MILK TOFFEE
907. MINI FLOUR MILL
908. MINI SUGAR PLANT
909. MISRI (PEARL SUGAR CANDIES)
910. MODERN RICE MILL
911. MURABBA
912. MUSTARD OIL EXTRACTION & REFINING
913. MUTTON TALLOW
914. NAMKEEN INDUSTRY (BHUJIA, CHANA CHUR ETC.)
915. NAMKEEN & SWEETS
916. NON-BASMATI RICE FROM PADDY
917. OLEORESIN, ESSENTIAL OIL, DYES & POWDER OF SPICES
918. OLEORESIN EXTRACTION FROM DIPTERO-CARPUT TURMINATUS AND PINUS KHASYANA
919. OLEORESIN EXTRACTION FROM CHILLI
920. PAN MASALA AND POUCH

1059. BUFFALO HORN TIP, HOOF
1060. BANQUET HALL
1061. BUTTON
1062. CALCINED PETROLEUM (C.P) COKE
1063. CANVAS SHOES
1064. CANVAS SHOES, JUNGLE BOOTS
1065. CARBON BRUSH, BRUSH HOLDER & SLIP RING
1066. CEMENT SHEETS WITH COIR FIBRE & OTHER SEGMENTS
1067. CERAMIC TILES (GLAZED) BY DOUBLE FIRING/HEATING
1068. CHILDREN RECREATION CENTRE
1069. COAL BRIQUETTES
1070. COLD STORAGE & ICE
1071. COLD STORAGE FOR FRUITS AND VEGETABLES
1072. COMPRESSOR (HERMETIC) FOR AIR CONDITIONER
1073. COSTUME JEWELLERY/ IMITATION JEWELLERY
1074. DECORATIVE LAMINATED SHEET (SUNMICA)
1075. DIAMOND CUTTING & EXPORTS
1076. DRINKING STRAW FROM PROPYLENE
1077. ENGINEERING COLLEGE
1078. ENTERTAINMENT CLUB
1079. FASHION TECHNOLOGY INSTITUTE
1080. FAST FOOD PARLOUR
1081. FAST FOOD (INSTANT FOOD & FAST FOOD PARLOUR)
1082. FIRE EXTINGUISHERS (SODA ACID TYPE)
1083. FISH NET
1084. FLORICULTURE (CUT FLOWER ROSE) WITH GREEN HOUSE
1085. FLOOR COVERING SHEET
1086. FILM STUDIO (VIDEO)
1087. FLUSH DOOR, CHIP BOARD, WOOD WOOL & OTHER INSULATING BOARDS
1088. GAS DETECTORS OF L.P.G
1089. GEMS MANUFACTURING
1090. GLASS BOTTLE BY SCRAP
1092. GOAT & SHEEP FARMING
1093. GOLD ELECTROPLATING
1094. GOLD JEWELLERY (E.O.U)
1095. GOLD PLATED SILVER JEWELLERY & CUTLERY
1096. GRANITE SLAB AND TILES
1097. GREEN HOUSE
1098. HARD CHROMIUM PLATING
1099. HEALTH CLUB AND BEAUTY PARLOUR CUM HAIR SALOON WITH SONA BATH
1100. HEALTH CLUB CUM BEAUTY PARLOUR TRAININGINSTITUTE
1101. HORN TIP,HOOVE BUTTON
1102. HOSPITAL
1103. HOSPITAL (100 BEDS)
1104. HOSPITAL (200 BEDS)
1105. ICE MAKING PLANT
1106. IMITATION AND COSTUME
1107. JEWELLERY (NECKLACE, EARRINGS EAR TOP ETC.)
1108. INITMATE SCENT CHEMICALS FROM ALL TYPES OF FLAVOUR
1109. INVESTMENT CASTING
1110. JUTE, COIR, GLASS ROPE/ SUTLI
1111. JUTE TWINE
1112. L.P.G BOTTLING PLANT
1113. L.P.G REGULATOR (DOMESTIC PURPOSE)
1114. LAMINATED PARTICLE BOARD & HARD BOARD
1115. LAMINATED SAFETY AND TOUGHENED GLASS
1116. LEASING & HIRE PURCHASE
1117. LICHEN (CHARILA)
1118. MANILA ROPES
1119. MEDICAL COLLEGE
1120. MATCH UNIT FROM WAXED PAPER
1121. MEDIUM DENSITY FIBRE BOARD
1122. MELAMINE CROCKERY
1123. MINERAL WATER
1124. MINI CEMENT PLANT
1125. MIRROR SILVER, GOLDEN, PINK, BLACK & SMOKES
1126. MODERN ADVERTISING AGENCY WITH DTP & FILM STUDIO
1127. MOTEL/SMALL HOTEL
1128. MULTI COLOUR PRINTING
1129. MULTI STOREY COMMERCIAL COMPLEX ALONGWITH RESIDENTIALAND DELUX FLATS FOR FOREIGN TOURISTS & REVOLVING RESTAURENT AT THE TOP
1130. MULTIPLE LAMINATION INDUSTRY
1131. MUSHROOM GROWING AND PROCESSING (BY DEEP FREEZING METHOD)
1132. NEWS PAPER PRINTING
1133. NICKEL LINED INDUSTRIAL SCREEN
1134. OFFSET COLOUR PRINTING PRESS (SIX COLOUR)
1135. OFFSET PRINTING PRESS
1136. P.C.C ELECTRIC POLES
1137. PHOTOGRAPHIC DEVELOPER & FIXER
1138. PVC EXTRUSION PROFILE (DOOR & WINDOWS)
1139. POP-CORN
1140. PHOTO ETCHING OF S.S.
1141. PRE STRESSED CEMENT CONCRETE PIPES
1142. PILFER PROOF CAPS
1143. PILFER PROOF CAPS AND CROWN CAP
1144. POUCH MAKING & GRAVURE PRINTING (ROTO PRINTING)
1145. POULTRY & FISH FARMING (INTEGERATED UNIT)
1146. PRINTING OF TIN SHEETS
1147. READYMADE GARMENTS
1148. RESTAURANT
1149. ROSE PLANTATION AND ROSE OIL EXTRACTION
1150. ROTOGRAVURE PRINTING
1151. SAFETY BELTS
1152. SAFETY MATCHES
1153. SHOE LACES
1154. SILK COCOON CULTIVATION (GROWING OF SILK COCOON WARM)
1155. SILK SCREEN PRINTING FORMULATIONS FOR PLASTIC, PAPER & CLOTH
1156. SPIKENARD (JATAMANSI)
1157. STENCIL COATING SOLUTION
1158. SUGAR CANDY (MISRI)
1159. SUGAR CANE PLANTATION
1160. SUGAR CANE JUICE PRESERVATION
1161. SURAT ZARI
1162. SYNTHETIC SHOES & SOLES
1163. TEA PACKAGING INDUSTRY
1164. TENNIS BALLS
1165. THREE STAR HOTEL
1166. TRAVELLING AGENCY
1167. TRAYS, TROLLEYS FOR HOSPITAL WITH SCRATCHLESS COATING
1168. WAX EXTRACTS (TANNING POWDER)
1169. WIRE ROPE SLINGS
1170. WOOD WOOL SLAB
1171. WOODEN CANE FURNITURE WITH EXPORT POTENTIAL
1172. WOODEN FURNITURE
1173. WOODEN PANEL INCLUDING KILN SEASONING
1174. WOODEN FURNITURE
1175. WATCH CASE BUFFING
1176. WATCH DIAL
1177. WRIST WATCHES
1178. WATCHES (ELECTRONIC)
1179. ZEDOARY (KACHUR)

EDIBLE OILS, ESSENTIAL OILS LURICATIING OILS, GREASES, VEGETABLE OILS, WAXES, CAMPHOR, PERFUMES & PERFUMERY COMPOUNDS AND REFINED OILS ETC.

1180. AROMATIC PERFUMERY COMPOUND
1181. AEROSOL
1182. AGARBATTI PERFUMERY COMPOUND
1183. BEES WAX MANUFACTURE
1184. CAMPHOR
1185. CARDANOL FROM CASHEW NUT SHELL LIQUID
1186. CASTOR OIL
1187. CASTOR OIL DERIVATIVE OLEORESINS
1188. CHILLI OIL
1189. CITRONELLA OILS
1190. CLOVE OIL
1191. CONCENTRATE OF ROSE JASMINE & LILY ETC.
1192. COLOURED FLAME CANDLE

1193. CANDLES (SEMI-AUTOMATIC)
1194. CORN OIL (MAIZE OIL)
1195. DEHYDRATED CASTOR OIL
1196. EUGENOL FROM CINNAMON LEAF OIL
1197. EXTRACTION OF ESSENTIAL OIL (CARDAMON, JEERA, AJOWAN, GINGER OILS ETC. & PACKAGING OF GROUND SPICES)
1198. EXTRACTION OF JASMINE ESSENCE
1199. EXTRACTION OF ESSENTIAL OILS BY SUPER CRITICAL FLUID METHOD FROM FLOWERS, HERBS & SPICES
1200. EUCALYPTUS OIL
1201. EXTRACTION OF OIL FROM OIL SEED EXPANDEREXTRUSION TECHNOLOGY)
1202. FAT LIQUOR SULPHATED OIL
1203. FLAVOURS FOR FOOD
1204. GARLIC OIL & POWDER
1205. GINGER OIL, SANDALWOOD OIL AND NAGARMOTHA OIL
1206. GINGER OIL
1207. GINGER OIL & GINGER DUST
1208. INTEGERATED WAX COMPLEX
1209. IONONE FROM LEMON GRASS OIL
1210. JASMINE & LILLY FLOWER OIL
1211. LEMON GRASS OIL
1212. LIQUID PARAFFIN
1213. LUBE OIL & GREASE
1214. LUBRICATING OIL
1215. MENTHOL CRYSTALS
1216. MENTHOL OIL & CRYSTAL
1217. MICRO CRYSTALLINE WAX
1218. MUSTARD OIL (EDIBLE OIL)
1219. OIL FROM ARTEMISIA HERBS
1220. PALM OIL CRUSHING UNIT
1221. PAN MASALA
1222. PARAFFIN WAX
1223. PARAFFIN WAX FROM SLACK WAX
1224. REFINED OIL-SUN FLOWER OIL, GROUNDNUT OIL, STAFF FLOWER OIL & COTTON SEED OIL
1225. REFINED VEGETABLE OIL
1226. RECLAMATION OF USED ENGINE OIL
1227. RICE BRAN OIL (R.B.O)
1228. ROSE OIL EXTRACTION
1229. SMOKE LESS CANDLE
1230. SPICE OIL & OLEORESINS
1231. SOLVENT EXTRACTION PLANT (OIL CAKE BASED)
1232. SYNTHETIC ALMOND OIL
1233. SYNTHETIC TALLOW
1234. SYNTHETIC GHEE
1235. VEGETABLE OIL EXTRACTION & REFINING
1236. WADDING OIL (100%) FOR WADDING OF COTTON HOSIERY CLOTH IN DYEING PROCESS
1237. WAX EMULSION FOR TEXTILE
1238. WAX FLOOR POLISH

PAINT, ENAMEL, SOLVENTS, THINNERS, INKS & VARNISH

1239. ACRYLIC EMULSION PAINTS
1240. ALUMINIUM PAINT
1241. AUTOMOBILE PAINTS
1242. BALL POINT PEN REFILL INK
1243. BITUMINIOUS ROAD EMULSION
1244. BITUMEN
1245. BITUMINIOUS FELTS FOR WATER & DAMP PROOFING
1246. BITUMINIOUS ROAD EMULSION RAPID MEDIUM & SLOW SETTING
1247. BUFFING & POLISHING
1248. CEMENT PAINT FOR WHITE & GREY CEMENT

1249. DISPERSANT
1250. DRY DISTEMPER
1251. DRY DISTEMPER & CEMENT PAINT
1252. DUPLICATING INK BLACK FOR GESTNER DUPLICATOR
1255. EMULSION PAINTS (WATER BASED)
1256. HAMMERTONE PAINT
1257. INSULATING VARNISH & WIRE ENAMEL
1258. IRON OXIDE PIGMENTS
1259. INSULATING VARNISH (POLY VINYL BUTYRAL BASED, FFC GRADE)
1260. LIME COLOUR (CEMENT COLOUR)
1261. SYNTHETIC RED OXIDE FOR FLOORINGS
1262. SOLVENT & THINNERS
1263. MARKING INKS (WATER PROOF)
1264. METAL NAPHTHANATE (AS DRIER FOR PAINTS)
1265. N.C.PUTTY
1266. OFFSET PRINTING INK
1267. OIL BOUND DISTEMPER PAINT
1268. PAINT BRUSHES
1269. PAINT REMOVERS
1270. PAINT INDUSTRY
1271. PAINT & VARNISH
1272. PICTURE VARNISH
1273. POWDER COATING PAINT
1274. PRINTING INKS (OFFSET, FLEXO & ROTO GRAVURE)
1275. PRIMER PAINT & ENAMEL PAINT
1276. PUTTY & WATER PROOFING PAINT
1277. PRINTING INKS (FLEXO-GRAPHIC INK)
1278. PUTTY (METAL CASEMENT)
1279. RED OXIDE PRIMER (ANTI CORROSIVE)
1280. REFRECTORY PAINT (GRAPHITE BASED)
1281. SCREEN PRINTING INKS
1282. SILK SCREEN PRINTING INK FORMULATION FOR PLASTIC, PAPER, CLOTH
1283. STAMP & PAD INK
1284. STOVING PAINT
1285. SPIRIT SOLUBLE MALEIC RESIN
1286. TEXTURE PAINT
1287. THINNERS AND ITS ALLIED PRODUCTS
1288. TONER INK
1289. VARNISH THINNER (SOLVENT)
1290. VACUUM METALLIZING LACQUERS
1291. WOOD PRIMER

PHARMACEUTICAL, DRUGS, AYURVEDIC/HERBAL COSMETICS & MEDICINES, HOMOEOPATHIC MEDICINES, DISPOSABLE SYRINGE, DENTAL COLLEGE & FINE CHEMICALS ETC.

1292. AROMATIC PILLS
1293. ASPIRIN
1294. AYURVEDIC PAIN BALM OINTMENTS
1295. AYURVEDIC CHURAN AND TABLETS
1296. AYURVEDIC TABLETS (HAJMOLA TYPE)
1297. AYURVEDIC/HERBAL PHARMACY
1298. AYURVEDIC SHERBATS
1299. AYURVEDIC PRODUCTS
1300. BULK DRUGS (E.O.U)
1301. BLOOD BAGS
1302. CALCIUM GLUCONATE
1303. CAPSULE, TABLET & INJECTION WITH MODERN INSTRUMENTS
1304. CASHEW FENI
1305. CHLOROQUINONE PHOSPHATE (BULK DRUGS)
1306. CLINICAL THERMOMETER
1307. DENTAL CLINIC

Above all the Detailed Project Report are available at *"ENGINEERS INDIA RESEARCH INSTITUTE"*. 4449, Nai Sarak (D), Main Road Delhi - 110 006
● Ph : 91-11-23918117, 2391 6431, 2392 0361, 31082370 ● Fax : 91-11-2391 6431
● E-Mail : eirisidi@bol.net.in

1308. DENTAL COLLEGE
1309. DENTAL GRADE EUGENOL
1310. DEXTROSE MONOHYDRATE, LIQUID GLUCOSE
1311. DEHYDRATED ONION & ONION POWDER
1312. DEXTROSE POWDER (ANHYDROUS FROM STARCH)
1314. DEXTROSE SALINE SOLUTION
1315. DISTILLERY (I.M.F.L)
1316. DISPOSABLE NEEDLES FOR SYRINGES
1317. DISPRIN
1318. DISTILLED WATER
1319. EMPTY HARD GELATINE CAPSULES
1320. FILLING & PACKING OF CAPSULES
1321. GLUCOSE - D - POWDER
1322. GLYCERINE
1323. HERBAL COSMETICS
1324. HERBAL SHAMPOO
1325. HERBAL HAIR OILS (AYURVEDIC)
1326. HOMOE & BIO-MEDICINES WITH MOTHER TINCTURE
1327. HOMOEPATHIC MEDICINES
1328. HYPODERMIC NEEDLES
1329. I.V. FLUIDS
1330. IBUPROFEN
1331. INFUSION & TRANSFUSION SETS (I.V. SET)
1332. INJECTABLE FOR PHARMACEUTICALS
1333. INJECTION AMPOULES PACKAGING BOX
1334. INTEGERATED SURGICAL COTTON
1335. ICE MAKING PLANT
1336. ICE & COLD STORAGE
1337. LACTOSE & BY PRODUCTS PROCESSING FROM MILK
1338. LICHEN (JATAMANSI CHARILA)
1339. LIQUID GLUCOSE AND ITS BY-PRODUCTS
1340. L-LYSINE MONOHYDRO CHLORIDE
1341. LIQUID GLUCOSE FROM POTATOES
1342. MEDICAL COLLEGE
1343. NICOTINE FROM TOBACCO WASTE
1344. OINTMENT-AYURVEDIC (YELLOW & WHITE)
1345. PHARMACEUTICAL AND FOOD GRADE GELATINE
1346. PHARMACEUTICAL INDUSTRY (TABLETS, CAPSULES, LIQUID, GEL, OINTMENT POWDER INJECTABLE)
1347. PHARMACEUTICAL UNIT (EOU) WITH FORMULA TIONS, INJECTABLES, ETC. PYRIDINE & DERIVATIVES
1348. SALT (IODIZED SALT)
1349. SALINE & INJECTION WATER
1350. SALINE WATER & DEXTROSE SOLUTION (I.V.FLUID IN PLASTIC BOTTLES)
1351. SORBITOL
1352. STARCH (MAIZE)
1353. SURGICAL ADHESIVE PLASTER
1354. SURGICAL BANDAGES
1355. SURGICAL GLOVES
1357. SURGICAL COTTON
1358. SURGICAL COTTON AND BANDAGE
1359. SYNTHETIC CAMPHOR POWDER
1360. TABLETS & CAPSULES
1361. TISSUE CULTURE
1362. TINCTURE FROM RECTIFIED SPIRIT
1363. TRIMETHOPIME
1364. VETERENARY MEDICINES (ONLY FORMULATIONS)
1365. VITAMIN 'C', SORBITOL' ANHYDROUS DEXTROSE, STARCH

PULP, PAPER, STRAW/GREY BOARD, KRAFT PAPER, PACKAGING, PAPER CARRY BAGE, PAPER FROM AGRO WASTE & STATIONERY ETC.

1366. AMMONIA PAPER
1367. AUTOMATIC BOOK BINDING
1368. ADHESIVE (FEVICOL TYPE)
1369. ALL PIN & GEM CLIPS
1370. CARBON PAPER
1371. CARD BOARD
1372. CARBON LESS PAPER
1373. CELLPHANE PAPER
1374. COMPUTER FORMS & SECURITY PRINTING PRESS
1375. CORRUGATED BOARD & BOX (PRINTED & LAMINATED)
1376. CORRUGATED BOARD AND BOXES FROM FROM CARD BOARDS
1377. CORRUGATED CARTONS FROM PLAIN PAPERS
1378. CORRUGATRED PACKING & MATERIAL (BULB & TUBES PACKING)
1379. DESK TOP PUBLISHING
1380. DEFOAMING AGENT FOR PAPER PLANT
1381. DRINKING STRAW PAPER
1382. D.T.P CUM OFFSET PRESS
1383. EGG TRAYS
1384. EXERCISE NOTE BOOK, REGISTER AND PAD
1385. FLEXOGRAPHIC INK
1386. GREETING CARD BY OFFSET PRESS
1387. HAND MADE PAPER FILTER PAPER
1388. HARD BOARD
1389. INJECTION AMPOULES PACKAGING BOXES
1390. INSULATIING PAPER
1391. KRAFT PAPER
1392. KRAFT PAPER FROM BAGASSE
1393. LAMINATED PACKAGING PAPER WITH PRINTING
1394. LAMINATION & COATING ON PAPER
1395. M.G. PAPER FROM WASTE PAPER
1396. MILL PAPER FROM WASTE PAPER
1397. MILL BOARD FROM RICE & WHEAT STRAWS
1398. MILL BOARD FROM WASTE PAPER
1399. MINI PAPER PLANT FROM SISAL
1400. MINI PAPER PLANT
1401. MULTI WALL PAPER SACKS
1402. NEWS PAPER FOR CHILDREN
1403. NEWS PRINT PAPER FROM RICE STRAW BAGASSE
1404. NEWS PAPER CHILDRENS
1405. NEWS PRINT PAPER
1406. OFFSET AND TREADLE TYPE PRINTING PRESS
1407. MILL BOARD BASED ON RICE STRAW
1408. PAPER AND BOARD FROM STRAW
1409. PAPER & PAPER PRODUCTS
1410. PAPER ENVELOPES
1411. PAPER CARRY BAGS
1412. PAPER BOARD CARTON
1413. PAPER CONES FOR LOUD SPEAKERS
1414. PAPER FROM AKRA
1415. PAPER FROM BAGASSE WITH CORRUGATED BOARD & BOXES
1416. PAPER FROM BAMBOO
1417. PAPER GLASSES FOR BEVERAGES
1418. PAPER FROM RICE HUSK & WHEAT HUSK
1419. PAPER FROM TREE BARK, EUCALYPRUS WOOD
1420. PAPER PRODUCTS
1421. PAPER PLANT (WHITE WRITING & NEWS PAPER FOR PULP & WASTE PAPER)
1422. PAPER PLATES, PAPER GLASS
1423. PAPER CONES & TUBES
1425. PAPER PLANT WITH DTP & PRINTING & PUBLISHING UNIT
1426. PAPER BASED PHENOLIC SHEET
1427. PAPER CUP FOR ICE CREAM
1428. PAPER TUBES SPIRAL WINDING COMPOSIT CONTAINER
1429. PAPER LABLE FOR BEER BOTTLES
1430. PARTICLE BOARD & BLACK BOARD WITH SANDING & LAMINATION OF PARTICLE BOARD
1431. PARTICLE BOARD FROM RICE HUSK
1432. POUCH FILLING & MAKING FOR TOMATO SAUCE
1433. POUCH MAKING &

GRAVURE PRINTING
1434. PROCESSING OF PAPER FOR FEEDING IN COMPUTER
1435. PULP FROM BAMBOO & WOOD
1436. PAPER FILES
1437. PLAYING CARDS
1438. ROSIN SIZING AGENT (FOR PAPER PLANT)
1439. SAND PAPER
1440. SANITRY NAPKINS
1441. SILICON COATED PAPER
1442. STENCIL PAPER
1443. STRAW BOARD AND GREY BOARD
1444. STRAW BOARD & MILL BOARD
1445. STRAW BOARD AND PAPER BOARD
1446. TISSUE PAPER FACIAL
1447. TISSUE MOIST TOILETERY CLEANSING TISSUE AND RELATED PRODUCTS
1448. TISSUE PAPER ROLLS
1449. TETRA PACK FOR MILK PACKAGING, GHEE & OTHER LIQUIDS
1450. TOILET PAPER ROLLS
1451. TOILET PAPER & NAPKINS
1452. WAX COATED PRINTED PAPER
1453. WET FACE FRESHNER TISSUE
1454. WHITE WRITING & PRINTING PAPER
1455. WRITING & PRINTING PAPER (PAPER MILLS)

PLASTIC, B.O.P.P, ACRYLIC, DISPOSABLE PLASTIC PRODUCTS, PET PRODUCTS, P.V.C, H.D.P.E, P.P, L.D.P.E., P.U, A.B.S, THERMOFOARMING, MASTER BATCHES, & POLYMER AND RUBBER PRODUCTS, TYRE, TUBE, ADHESIVE, SHEET, COIR & MANY OTHERS

1456. ABS GRANULES FROM ABS SCRAPS FROM OLD T.V. CABINETS, WHITE GOODS ETC.
1457. ACRYLIC BEADS
1458. ACRYLIC COPOLYMER EMULSION
1459. ACRYLIC LATEX
1460. ACRYLIC SHEET
1461. ACRYLIC SHEET & MOULDED PRODUCTS
1462. ACRYLIC TEETH
1463. AUTO TUBES
1464. AUTO FLAPS FOR TRUCKS & BUSES
1465. AUTO TYRES & TUBES
1466. BABY BOTTLES (PLASTIC) WITH WHITESILICON RUBBER NIPPLES
1467. B.O.P.P. FILM
1468. B.O.P.P. PRESSURE SENSITIVE SELF ADHESIVE TAPE
1469. BABY NIPPLE (SILICON)
1470. BABY NIPPLE (BIG SIZE)
1471. BALLOON PLASTIC ADVERTISING
1472. BLISTER FILM PVC
1473. BLISTER PACKAGING & POUCH PAKAGING
1474. BLOW MOULDING PLASTIC CONTAINER
1475. COATING ON METALIZED POLYESTER FILM/METALISED PAPER/ ALIMINIUM FOIL
1476. COATING ON PLASTIC (ELECTROLYSIS) & GLASS
1477. COIR FOAM (RUBBERISED)
1478. COLOUR COATING ON PLASTICS
1479. COLOUR MASTER BATCHES FOR VARIOUS PLASTICS
1480. CYCLE TYRES AND TUBES
1481. DISPOSABLE PLASTIC CUPS GLASSES, ETC.
1482. DISPOSABLE PLASTIC SYRINGES & NEEDLES
1483. DISPOSABLE PLASTIC SYRINGES
1484. DOUGH MOULDING COMPOUND (D.M.C)
1485. EPOXY RESIN
1486. EXPANDED POLYESTRENE MOULDING (THERMOCOLE)
1487. F.R.P AUTO,SCOOTER ROOFS & CEILINGS
1488. F.R.P PRODUCTS (HELMET, WASHBASIN SHEETS, ROOFING SHEETS)
1489. FIBRE REINFORCED PLASTIC (HIGH PRESSURE MOULDING WITH SMC BMC AND DMC)
1490. FIELD RUBBER CONVERTED TO THE 60% LATEX RUBBER
1491. FLEXIBLE P.U. FOAM
1492. FORMALDEHYDE CROCKERY & OTHER ITEMS
1493. FORMALDEHYDE RESIN (UREA, PHENOL,MELEMINE)
1494. GASKET SHEET
1495. GUM BOTTLE (PVC)
1496. GLASS BEADS
1497. HDPE COATED PAPER SACK
1498. H.D.P.E. BAGS
1499. H.D.P.E. CONTAINERS (BLOW MOULDING)
1500. H.D.P.E. CONTAINER, POLY JARS BY INJECTION MOULDING (FOOD GRADE)
1501. H.D.P.E. JERRY CANS
1502. HDPE MANUFACTURING FROM ETHYLALCOHOL
1503. H.D.P.E PIPE AND FITTINGS
1504. H.D.P.E. PIPES
1505. H.D.P.E PRINTED BAGS
1506. H.D.P.E TWINES AND ROPES
1507. H.D.P.E. & L.D.P.E PIPES AND FITTINGS
1508. H.D.P.E/PP BOX STRAPPING
1509. H.D.P.E/PP WOVEN SACKS USING PLAIN LOOMS
1510. HOLOGRAM STICKERS-3D
1511. H.M BAG PLANT WITH PRINTING UNIT
1512. HAWAI CHAPPALS (RUBBER)
1513. I.V PLASTIC BOTTLE
1514. ICE CREAM CUP (PLASTIC)
1515. INJECTION MOULDED AUTO COMPONENTS
1516. INJECTION & BLOW MOULDED PLASTIC PRODUCTS
1517. INJECTION MOULDED PLASTIC PRODUCTS
1518. INTEGERATED COMPLEX ESTER'S & ALLIED PRODUCTS (D.O.P,D.B.P, & ETHYL ACETATE, BUYTL ACETATE, WIRE ENAMELS, JELLY CABLE COMPOUND)
1519. L.D.P.E. (LOW DENSITY POLY ETHYLENE) GRANULES FROM VIRGIN (L.D.P.E. RESIN)
1520. INTEGERATED SURGICAL RUBBER GOODS INDUSTRY
1521. INJECTION MOULDED PLASTIC BALLS
1522. L.D.P.E FROM ETHYL ALCOHOL
1523. LDPE MOULDED PRODUCTS
1524. LAMINATION OF COEXTRUSION MULTILAYER FILM IN ROLL FORM
1525. LATEX RUBBER
1526. LATEX RUBBER CONDOM
1527. MASTER BATCHES (COLOURED, P.V.C, L.D.P.E, H.D.P.E, ETC.)
1528. MELAMINE FORMALHYDE RESIN
1529. MOULDED LUGGAGE
1530. MULTI-LAYER (3 LAYER BAGS)
1531. MULTI-LAYER (3 LAYER) FILM WITH LAMINATION & PRINTING
1532. OIL SEAL
1533. PET BOTTLE/CONTAINERS
1534. PET BOTTLES FROM PRE FORM
1535. PET BOTTLE & MINERAL WATER
1536. PET PRE-FORM FROM PET RESIN
1537. PET PRE-FORM CUM PET BOTTLES
1538. PET PRE-FORM PET BOTTLES CUM MINERAL WATERS
1539. POLY CARBONATE RESIN
1540. PTFE COMPONENTS
1541. PU/PVC SOLE FOR SPORT SHOE BY IMPORTED M/C.
1542. PVC BATTERY SEPARATOR
1543. P.V.C COMPOUNDS (FRESH)
1544. P.V.C COMPOUNDS (SCRAP)
1545. P.V.C ELECTRICAL INSULATING TAPE
1546. P.V.C. EXTRUSION PROFILES
1547. P.V.C FITTINGS
1548. P.V.C FLEXIBLE FUSIBLE POWDER HEAT FUSIBLE POWDER
1549. P.V.C GRANULES (FOR

INSULATION & SHEETS GRADES)
1550. P.V.C GRANULES FROM PVC SCRAPS (WITH POLLUTION CONTROL)
1551. P.V.C HOSES
1552. P.V.C LEATHER CLOTH
1553. P.V.C FLEXIBLE PIPES
1554. P.V.C PIPES AND FITTINGS
1555. POLYTHENE BAGS (PRINTED)
1556. PVC PLASTICS FILM SHEET SOFT/RIGID
1557. PVC RESIN AND COMPOUND
1558. PVC RULAR
1559. PVC STABLIZERS (SINGLE PACK SYSTEM)
1560. PVC WIRE AND CABLES
1561. PAPER BASED PHENOLIC SHEET FOR ELECTRICAL
1562. PHENOL FORMALDEHYDE RESIN
1563. PHENOLIC RESIN
1564. PLASTIC BEADS FROM PLASTIC SCRAPS
1565. PLASTIC BUTTONS
1566. PLASTIC CANS
1567. PLASTIC COLLAPSIBLE TUBE
1568. PLASTIC CORRUGATED SHEET & BOXES
1569. PLASTIC FILM AND SHEETS WITH PRINTING FLEXO & ROTO/LDPE/HDPE/PP/HM/PVC
1570. PLASTIC FILTER MASTER BATCH & OTHER MASTER BATCHES FOR VARIOUS PLASTICS
1571. PLASTIC JERRY CANS
1572. PLASTIC GRANULES OR POWDER FROM PLASTIC SCRAP
1573. PLASTIC INJECTION MOULDED T.V. CABINETS
1574. PLASTIC ITEMS MANUFAC TURE FROM POWDER MELAMINE
1575. PLASTIC GOODS
1576. PLASTIC PIPES & TARPAULINES
1577. PLASTIC SHEET FROM SCRAP
1578. PLASTIC PLANT (BLOW MOULDING & INJECTION MOULDING)
1579. PLASTIC PRODUCTS (GOLD, SILVER, NICKEL)
1580. PLASTIC TOYS
1581. POLYESTER BEADING
1582. POLYESTER FILM
1583. POLYTHENE BAGS & AUTOMATIC PRINTING
1584. POLYTHENE PRINTED BAGS
1585. POLYURETHANE FOAM AND ITS PRODUCTS
1586. PROPYLENE FILM (PRINTED) & BAG MANUFACTURING
1587. PLASTIC MATS
1588. RAINBOW COLOUR ON PVC FILM & SHEET
1589. RED MUD PVC PIPES AND FITTINGS
1590. RE-RUBBERISED OF SOLID TYPE
1591. RESIN COATED SAND REXINE
1592. REXINE CLOTH & ALLIED PRODUCTS
1593. RUBBER ADHESIVE
1594. RUBBER AUTO PARTS
1595. RUBBER BELTING
1596. RUBBER MOULDING UNIT INCLUDING LINING RUBBER SHEETING
1597. RUBBER RECLAIMING
1598. RUBBER ROLLERS FOR TEXTILE MILLS & PAPER INDUSTRIES
1599. RUBBER & PLASTIC SHEETS, MATS & FLAPS
1600. RUBBER SHEET AND ALLIED HOSPITAL RUBBER GOODS
1601. RUBBERIZED PVC GASKET
1602. RUBBERISED COIR
1603. RUBBER COMPOUND FOR AUTOMOBILES
1604. SAFETY BELTS
1605. SILVER AND GOLD PLATING ON PVC AND NYLON-6
1606. SILICONE RUBBER NIPPLES/ TEATS
1607. SPECTACLE FRAMES (PLASTIC)
1608. SPUNGE RUBBER
1609. SURGICAL EXAMINATION GLOVES
1610. SYNTHETIC PEARL COATING ON POLYSTYRENE BEADS
1611. SYNTHETIC RUBBER ADHESIVE
1612. TEFLON MANUFACTURING
1613. TEFLON TAPE
1614. TEFLON TAPES & CABLES
1615. THERMOCOLE SHEET AND MOULDED PRODUCTS EXPANDED POLYESTERENE EXTRUSION PROFILES
1616. THERMOFORMED PACKAGING (BLISTER PACKAGING & POUCH PACKAGING)
1617. THERMOPLASTIC POLYURETHANE
1618. THERMOFORMED CUPS, PLATES & GLASS WITH HIPS SHEET
1619. THERMOCOLE
1620. THERMOCOLE BASED DISPOSABLE GLASS, CUPS & PLATES
1621. TOOTH BRUSHES
1622. TOY BALLOON, DECORA TIVE & INDUSTRIAL BALLOONS
1623. TREAD RUBBER
1624. TYRE RETREADING (HOT)
1625. TYRE RETREADING BY COLD PROCESS
1626. TYRE TUBES & FLAPS
1627. TYRE & TUBES
1628. UNSATURATED POLYESTER FOR REXINE
1629. V-BELT AND FAN BELT
1630. VINYL ASBESTOS AND PVC WALL PAPER
1631. VITON (FLUORO ELASTOMER)

SOAP, COSMETICS & PERFUMS

1632. ACID SLURRY, SYNTHETIC DETERGENT POWDER
1632. ACID SLURRY
1633. AGARBATTI SYNTHETIC PERFUMERY COMPOUND
1634. AFTER SHAVE LOTION
1635. ANTISEPTIC CREAM
1636. BETA IONONE
1637. BLEACHING POWDER
1638. BLUE DETERGENT POWDER
1639. CLEANING POWDER (VIMTYPE)
1640. COLD CREAM
1641. COLOURED FLAME & PERFUMED CANDLES (RED, BLUE, GREEN FLAME)
1642. COSMETIC INDUSTRY (MODERN)
1643. COSMETIC INDUSTRY (SHAMPOO, SPRAY PERFUME, TALCUM POWDER
1644. DETERGENT POWDER (ARIEL TYPE)
1645. DETERGENT POWDER (NIRMA TYPE) FULLY AUTOMATIC PLANT
1646. DETERGENT WASHING POWDER
1647. FISH OIL SOAP
1648. GLYCERINE TRANSPARENT SOAP
1649. HAIR REMOVING CREAM
1650. HERBAL COSMETICS
1651. HERBAL SHAMPO & CREAM
1652. HERBAL/AYURVEDIC COSMETICS
1653. INCENSE POWDER, INCENSE STICKS & INCENSE CAKE
1654. OPTICAL WHITENERS
1655. ROSE OIL EXTRACTION
1656. SHAMPOOS (COCONUT OIL BASED COLD PROCESS)
1657. SHAVING CREAM
1658. SINDUR (KUMKUM)
1659. SOAP COATED PAPER
1660. SPRAY DRIED DETERGENT POWDER
1661. STAIN REMOVER
1662. TALCUM POWDER (FACE & TOILET POWDER)
1663. TOILET AND HERBAL SOAP
1664. TOOTH PASTE & POWDER
1665. WASHING DETERGENT POWDER AND WASHING SOAP
1666. WASHING POWDER LIQUID DETERGENTS LOTION & SHAMPOO

Above all the Detailed Project Report are available at *"ENGINEERS INDIA RESEARCH INSTITUTE"*. 4449, Nai Sarak (D), Main Road Delhi - 110 006
● Ph : 91-11-23918117, 2391 6431, 2392 0361, 31082370 ● Fax : 91-11- 2391 6431
● E-Mail : eirisidi@bol.net.in

TEXTILE INDUSTRIES, READYMADE GARMENTS, COTTON, DYEING, BLEACHING, CLOTH, HOSIERY, POWER LOOM, HAND LOOM, WOOLLEN, SILK, SOCKS, SURGICAL COTTON & MANY OTHERS

1667. ANGORA RABBIT WOOL
1668. BUCKRAM
1669. CANVAS SHOES, JUNGLE BOOT, BOOT RUBBER KNEES & BOOT COMBAT
1670. CARPET FROM COTTON WASTE
1671. CERAMIC THREAD GUIDE
1672. COTTON BUDS/SWABS
1673. COTTON FROM WASTE YARN
1674. COTTON ROLLS
1675. COTTON SPIDERS FOR LOUD SPEAKERS
1676. DENIM CLOTH
1677. DENIM CLOTH (INTEGERATED UNIT WITH BLEACHING, DYEING AND PRINTING)
1678. DISPERSENT FOR TEXTILE
1679. DYEING & BLEACHING
1680. DYEING OF HANK YARN
1681. EMULSIFIER FOR WOOL BATCHING OIL
1682. EMBROIDERY ON FABRICS
1683. GARMENT DYEING, WASHING & STITCHING (JEANS, JACKETS, SKIRTS & SHIRTS)
1684. GOVES KNITTING
1685. GUNNY BAGS
1687. HDPE WOVEN SACKS
1688. HDPE TARPAULINS USING PLAIN LOOM WITH LAMINATION
1689. HDPE/PP WOVEN SACKS USING CIRCULAR LOOMS
1690. HOSIERY CLOTH (COTTON) PROCESSING (BLEACHING, DYEING, FINISHING OF CLOTH)
1691. HOSIERY INDUSTRY
1692. HOSIERY MERCERISING
1693. HOSIERY PRODUCTS LIKE VEST, BRIEF, T-SHIRTS & SOCKS
1694. JACQUARD FABRICS
1695. JUTE COIR, GRASS ROPE/ SUTLI MAKING
1696. JUTE FELT
1697. JUTE TWINES
1698. KNITTED FABRICS
1699. LAMINATED JUTE BAGS
1700. LAMINATION OF HDPE WOVEN CLOTH (JUTE,COTTON, PAPER)
1701. NYLON YARN CRIMPING, DOUBLING AND BLEACHING
1702. PIGMENT BINDER FOR TEXTILE PRINTING
1704. POLYESTER RESIN FOR WIRE ENAMEL
1705. POLYESTER RESIN
1706. POLYESTER YARN FROM WASTE POLYESTER ZIP FASTENERS
1707. POWER LOOM
1708. READYMADE GARMENTS & HOSIERY
1709. READYMADE GARMENTS MERCHANDISE
1710. READYMADE GARMENTS & COVERS
1711. READYMADE GARMENTS & EMBROIDERY OF GOWNS, SHIRTS, BLOUSES, T-SHIRTS ETC. (ONLY LADIES)
1712. READYMADE SALWAR SUIT
1713. RECOVERY OF NYLON FROM NYLON WASTE
1714. ROTARY PRINTING AND DYEING ON COTTON, SYNTHETIC TEXTILE
1715. SANITARY NAPKINS
1716. SCREEN PRINTING ON COTTON CLOTH
1717. SEWING THREAD REELS & BALLS MAKING INDUSTRIES
1718. SCREEN PRINTING ON COTTON, POLYESTER & ACRYLIC
1719. SHAWLS (WOOLLEN)
1720. SHOE LACES
1721. SILK FABRICS ON HANDLOOM
1722. SOCKS KNITTING
1723. SPINNING, DOUBLING DYEING MERCERISING & BLEACHING OF COTTON YARN
1724. SPINNING & CARDING OF WOOL INTO YARNS
1725. STARCH BOOK BINDING CLOTH
1726. SURAT JARI
1727. SURGICAL COTTON & BANDAGE
1728. SYNTHETIC TEXTILE INDUSTRY(SUITING, SHIRTING, SAREES) TERRY CLOTH
1729. T-SHIRTS
1730. TOWELS, BED SHEET COVERS
1731. TERRY TOWEL
1732. TERRY FABRICS WEAVING UNIT
1733. TEXTILE AUXILLIARIES & CHEMICALS
1734. TEXTILE BLEACHING, DYEING & FINISHING & PRINTING OF COTTON FABRICS
1735. TEXTILE (HOSIERY)
1736. TEXTILE MILL
1737. TEXTILE DYEING & PRINTING
1738. TEXTILE PRINTING (JOB WORK)
1739. TEXTILE PIGMENT PRINTING BINDER
1740. TOWEL (TERRY)
1741. VELVET CLOTH BY FLOCKING PROCESS
1742. VISCOSE STAPLE FIBRE
1743. WADDING OIL (100%) FOR WADDING OF COTTON HOSIERY CLOTH IN THE DYEING PROCESS
1744. WEAVING OF DASUTI CLOTH WITH PRINTING, DYEING, EMBROIDERY & FINISHING
1745. WASHING OF JEANS & OTHER GARMENTS
1746. WORSTED WOOLLEN YARN CLOTH
1747. ZARI GLITTER SALMA SITARA OF PLASTIC FILM

INFOTECH/IT, HOSPITALITY, HOSPITAL, COLLEGE, SCHOOL, MEDICAL, ENTERTAINMENT CLUB, WARE HOUSING & REAL ESTATE, PROJECTS

1748. AMUSEMENT PARK
1749. AMUSEMENT PARK CUM WATER PARK
1750. BANQUET HALL
1751. CALL CENTER (DOMESTIC)
1752. CALL CENTER (INTERNATIONAL)
1753. CHILDREN RECREATION CENTRE
1754. COLD STORAGE
1755. COMMUNITY HALL
1756. COMPUTER EDUCATION INSTITUTE
1757. COMPUTER SOFTWARE
1758. COLLEGE
1759. CYBER CAFE
1760. DENTAL CLINIC
1761. DENTAL COLLEGE
1762. DIAGONOSTIC CENTRE
1763. E-COMMERCE/BUSINESS
1764. E-SCHOOL (Rs. 5000/-)
1765. ENGINEERING COLLEGE
1766. ENTERTAINMENT CLUB
1767. ENTERTAINMENT CLUB, HOLIDAY RESORT, 4 STAR HOTEL, AMUSEMENT PARK CUM WATER PARK, MUSHROOM & ITS PRODUCTS, FISH FARMING, LAKE FOR BOATING, DEER PARK
1768. FASHION TECHNOLOGY INSTITUTE
1769. FAST FOOD PARLOUR
1770. FIVE STAR HOTEL
1771. FOOD PARLOUR
1772. FRANCHISE TRAINING PROGRAMME FOR IIT & ENGINEERING ENTRANCE EXAMS.
1773. GOLF COURSE
1774. HEALTH CLUB, BEAUTY PARLOUR
1775. HEALTH CLUB AND FITNESS CENTER
1776. HEALTH RESORTS
1777. HOLIDAY RESORTS
1778. HOLIDAY RESORT CUM

ENTERTAINMENT CLUB WITH 4 STAR HOTEL
1779. HOSPITALS
1780. ICE CREAM PARLOUR
1781. INTERNET SERVICE PROVIDER (I.S.P.)
1782. MEDICAL COLLEGE
1783. MEDICAL COLLEGE, HOSPITAL & RESEARCH INSTITUTE
1784. MEDICAL TRANSCRIPTION CENTRE
1785. MENTAL RETARDATION HOSPITAL & CEREBRAL PALSY
1786. MOTEL/SMALL HOTEL
1787. MULTISTOREY COMMERCIAL COMPLEX
1788. MULTISTOREY RESIDENTIAL COMPLEX
1789. NURSERY SCHOOL
1790. NATURE CARE CENTRE
1791. NURSING HOME
1792. ONLINE SHOPPING MALL (RS. 5000/- REPORT)
1793. PORTAL
1794. REHABILITATION CENTRE FOR AGED & NEEDY PERSONS
1795. RESIDENTIAL CUM COMMERCIAL COMPLEX
1796. RESTAURANT
1797. RESTAURANT WITH PUB
1798. SCHOOL (PRIMARY)
1799. SCHOOL (HIGHER SECONDARY)
1800. THREE STAR HOTEL
1801. TOURIST CLUB
1802. TRAINING INSTITUTE FOR MEDICAL TRANSCRIPTION
1803. VIDEO FILM STUDIO
1804. WARE HOUSE
1805. WEBSITE DESIGN & E-MAIL REGISTERING

AGRO BASED INDUSTRIES

1806. COAL BRIQUETTES FROM AGROWASTE
1807. FURFURALFROM RICEHULL
1808. MUSHROOM CULTIVATION & PROCESSING (BUTTON)
1809. MUSHROOM GROWING & PROCESSING WITH AIR CONDITIONING
1810. MUSHROOM CULTIVATION & PROCESSING UNIT DEHYDRATION & PACKAGING OF OYSTER & PADDY STRAW MUSHROOMS
1811. ORGANIC MANURE
1812. PAPAYA CULTIVATION
1813. PAPAYA & TOMATO CULTIVATION
1814. PROCESSING & UTILISATION OF COCONUT
1815. PROCESSING OF SHEEP HAIR TO PRODUCE WOOL

BAKERY, CONFECTIONERY & FOOD PRODUCTS

1816. AGROLACTOR SOYA MILK
1817. APPLE FRUIT JUICE WITH CANNING BOTTLING
1818. AYURVEDIC SHARBAT
1819. BAKERY UNIT (PASTRIES, BREAD, BUNS, CAKE, TOFFEE ETC.)
1820. BAKING POWDER
1821. BANANA & ITS BY PRODUCTS
1822. BANANA POWDER
1823. BANANA WAFERS
1824. BANANA CULTIVATION
1825. BEER INDUSTRY
1826. DEHULLING OF JAUN FOR BEER
1827. BEER & WINE
1828. BEER, ALCOHOL, IMFL
1829. BESEN PLANT
1830. BISCUIT PLANT
1831. BREAD & BISCUIT PLANT
1832. BOTTLING PLANT COUNTRY LIQUOR FROM RECTIFIED SPIRIT
1833. BRANDY
1834. BREAD RUSKS
1835. CANNED FRUITS & VEGETABLES
1836. CANNING & PRESERVATION OF MEAT
1837. CANNING & PRESERVATION OF VEGETABLES
1838. CANNING OF MANGO PULP & MANGO SLICES
1839. CARBONATED BEVERAGS
1840. CASHEW FENI
1841. CASHEW NUT (DRIED & FRIED)
1842. CATTLE BREEDING
1843. CATTLE BREEDING & DAIRY FARM TO PRODUCE MILK
1844. CATTLE FEED FROM TAPIOCA
1845. CHEWING GINGER & AMLOKI
1846. CHEWING GUM
1847. CHILLI SAUCE
1848. CHILLI POWDER
1849. CHOCOLATE
1850. CIDER PLANT
1851. COCOA POWDER
1852. COCOA BUTTER & COCOA POWDER
1853. COCONUT SHELL POWDER
1854. COCONUT WATER
1855. COCONUT SWEET (WATERY)
1856. COCONUT MILK POWDER (DEHYDRATED)
1857. COCONUT PRODUCTS & BY PRODUCTS (INTEGRATED PLANT)
1858. COLD DRINK
1859. CURRY POWDER
1860. DAIRY FOR MILK PROCESSING (GHEE, BUTTER & PANEER)
1861. DAIRY PRODUCTS
1862. DAIRY PRODUCTS MILK PACKAGING IN POUCH (GHEE, BUTTER, ETC.
1863. DAIRY FARM TO PRDUCE MILK WITH PACKAGING (COW)
1864. DAIRY FARM TO PRDUCE MILK WITH PACKAGING (BUFALLOE)
1865. DAIRY FARM & MILK PRODUCTS
1866. DAL MOTH, CHANACHUR & BHUJIYA
1867. DEHYDRATION OF FRUITS & VEGETABLE
1868. DESICCATED COCONUT POWDER FROM COCONUTS
1869. DEHYDRATION & CANNING OF FRUITS & VEGETABLES
1870. DRY FRUIT ROASTING & PACKAGING
1871. DRYING OF RED CHILLIES, HALDI, DHANIYA, PEAS & GROUND NUT
1872. EGG POWDER
1873. FISH CANNING IN TIN & POUCHES
1874. FISH DEHYRATION (DRYING OF FISH)
1875. FISH MEAL
1876. FISH PROCESSING (BEAST FREEZING PROCESSES)
1877. FLAVOURS FOR FOOD INDUSTRIES
1878. FLOUR MILL (ROLLER)
1879. FROZEN MEAT
1880. FOOD DEHYDRATION (FRUITS & VEGETABLES)
1881. FRIED & ROASTED GROUND NUT, GRAMS, PEAR ETC.
1882. FRUIT JUICE MAKING & PACKAGING IN PLASTIC CONTAINER
1883. FRUIT JUICE IN TETRA PACK (DRINKS)
1884. FRUIT JUICE, SQUASHES, SAUCE & KETCHUP, JAM, JELLY, VINEGAR ETC.
1885. GARLIC FLAKES
1886. GARLIC POWDER
1887. GHEE & BUTTER
1888. GINGER (PULVERISED)
1889. GINGER GLAZING & PRESERVATION
1890. GINGER STORAGE
1891. GINGER PROCESSING
1892. GINGER OIL & GINGER DUST
1893. GINGER POWDER (DRY) & OLEORESIN
1894. GRAPE DEHYDRATION
1895. GRAPE CULTIVATION
1896. GRAPE JUICE
1897. HONEY PROCESSING & PACKAGING
1898. ICE CREAM & ICE CANDY
1899. ICE CUBE
1900. INVERT SUGAR
1901. IDLI MIX, DOSA MIX SAMBHAR MIX, VADA MIX, GULAB JAMUN MIX
1902. INSTANT COFFEE & INSTANT TEA

1903. INSTANT NOODLES
1904. INSTANT SOUPS
1905. IODIZED SALT FROM CRUDE SALT
1906. JAM CHUTNEY PICKLES & SQUASHES
1907. KATHA MANUFACTURING
1908. LECITHIN (SOYA BASED)
1909. LEMON & ITS PRODUCTS
1910. MACARONI MANUFACTURING
1911. MACARONI, SPAGHETTI, VERMICELLI & NOODLES
1912. MAIZE & ITS BY PRODUCTS MALTING PLANT
1913. MANGO PAPPAD (AAM PAPPAD)
1914. MANGO POWDER RIPE
1915. MANGO POWDER
1916. MANGO PROCESSING & CANNING (MANGO PULP)
1917. MEAT PROCESSING (CHICKEN MUTTON)
1918. MEAT PROCESSING (BUFFALO)
1919. MENTHOL BOLD FROM MENTHOL FLAKES
1020. MILK POWDER
1921. MILK POWDER & GHEE
1922. MILK POWDER, GHEE & SPICES
1923. MILK PRESERVATION & MARKETING TO WHOLE SELLERS
1924. MILK PRESERVATION & MARKETING TO WHOLE SELLERS (IN POUCHES)
1925. MILK TOFFEE MANUFACTURES
1926. MINERAL WATER
1927. MINERAL WATER IN POUCHES
1928. MINI FLOUR MILL ATTA MAIDA, SUJI & WHEAT BRAN
1929. MITHAI/HALWAI (SWEET & NAMKEEN)
1930. MUTTON PROCESSING
1931. PAN MASALA (MEETHA, SADA, ZARDA) MAKING & PACKING
1932. PAN MASALA AND POUCH MAKING
1933. PANEER (CHEESE)
1934. PAPAD & BARIYAN
1935. PAPAD PLANT
1936. PEPSICOLA IN POLYTUBES
1937. PETHA PACKAGING
1938. PICKLES
1939. PIGGERY/MEAT/CHICKEN PROCESSING
1940. PINE APPLE JUICE CANNING
1941. POTATO & ONION POWDER
1942. POTATO & ONION FLAKES
1943. POTATO CHIPS
1944. POTATO GRANULES
1945. POUCH FILLING FOR SAUNF SUPARI ILAICHI ETC.
1946. PRESERVATION OF RAWS MANGO JUICE
1947. PROCESSED CHEESE & MARINE PDTS.
1948. PULP FROM TARMARIND
1949. READYMATE PROCESSED FOOD
1950. RICE & CORN FLAKES
1951. RICE BASMATI (TRADING)
1952. RICE POLISHING & PACKAGING IN POUCH
1953. ROASTED/SALTED/MASALA/ CASHEW NUTS ALMONDS & PEA NUT
1954. ROLLER FLOUR MILL

INFOTECH/IT PROJECTS

1955. MEDICAL TRANSCRIPTION
1956. E-COMMERCE
1957. CYBERCAFE
1958. INTERNET SERVICE PROVIDER (ISP)
1959. COMPUTER EDUCATION CENTRE
1960. PORTAL (WEBSITE DESIGN)
1961. CALL CENTRE

TERMS AND CONDITIONS

FOR INDIA

1. Please ask for Quotations of Each *Market Survey Cum Detailed Techno Economic Feasibility Report.* Payable in advance through Draft/M.O./Cash in favour of 'ENGINEERS INDIA RESEARCH INSTITUTE', Delhi. Delivery by Regd.post within 2 Days. (Postage Free)

2. Ask for the Hi-Tech Projects Monthly magazine. Each Magazine covers many Project Profiles for selection of Industry.

FOR OVERSEAS

1. Please ask for Quotations in US $ of Each *Market Survey Cum Detailed Techno Economic Feasibility Report.* Payable in advance through Draft/M.O./Cash in favour of 'ENGINEERS INDIA RESEARCH INSTITUTE', Delhi. (Payable in India) Delivery by Regd.post within 4 Days.

2. Ask for the Hi-Tech Projects Monthly magazine. Each Magazine covers many Project Profiles for selection of Industry.

ENGINEERS INDIA RESEARCH INSTITUTE

4449, Nai Sarak (D), Main Road, Delhi - 110 006 (India)
Ph:. 91-11-23918117, 23916431, 23840361, 31082370
Fax: 91-11-23916431 E-Mail : eirisidi@bol.net.in
Website:www.startindustry.com
Also at : 4/27, Roop Nagar, Near Roop Nagar No. 1 School, Delhi - 110 007 (India) Ph:. 23840361

JUST PUBLISHED-NEW BOOKS

HAND BOOK OF AGRO CHEMICAL INDUSTRIES (INSECTICIDES & PESTICIDES)

By : EIRI BOARD

ISBN. 81-86732-46-2 + Rs. 900/-

The Book has just published and covers following Contents : Agro Chemical Industries, Pesticides, Insecticides, Fungicides, Nematicide, Rodenticides, Molluscicides, Fumigants, Acaricides, Herbicides, Plant Growth Regulators, Repellents Attractants, Pheromones, Synergists, Synthetic Inhibitors and Proinsecticides, Toxicoligy & Safe use of Pesticides, Insecticide Act, Pesticide Formulations, Pesticide Mixtures, Modern Equipments for a Pesticide Formulation Labiratory & Pilot Plant, Aerosol Formulations, Advances in Pesticides Formulations Packaging, Aerosol Packaging Technology, Packaging In Pesticides, Emulsifier for Pesticides, Pesticide by Neem Fruits & Seed, Mosquito Coils and mats, Air Freshner (Odonil Type), Insecticide from Neem Seed & Oil, Phenyl, Recent Developments in Pesticide Formulations, Allethrin Mosquito Repellent Oil, Mosquito Repellent Agarbatti, Aerosol & Mosquito Repellent Spray (Baygon, HIT & Mortein Type), Suppliers of Plant & Machinery and Raw Materials etc.

HAND BOOK OF SPICES & PACKAGING WITH FORMULAES

By : EIRI BOARD

ISBN. 81-86732-31-4 + Rs. 650/-

The Book covers new formulaes of various kinds of Spices. The major chapters of the book are Ajowan, Amchur, Aniseed, Asafoetida, Chilli, Caraway, Cardamom, Cassia, Celery Seed, Cinnamon, Clove, Coriander, Cumin Seed, Fennel, Garlic, Ginger, Pepper, Drying of Red Chilli, Dry Ginger, Onion Dehydration, Garlic Powder, Formulaes of Different Kinds of Ground Spices, Packaging of Spices, Methods of Tests, Agmark, Details of Machinery, National Standards, Importers/Exporters of Spices, Plant & Equipment Suppliers & Manufacturers of Spices

MANUFACTURE OF SNACKS FOOD, NAMKEEN, PAPPAD & POTATO PRODUCTS

By : EIRI BOARD

ISBN. 81-86732-37-3 + Rs. 650/-

Extruded Snacks, Health Food Snacks, Snack Food Preservatio & Packaging, Details of Plant, Machinery & Equipments, Instant Noodles, Namkeen, Namkeen & Sweets, Potato Products. Manufacturers of Plants & Machineries of Snacks Food, Manufacturers of Machineries of Papped Plants, Manufacturers of Plant & Machineries of Namkeen, Manufacturers of Raw Materials, Suppliers of Packaging Materials. Potato, Pappad & Barian Plant, Potato Waffers, Potato Chips, Packaging of Snack Foods.

ENGINEERS INDIA RESEARCH INSTITUTE Mobile : 9811437895
4449, Nai Sarak, Main Road, Delhi - 110 006 (INDIA) Ph./Fax : 91-11- 23918117, 23916431, 23840361